Programming in BASIC for Business

SECOND EDITION

Bruce Bosworth
Harry L. Nagel
St. John's University, New York

SCIENCE RESEARCH ASSOCIATES, INC.
Chicago, Palo Alto, Toronto
Henley-on-Thames, Sydney
A Subsidiary of IBM

Acquisition Editor	Terry Baransy
Project Editor	James C. Budd
Compositor	Interactive Composition Corporation
Illustrator	Rogondino and Associates
Cover and Text Designer	Barbara Ravizza
Cover Photo	Lee Youngblood

Library of Congress Cataloging in Publication Data

Bosworth, Bruce.
  Programming in BASIC for business.

  Includes index.
  1. Basic (Computer program language) 2. Business—Data processing. I. Nagel, Harry L., joint author. II. Title.
HF5548.5.B3B67 1981 001.64'24 80-23195
ISBN 0-574-21325-2

10 9 8 7 6 5

Contents

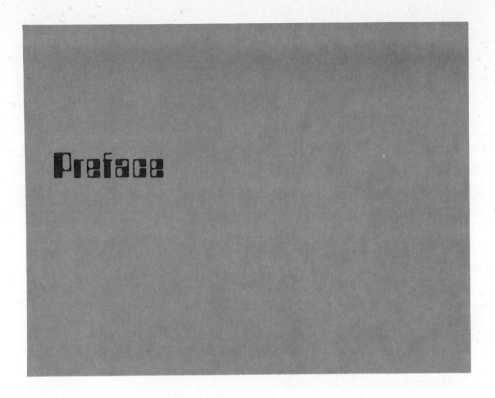

Preface

This book was written to introduce students to the BASIC programming language. There are other texts about BASIC, but they are general in their approach and seldom cover business applications. This book fills the need for a comprehensive treatment of the BASIC language with a business orientation. Specific chapters of the book are designed to explain completely selected BASIC statements. Each statement is presented in illustrative programs, complete with output. Small cases reinforce the meaning of each statement. Students will find numerous programming exercises of varying difficulty at the end of each chapter. These exercises test their understanding of the concepts introduced thus far. After mastering the first nine chapters, students can design, code, and test the larger application programs to solve the business problems in Chapter 15.

Many aspects of the BASIC language differ from computer system to computer system. However, a subset of the BASIC language has been standardized. The subset is known as ANSI minimal BASIC. Programs in Chapters 1–10 of this book were prepared using ANSI minimal BASIC.

This book can be used in a course completely devoted to computer programming. It can also be used as a supplement in a course on data processing. Basic business courses in which students are introduced to the computer as a tool in today's business world will find this text very helpful.

Much of the material in the book has been used in college classrooms over a period of several years. All of the programming exercises and the larger case problems in Chapter 15 have been class-tested and were well received by students.

Following a brief introduction to programming, flowcharting, and time-sharing in Chapter 1, a complete set of chapters (2 through 9) sufficient for a short course in BASIC is presented. Chapters 10 through 14 provide advanced aspects of BASIC, including string variables, PRINT USING, matrices, and data files. The BASIC language elements covered in these chapters will differ from system to system. Individual "advanced" chapters may be omitted, as the particular situation dictates.

We have added several new topics in this edition, in part reflecting new programming developments that have grown in importance in recent years. These additions serve to keep the text current and provide more options for instructors in meeting the needs of their particular courses and students. Topics added in this edition include:

- program development
- concepts of structured programming
- alphabetic and numeric sorting
- programmmed processing controls
- direct access file operations

In order to enhance the readability and pedagogy of the first edition, we have made several refinements and modifications. They include a:

- separate chapter for the GO TO statement
- separate chapter for the IF/THEN statement
- treatment of string variables, first as ordinary strings, and then as subscripted strings
- separate chapter for sorting

When preparing a new edition, authors are often faced with the dilemma of how to handle new developments in a particualr field. We recognize that programming in general has been experiencing a trend toward structured programming and related concepts. We have seen texts that do a splendid job of putting structure into COBOL and other high-level programming languages. We have seen texts that promise to put structure into BASIC but never deliver. We have decided to follow a more conservative approach. In this text we indicate that structured programming and related concepts can serve a useful purpose in program development and in furthering the understandability of code. We point out that well-defined control structures exist, and that proper use of them can facilitate program development in general and within the BASIC language specifically.

What we have *not* done is rewrite this edition as a structured BASIC text. Instead we have carefully retained proven features of the first edition. Clear explanations are given for each BASIC statement. These are followed by actual program listings. Each concept is further developed in case-application problems. Every chapter concludes with a summary and a large variety of graduated exercises and programming assignments. Selected solutions are also included at the end of the text. Asterisks indicate the exercises that have text solutions.

We have added seventy new exercises/programming problems, representing a 40 percent increase over the first edition. Also, twenty new application cases have been added to this edition.

With the current growth of microcomputers and the recognition that all users of such hardware would like a BASIC text to be specific to their hardware, we have chosen to cover American National Standards Institute Minimal BASIC concepts in this text. Chapters 2 through 10 follow ANSI minimal BASIC. The chapters beyond those reflect concepts that can generally be found on most systems but do not meet any standard as of yet.

Those chapters dealing with ANSI minimal BASIC (Chapters 2–9 and ordinary strings in Chapter 10) can be adapted to the vast majority of microcomputers available without major changes. That includes the following:

Radio Shack—TRS-80
Apple Computer, Inc.—Apple II
Commodore Business Machines—PET
Texas Instruments, Inc.—TI-99/4
Warner Communications Co.—ATARI

In stressing the interchangeability of ANSI minimal BASIC among microcomputers, we have added an appendix for the popular Radio Shack TRS-80. It indicates how the text material compares with Radio Shack Level II BASIC.

We would like to express our appreciation to Marilyn Bohl of IBM for her detailed review of the manuscript and the many helpful suggestions she made. Several other persons participated in the review of our manuscript and also helped improve it by their comments: Richard N. Bialac, Xavier University; William T. Bounds, Jr., University of Central Arkansas; Franklin P. Chinn, Brevard Community College; Frank M. Clamon, Jr., Davidson County Community College; Floyd E. Eaves, Chattanooga State Technical Community College; Jerry Elam, St. Petersburg Junior College; Gregory W. Jones, Utah State University; Beverly B. Madron, Western Kentucky University; James A. Pope, Guilford College; W. L. Staats, Hudson Valley

Community College; Charles W. Strickland, Surry Community College; Michael J. Walton, Miami-Dade Community College.

Special thanks to Seyed-Hassan Fonouni, our graduate assistant, who prepared and executed numerous BASIC programs for us. In addition, we are especially indebted to Mary Giuntini and Karen Seldon for their assistance in typing and retyping the drafts of this book.

chapter 1

Introduction to Timesharing and BASIC

Ever since the early 1950s we have witnessed a rapid increase in the use of computers in our everyday lives. Today, computers are common in government, education, and business. Look at your driver's license or telephone bill. In all probability it was processed by computer. Examples like this are all around us.

To be useful, computers must be told not only what to do but also how to do it. This is the purpose of programming. A *program* is a detailed set of instructions that direct the computer to do its job. A *programmer* is a person who prepares such programs. Programs are typically referred to as *software*. *Hardware* constitutes the physical components of a computer system; i.e., the equipment.

COMPUTER LANGUAGES

There are a number of computer languages in which a programmer can write the detailed instructions needed to get the computer to work. The names of some of these languages are BASIC, FORTRAN, COBOL, Assembler, PL/I, APL, PASCAL, and RPG.

Learning how to program a computer is similar to learning a foreign language. In the BASIC language, however, there are about 30 verb-words, so vocabulary is no problem. Programming is like playing chess. There are only six different kinds of pieces on a chessboard but an infinite number of combinations of moves. Thus with the verb-words in the BASIC language we can write programs to do such diverse things as:

1. Help a person find a mate.
2. Prepare a payroll for a company including the writing of the checks, determining the appropriate federal, state, and local tax deductions, social security tax, pension deductions, insurance deductions, etc.
3. Process applications for credit cards to determine who is eligible.
4. Maintain a running balance of the inventory of a company with many products.
5. Explore different marketing strategies by creating a hypothetical environment to test them in.

PROGRAMMING WITH DATA CARDS

The most common approach used to enter data and programs into a computer is by means of punched data cards. Processing data and programs

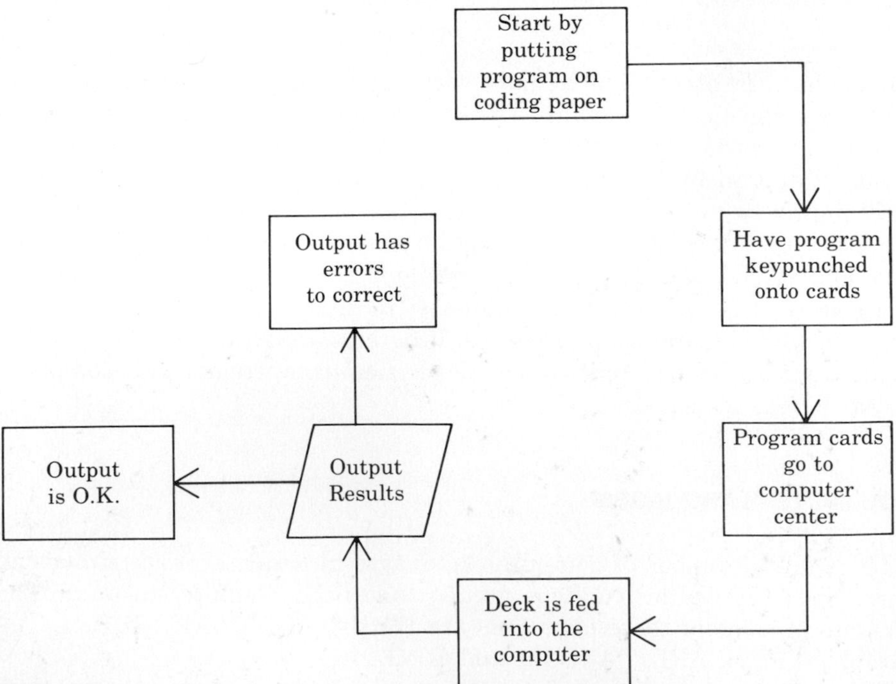

FIGURE 1.1 Sequence for Programming with Punched Cards

punched on cards generally follows this sequence: (1) write your program on special coding paper; (2) submit it to a keypunch operator to have a deck of cards produced; (3) submit the completed deck to the computer center, where it is placed on top of a batch of other decks waiting to be fed into the computer; (4) later in the day, or tomorrow or maybe next week, pick up your results, the *output.*

If you are lucky, the output is okay. If the program had an error in it, you have to correct it and start the sequence over again. Figure 1.1 illustrates the sequence described above.

TIMESHARING

A major problem with the punched card approach is that users do not have ready access to the computer. This means that fast and immediate results cannot be obtained. In the 1960s timesharing systems were developed to overcome the problem of getting access to the computer and obtaining output results. Such systems consist of terminals (which often look like typewriters) connected by telephone lines to computers in other locations. In this manner many people can be connected to one computer. Figure 1.2 shows the general scheme of a timesharing system.

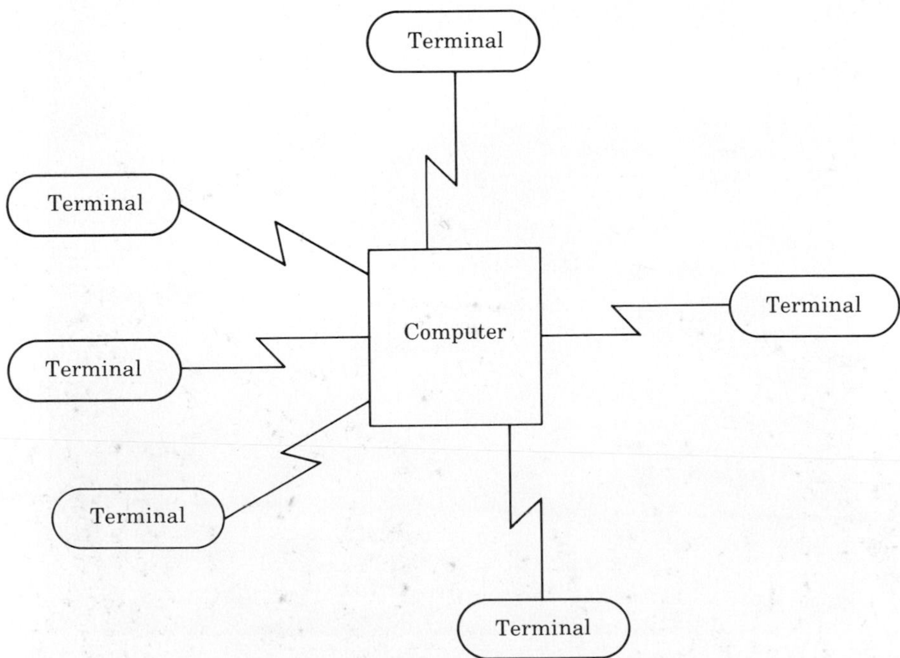

FIGURE 1.2 A Timesharing System Scheme

The computer, which works very quickly, can process many people's instructions in much the same way that a chess master can play "simultaneously" many players. He makes one move against each opponent, and by the time he has moved against all his opponents, the first player is ready again with his next move.

With timesharing, programs can be processed almost immediately. Obvious errors can be corrected on the spot. Output can be obtained in minutes, rather than hours or days.

Because timesharing is a convenient and easy method of interacting with a computer, the use of such systems is on the rise. Typical timesharing users are in banking, health and medical care, airline, hotel, and car rental reservations, and other areas where a speedy response is required.

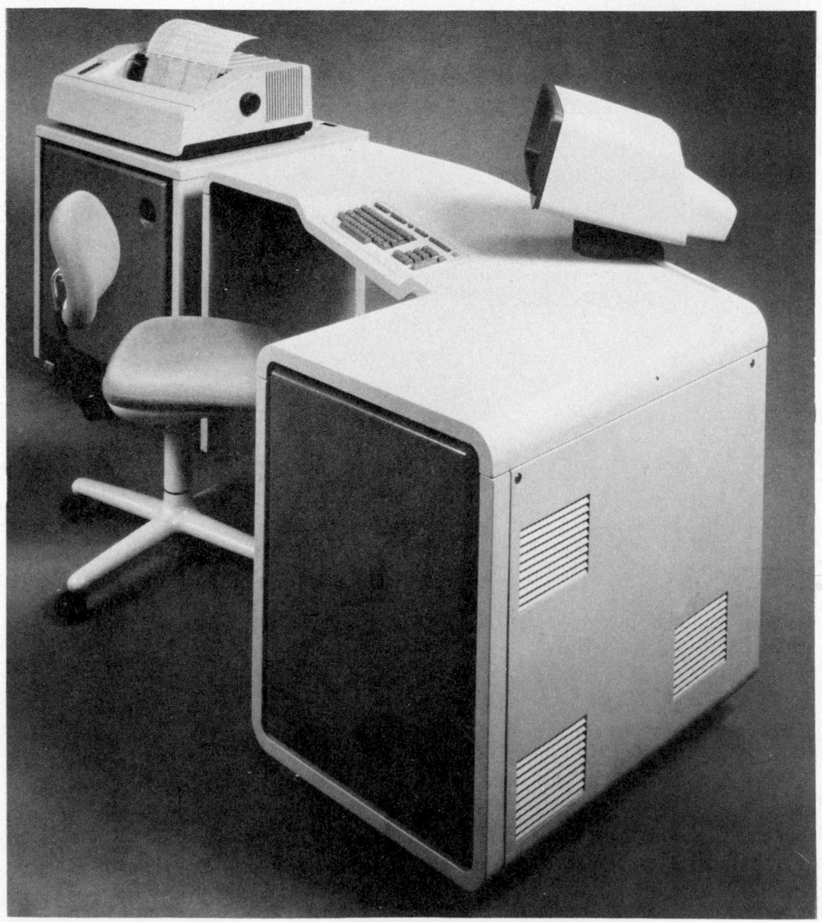

FIGURE 1.3 Minicomputer (Courtesy of Hewlett-Packard)

RECENT COMPUTER DEVELOPMENTS

In recent years computers and computer systems have become smaller and less expensive. Some computers are portable, weighing less than 50 pounds, and can rest on an office desk. The most rapidly developing segment of the business computer market consists of *minicomputers*. These computers have many of the capabilities of any full-size large computer. Generally their size and storage capacity are smaller, and prices range from $2000 to $100,000, depending on how complex the system is. Such minicomputers support high-level programming languages such as FORTRAN, COBOL, RPG, and BASIC. Figure 1.3 shows a minicomputer.

Another area of computer growth is the home and hobby market. More and more *microcomputers* are being bought as "personal computers." These computers have limited storage capabilities but are being used by students, lawyers, engineers, and educators. Generally, a microcomputer sells in the price range of $500 to $10,000, depending on storage capability. With additional equipment, many microcomputer systems are finding their way into businesses. The language used with most microcomputers is BASIC. A typical microcomputer is shown in Figure 1.4.

FIGURE 1.4 Microcomputer, Radio Shack, TRS-80 (Courtesy of Tandy Corp.)

PURPOSE AND PLAN

As noted above, the programming language BASIC (*B*eginners *A*ll-purpose *S*ymbolic *I*nstruction *C*ode) is used with both minicomputers and microcomputers. It is also the language most commonly used in terminal-oriented timesharing environments. This book introduces the student to the BASIC language, one step at a time. The early chapters introduce simple programming concepts that, when applied, will build up the student's confidence and his ability to go on. In this way BASIC is easy to learn. If the time is taken to study each chapter and to do the many exercises at the end of each one, the student can easily move forward.

ANSI BASIC

The BASIC language discussed in this text conforms to the specifications as stated in the *American National Standard for Minimal BASIC,* X3.60-1978*. Chapters 2–9 and the first part of Chapter 10 represent minimal BASIC. There are 26 keywords in minimal BASIC. They are: BASE, DATA, DEF, DIM, END, FOR, GO, GOSUB, GOTO, IF, INPUT, LET, NEXT, ON, OPTION, PRINT, RANDOMIZE, READ, REM, RESTORE, RETURN, STEP, STOP, SUB, THEN, and TO.

Other topics treated in Chapters 10–14 are extensions of the BASIC language. They may differ from system to system. Many of these differences are noted throughout the text. Students are advised to refer to the appropriate system manual so that they can understand any differences encountered.

Developing a Program

In order to develop a program and get it to work correctly, a series of steps should be followed. These steps are outlined below.

1. Defining the Problem. What is the task to be done? What information and data must I collect to do the specified task? What is the output required?
2. Planning. Break the problem down into small components. Think about the steps that have to be taken to solve it. Develop a rough flowchart to show the sequence of the steps to be taken.

* The purpose of the standard is "to promote the interchangeability of BASIC programs among a variety of automatic data processing systems" (p. 7). It is published by the American National Standards Institute, 1430 Broadway, New York, N.Y. 10018.

3. Coding. Use BASIC statements to write out the step-by-step instructions needed in your program.

4. Desk checking. Go over your program, checking for errors and "bugs." There are two types of errors that can affect the execution of your program. These are syntax errors and logic errors. A syntax error might be a misspelled BASIC keyword or a missing punctuation mark. Such errors, if not discovered when desk checking, will be flagged by the computer–in the form of error messages–when you process or run your program. A logic error may involve the incorrect sequence of your program statements or the incorrect formulation of a processing expression. It is important to find these logic errors or others when desk checking, because the computer will not necessarily spot this kind of error. As a result, erroneous output may be produced.

5. Program Testing. Enter your program into the computer and run it. You might use test data for which you already know the answer. In this way you can compare output results with the known answer. Generally, most programs do not run successfully the first time. Possibly all of the errors were not discovered when desk checking. Also, new errors may have developed as you typed your program in. This is a good reason to check over your program before running it.

6. Debugging. While at the terminal, it may be possible to correct errors as indicated by the error messages–as well as to clear up any logic problems. You may cycle back to step 5 until you are satisfied with the results.

7. Documentation. Once the program is complete and runs correctly, it should have support information for anyone else who may use it. This supporting documentation may include a final flowchart showing the sequence and logic of the program, a written description of the program outlining what it does and any special features it has, special instructions for using the program, a listing of the variables used in the program and what each one represents, and so on.

CASE 1.1 The proper pricing of goods or service is essential for a business to be successful. To arrive at a selling price it is a common practice in many businesses to add a markup to the original cost of an item. The markup can be a percent of the item cost, sufficient to provide a satisfactory profit after covering all expenses. A program can be written to derive the selling price of an item as the sum of its cost and markup. Following the steps described above, such a program can be developed as shown.

1. Define the Problem. Write a program to find the selling price of an item, given the item cost and the markup percent.
2. Planning. Let

$$S = \text{selling price}$$
$$C = \text{item cost}$$
$$M = \text{markup percent}$$

then $S = C + M \times C$

Data inputs include values for C and M. Compute the following in sequence:

a. markup $= M \times C$
b. add markup to the cost C
c. derive the result S

What should be printed out? Output could be S, C, and the markup. In what order should it be generated? On the output, print the item cost, markup, and then the selling price.

Should the output have a heading? Form the output as follows:

Item Cost	Markup	Selling Price
—	—	—

The rough flowchart is shown in Figure 1.5. The symbols shown are explained in Figure 1.10.

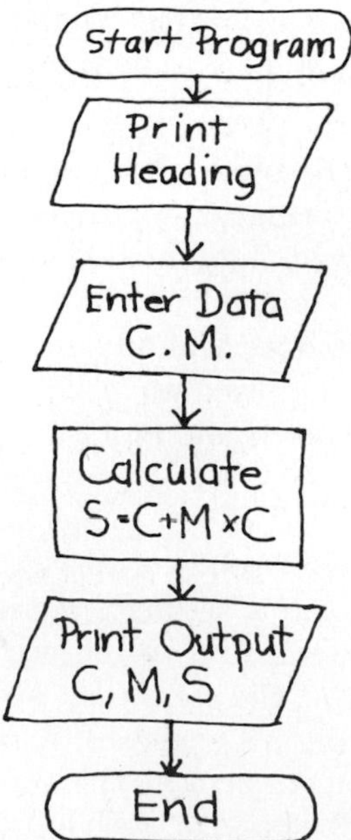

FIGURE 1.5 Case 1.1, Price Markup, Rough Flowchart

```
10 PRINT "ITEM COST", "MARKUP", "SELLING PRICE"
20 READ C, M.
30 LET S = C+M×C
40 PRINT C,M,S
50 END
60 DATA 50%, $35
```

FIGURE 1.6 Case 1.1, Handwritten Price Markup Program

3. Coding. Following the development outlined in step 2, a BASIC program is written. (See Figure 1.6.)
4. Desk Checking. Carefully go over your hand written program looking for syntax and logic errors. The program in Figure 1.6 has the following syntax errors:

30 LET $S = C + M \times C$	$\times$ is not the multiplication symbol; * is.
60 DATA 50%, $35	the symbols % and $ cannot be used with numeric data.

The program also has the following logic errors:

50 END	the END should be the highest line in the program; say, 70 END, and be after the DATA line.
60 DATA 50%, $35	is not logically consistent with line 20 READ C, M. Line 60 should be 60 DATA 35, 50.
60 DATA 50%, $35	in addition to the above error, the value for *M* should be a decimal one of .50 (=50%), not 50.

5. Program Testing. Enter your desk-checked program into the computer using the test data C = \$35, M = 50%, to see if S = \$35 + .50 × \$35 = \$52.50.
Run the program to see if it processes everything correctly. Figure 1.7 shows the above program with the resulting output. Note that the answer is not correct. Why not? Because when the data was entered, 50 percent was typed as 5.0, and not .50.

```
10 PRINT "ITEM COST","MARKUP","SELLING PRICE"
20 READ C,M
30 LET S = C + M*C
40 PRINT C,M,S
60 DATA 35, 5.0
70 END


RUN
ITEM COST        MARKUP          SELLING PRICE
 35               5               210
```

FIGURE 1.7 Program Testing, Case 1.1, Price Markup

6. Debugging. The data entry error has been resolved by correcting line 60, and a new program run was produced. This time the output is correct. (See Figure 1.8.)

```
5 REM PROGRAM FOR PRICE MARKUP
3 REM DEVELOPED 9-27-80 BY J.B. MACEY
10 PRINT "ITEM COST","MARKUP","SELLING PRICE"
15 REM S= SELLING PRICE, C= ITEM COST, M= % MARKUP
20 READ C,M
30 LET S = C + M*C
40 PRINT C,M,S
60 DATA 35, .50
70 END


RUN
ITEM COST      MARKUP          SELLING PRICE
 35             .5              52.5
```

FIGURE 1.8 Final Program, Case 1.1, Price Markup

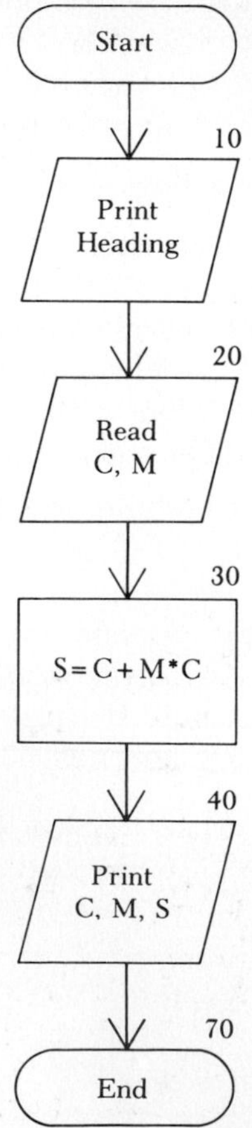

FIGURE 1.9 Flowchart for Program 1.8, Case 1.1, Price Markup

7. Documentation. A flowchart based on the completed program (Figure 1.8) has been produced, as shown in Figure 1.9. Comments in the form of remarks (REM statements) have been added to the program to describe it to other possible users.

FLOWCHARTING

A useful aid in understanding the logic of a program is a diagram showing the logic, called a program flowchart. For simple programs a flowchart is not necessary since the logic is apparent. The more involved the program, the more necessary the flowchart.

Typically, a programmer will make a rough diagram (Figure 1.5) as a flowchart to help with the writing of the program. Ultimately, a final flowchart (Figure 1.9) will be developed showing the logic of the final program. This final flowchart serves as documentation so that at some later date you, or other programmers, can understand the program it represents.

The standard flowcharting symbols used in this book are defined in Figure 1.10. These symbols are part of a set of flowcharting sysmbols adopted by the American National Standards Institute (ANSI) to encourage common practices in program documentation.

STRUCTURED PROGRAMMING

As programs get larger and more involved, the logic of a program often gets so confused that even the programmer is not sure how it works. To encourage good programming techniques, a widely publicized concept, called *structured programming*, has emerged. The objectives of structured programming are to:

1. Increase program clarity by reducing complexity.
2. Reduce program testing time.
3. Increase the programmer's productivity.

These objectives can be accomplished in part by developing a program through logic that is well thought out. Structured programming encourages a *top-down modular approach* when designing a program. This approach is nothing more than good planning. That is, to solve a problem you have to break it down into steps or modules to be performed. A structured program should incorporate these modules by using three basic control patterns, which will be explained in Chapter 7. It is at that point in the text that you will have covered enough material to see how the three control patterns work.

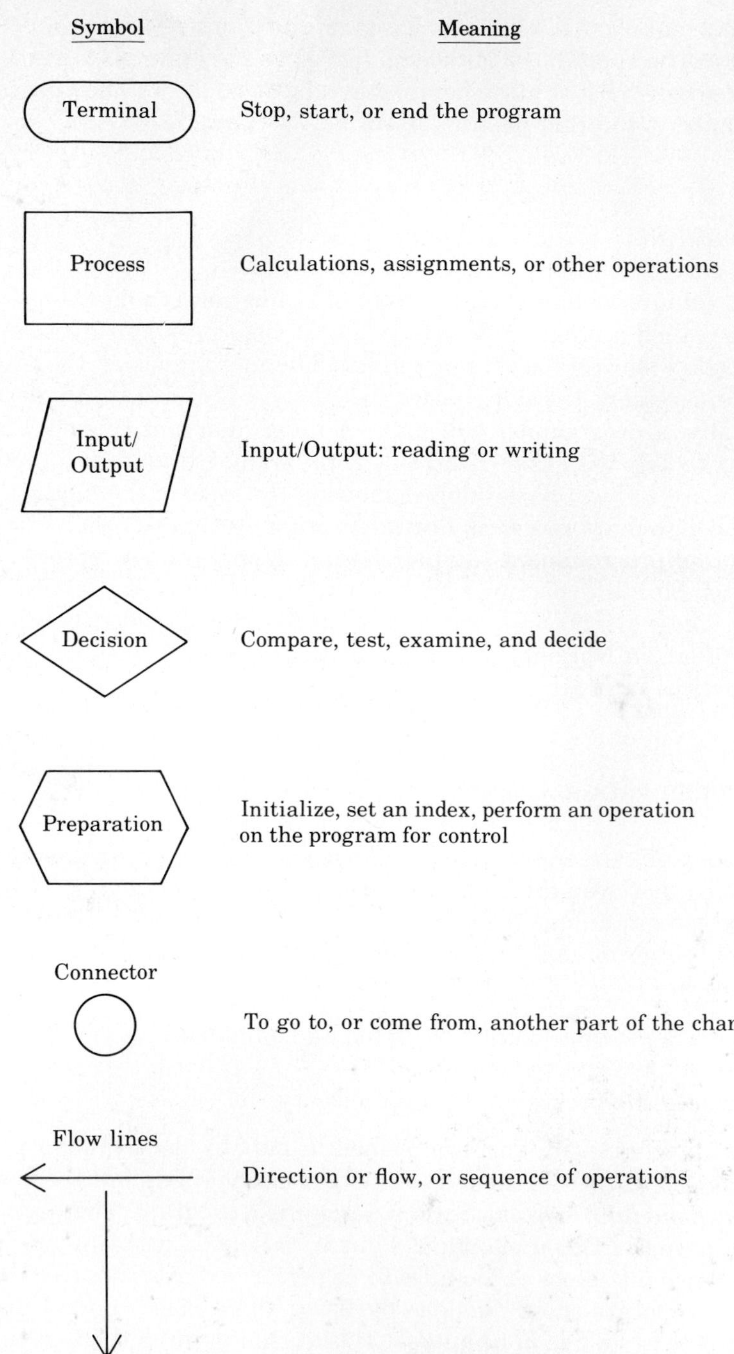

FIGURE 1.10 Flowchart Symbols and Meanings

Not every programming language lends itself completely to the control patterns of structured programming. But even though programming languages such as BASIC and FORTRAN lack some of the features that are suggested by structured programming, it is still possible to write a BASIC program using the ideas of structured programming. Currently, PASCAL and PL/I are the most suitable languages for structured programming.

SUMMARY

In the last twenty-five years, computers have become a common device in government, education, and business. With the development of minicomputers and microcomputers, they have also become "personal" items in the home.

All computers process data by following the steps of a program written in a specific language. The BASIC language first developed for timesharing systems and now widely used in smaller computer systems is an easy one to learn. An indication of the growth in use of the BASIC language is the fact that it is being standardized.

Writing a program requires: defining the problem, planning the sequence, coding, desk checking, testing, and documentation. Structured programming concepts can be used to develop good programming practices.

QUESTIONS

1. What are some applications of computers that you are aware of?
2. Discuss the advantages and disadvantages of timesharing.
3. What is meant by the term *computer program*?
4. What is meant by the terms *hardware* and *software*?
5. Do all computers accept the same programming languages?
6. Why is a "standard" BASIC programming language desirable?
7. What steps should be followed to develop a program?
8. What is a syntax error? a logic error?
9. What is the purpose of program flowcharting?
10. What are the objectives of *structured programming*?

chapter 2

END, PRINT, and REM

You can begin writing programs in the BASIC language almost immediately. Only two statements are required to generate output. This chapter shows how it is possible, with the use of the PRINT and END statements, to start programming. The third statement described in this chapter (REM) does not generate output.

PROGRAM STRUCTURE AND STATEMENT NUMBERS

A program in BASIC consists of a series of statements. Each statement is an instruction that stands alone as a single line. Each line in the program starts with a line number. These numbers are necessary to tell the computer the sequence of the program statements. A simple program illustrating some statements in BASIC and the idea of line numbering is shown in Program 2.1.

PROGRAM 2.1 Line Numbering in a BASIC Program

```
10 REM AN ILLUSTRATION OF A BASIC PROGRAM
20 PRINT "BASIC IS NOT A DIFFICULT LANGUAGE TO LEARN"
30 READ A
40 DATA 573.8
50 PRINT A
60 END
```

Notice that every line in Program 2.1 has a different number. The numbers go from low to high. The available range is from 1 to 99999.* Typically, spacing is suggested when numbering so that additional programming statements can be inserted if necessary. Line numbering such as

1
2
3
4
5

does not allow changes or additions to the program to be made easily. For example, a line cannot be added between lines 3 and 4. If the line numbering had been:

10
20
30
40
50

then a line could be added between existing lines if desired. For example, a line 25 can be inserted between the above lines 20 and 30. Line numbers are integer values only. Each line number is followed by a BASIC statement as shown in Program 2.1.

THE END STATEMENT

Every program written in BASIC must conclude with a statement indicating termination. The END statement does this. It is assigned the highest line number in the program.

The general form of this statement is

line # END

For example, 999 END is a complete END statement.

THE PRINT STATEMENT

The PRINT statement produces printed output. In general this statement can be used within a program in three different ways: (1) labeling and providing headings, (2) carrying out computations where it is not necessary to

*On some systems the range can start at zero: on others the range is larger.

store and identify the computation, and (3) showing the end result of the computation carried out as a separate operation using a LET statement.* In this chapter, only items (1) and (2) will be covered.

The PRINT statement has the general form

$$\text{line \# PRINT} \begin{Bmatrix} \text{labels or headings} \\ \text{computations} \\ \text{values or numbers} \end{Bmatrix}$$

Printing Literals

A literal is an expression, label, heading, or term made up of alphabetic or numeric characters or a combination of both. For example, a description of a part and the number of units in stock could be made up by alphabetic and numeric characters as illustrated by the following:

Alphabetic	*Numeric*	*Combination*
Red Pins: Stock	1458	Red Pins: Stock 1,458

Both alphabetic and numeric literals can be printed by placing the items to be printed in quotes. For example,

5 PRINT "RED PINS:STOCK 1,458"

A numeric can also be printed without being placed in quotes as long as it does not include any special characters such as commas. For example,

5 PRINT 1458

Programs 2.2 through 2.4 illustrate literal printing.

The output for each program is found after the word RUN. This word is a system command that is typed on the computer terminal and causes the program to be executed, that is, to have the program processed by the computer.**

PROGRAM 2.2 Printing Alphabetic Literals

```
5 PRINT "RED PINS:STOCK"
9 END


RUN
RED PINS:STOCK
```

*See Chapter 4.

**Appendix A describes some of the system commands that appear in this text. These commands are generally similar to those in most other systems. It is always a good idea to read the appropriate system manual so that you understand all system commands.

PROGRAM 2.3 Printing Alphabetic and Numeric Literals

```
5 PRINT "RED PINS:STOCK 1,458"
9 END

RUN
RED PINS:STOCK 1,458
```

PROGRAM 2.4 Printing a Numeric Literal without Quotes

```
5 PRINT "RED PINS:STOCK"
7 PRINT 1458
9 END

RUN
RED PINS:STOCK
 1458
```

Program 2.2 shows the alphabetic literal. Program 2.3 presents the combined alphabetic and numeric literal. Program 2.4 illustrates that a numeric does not have to be quoted to be printed.

It is a common error to forget the closing quotes when using the PRINT statement. An error message, such as "ILLEGAL EXPRESSION," may indicate that this has occurred.* Check all PRINT statements if such a message appears.

Blank spaces can improve the appearance of a BASIC program. Since blanks outside of the quotes are ignored by the computer, it would be better from a reading standpoint to have

5 PRINT "XYZ COMPANY FINANCIAL STATEMENT"

rather than

5PRINT"XYZ COMPANY FINANCIAL STATEMENT"

even though both statements are the same to the computer.

Those blanks that are included in the quotes are *not* ignored; they result in a space for each blank as part of the output. To see this effect, refer back to Programs 2.2 and 2.3 and the resulting output.

CONSTANTS

A *constant* is a value that remains fixed. Many computations use formulas that incorporate constant values. For example, compound interest is found

*After running a program, you may find that the output contains a message indicating that something is wrong with your program. Such error messages direct you to correct whatever is wrong. Since messages differ from system to system, the system manual should be studied for the appropriate error messages and their meanings.

using the formula $A = P(1 + r)^n$, where P is the principal or starting amount, r is the interest rate, n is the number of time periods, and A is the final result. The "1" in this formula is a constant. Examples of what constants can look like in BASIC are:

−6.345	.005214	3.1416
105138	2.71828	2

Program 2.5 illustrates the use of the above compound interest formula (with constants in the formula) to determine the total cost of a $3000 loan, at 9 percent interest, compounded yearly for 6 years.

PROGRAM 2.5 Finding Compound Interest: Constant Values

```
10 LET A = 3000*(1.0 + .09)↑6
20 PRINT A
30 END
```

When processing numerical data in BASIC, leading plus and minus signs and decimal points appropriate to the numbers being used are acceptable. Here are some unacceptable data values:

$100	... the dollar sign is not permitted
−58.32.6	... two decimal points are not allowed
4,365	... a comma between characters is not allowed
228−	... the minus sign should not be at the end

E Format

When values are printed out, they are generally limited to six character spaces, plus a decimal point if required.* For numbers that exceed these space limits, the *E format* may result. This scientific format indicates that the number to the left of the *E* should be multiplied by 10 raised to the power of the number after the *E*. For example, the value 2,000,000 in *E* format is 2.0*E*6. The interpretation, 2×10^6, tells us to multiply the 2 times 10 raised to the 6th power, which is the same as adding six zeros after the 2 to give 2,000,000.

If the *E* format is positive, to return to the full value equivalent move the decimal point to the right the number of places shown after the *E*. So for 2.0*E*6 we have

2.000000.

in which the decimal point is moved to the right six places. A value such as .00000456 in *E* format would be expressed as 4.56*E*−6. The *E* followed by

*Space limits differ from system to system.

a minus sign means that the value on the left is divided by 10 raised to the power to the right of the minus sign. In this example we have

$$\frac{4.56}{10^6} \quad \text{or} \quad \frac{4.56}{10000000}$$

To return from an E minus format to the full decimal equivalent, move the decimal point to the left the number of places indicated by the number after the E minus. So for $4.56E-6$ we have

$$.000004.56$$

where the decimal point is moved to the left six places.

Numerical data in E form can be included in a PRINT statement. Program 2.6 shows data in line 5 that is in E form; lines 10 and 20 show data that are very large and very small in value. The output illustrates what happens when these types of data are printed. A blank space after the E occurs in place of a "+" sign, which is not printed,

PROGRAM 2.6 Printing with *E* Format

```
5 PRINT 5.5E4,.283E-2
10 PRINT 1000000,2500000
20 PRINT .0000456,.052146721
99 END

RUN
 55000             .00283
 1E 6              2.5E 6
 4.56E-5           5.21467E-2
```

COMPUTATIONAL OPERATIONS

To direct the computer to perform a computation, the symbols for such computation must be used. These symbols in BASIC are as follows:

Operation	BASIC Symbol	Arithmetic Examples	BASIC
Exponentiation	↑	$X^2, 17^{1/2}$	X↑2,17↑.5
Multiplication	*	$A \times B, 2.14 \times D$	A*B,2.14*D
Division	/	$\frac{50}{Z}, L \div M$	50/Z,L/M
Addition	+	$A + B + C, 15 + X$	A+B+C, 15+X
Subtraction	−	$X - Y, B - 1.5$	X−Y,B−1.5

Besides knowing the symbols for computations, the programmer must know how expressions are evaluated by the computer. The order of priority is to do first any exponentiations; second any multiplications or divisions; and third any additions or subtractions. An expression is evaluated from left to right, following the order just described. Some examples are:

Expression	BASIC	Sequence of Operation
1. $A^2 - B + 4$	A↑2−B+4	[1] [2] [3] A↑2−B+4
2. $X + Y^2/Z^3$	X + Y↑2/Z↑3	[4] [1] [3] [2] X + Y↑2/Z↑3
3. $3/P - A \times C$	3/P − A*C	[1] [3] [2] 3/P − A*C

Notice in example 1 that subtraction is done before the addition. This sequence is because they are on the same level and, going from left to right, whichever comes first is done first.

In example 2, going from left to right and by order of priority, the exponentiation operations are carried out first and second, the division third, and the addition last. In example 3, going from left to right, the division is done first, the multiplication next, and the subtraction last.

Another concept that needs to be understood is the use of parentheses, or brackets, in an expression. Operations that are placed within parentheses will be performed before those that are not in parentheses. The sequencing described above will still apply to items in the parentheses. Below are several examples:

Expression	BASIC	Sequence
1. $a^2 + \frac{b}{2a}$	A↑2+B/(2*A)	[2] [4] [3] [1] A↑2+B/(2*A)
2. $P \times (1 + r)^n$	P*(1+R)↑N	[3] [1] [2] P*(1+R)↑N
3. $(2 + X) \times (Y - 4)$	(2+X)*(Y−4)	[1] [3] [2] (2+X)*(Y−4)
4. $K \times \frac{(L + M)^2}{4}$	K*((L+M)↑2/4)	[4] [1] [2] [3] K*((L+M)↑2/4)

Notice in each example that if the parentheses were not present the sequence of evaluation would change. Here is what the interpretation by the computer would be:

1. $a^2 + \frac{b}{2} \times a$
2. $P \times 1 + r^n$
3. $2 + X \times Y - 4$
4. $K \times L + \frac{M^2}{4}$

Each expression is now something very different from the original form.

Note that in the earlier BASIC example 4, K*((L+M)↑2/4), the items L+M that are contained within parentheses are themselves within parentheses. This inner expression L+M is evaluated first, followed by the remaining items within the outer parentheses.

Computational Printing

The PRINT statement can be used to direct the computer to perform computations. All of the symbols and operations described above can be incorporated in a PRINT statement. Programs 2.7–2.9 demonstrate computational printing using the information from Case 2.1.

CASE 2.1 The tax on sales in a certain state is 5 percent of the total value of the items purchased. Suppose two items were purchased for $5 and $10, respectively.

PROGRAM 2.7 A Single Computational PRINT Statement

```
2 PRINT (5+10)*.05
10 END


RUN
 .75
```

The output of Program 2.7 is a result of the computation performed based on line 2 of the program. Only the tax on the total is printed out. Note the use of parentheses to ensure the addition is carried out first, then followed by the multiplication.

Typically, the output desired has headings or labels. Programs 2.8 and 2.9 show how headings and labels can be printed. Observe that both programs show that more than one computation is possible in the PRINT statement (line 40).

PROGRAM 2.8 Printing Headings, Multiple PRINT Computations

```
10 PRINT "TOTAL","TAX"
20 PRINT "SALES","TOTAL"
40 PRINT (5+10),(5+10)*.05
50 END

RUN
TOTAL          TAX
SALES          TOTAL
 15             .75
```

PROGRAM 2.9 Underlining Headings, Multiple PRINT Computations

```
10 PRINT "TOTAL","TAX"
20 PRINT "SALES","TOTAL","GRAND TOTAL"
30 PRINT "-----------------------------------------------"
40 PRINT (5+10),(5+10)*.05,(5+10)+(5+10)*.05
50 END

RUN
TOTAL          TAX
SALES          TOTAL          GRAND TOTAL
-----------------------------------------------
 15             .75            15.75
```

Observe that none of the computations carried out with the PRINT statement in Programs 2.8 and 2.9 has quotes around it. A computation placed in quotes would result in the quoted expression being treated as a literal, not a computation.

Many times a computer output should have blank lines to improve the appearance of the output. Such a blank line can be obtained by inserting a PRINT statement as shown in Program 2.10, line 60.

PROGRAM 2.10 Skipping Lines Using the PRINT Statement

```
20 PRINT "TOTAL SALES"
40 PRINT "------------"
60 PRINT
80 PRINT "    $";(5+10+20)
90 END

RUN
TOTAL SALES
------------

    $ 35
```

For every blank PRINT in a program, a line is skipped. By properly inserting these PRINT statements, as many lines as desired may be skipped.

OUTPUT SPACING

A timesharing terminal output page commonly has a capacity of 75 character spaces between the left and right margins. When a PRINT statement indicates that more than one item will be printed on a line, the spacing is regulated by the computer. Two punctuation marks can be used in the PRINT statement to control how the output is spaced. These punctuation marks are the comma and the semicolon.

The Comma

In a PRINT statement, the comma sets the spacing at a field width of 15 spaces.* If you look back at the output of Programs 2.8 and 2.9, you will see spacing based on the commas in lines 10, 20, and 40 of both programs. In each program the literal headings and computational prints have been separated by commas.

With 75 character spaces to a line, the use of the comma permits up to five fields of 15 spaces for output. Program 2.11 has generated output that shows all five print fields being used.

PROGRAM 2.11 Print Field Positions Using Commas

```
5 PRINT "PRINT POSITION SHOWN BY NUMBERS BELOW"
10 PRINT
20 PRINT"1234567890123456789012345678901234567890123456789012345678901"
30 PRINT"FIELD 1","FIELD 2","FIELD 3","FIELD 4","FIELD 5"
40 END

RUN
PRINT POSITION SHOWN BY NUMBERS BELOW

1234567890123456789012345678901234567890123456789012345678901
FIELD 1        FIELD 2        FIELD 3        FIELD 4        FIELD 5
```

The output from Program 2.11 shows the location of each of the five print fields. This can be summarized as follows:

Print Field	From Left Margin Starting Position
1	1
2	16
3	31
4	46
5	61

*Some systems may set spacing in a slightly smaller or slightly larger field width.

Literals and negative values will be printed starting in these positions. Positive values are printed one space farther to the right to allow for the fact that a + sign was not printed (but can be assumed). The output of Program 2.9 illustrates where literals and numerics have their starting positions.

It may be desired to skip a field so as to have output spaced across the entire page. Such field skipping can be accomplished by using a blank quote as shown in line 5 of Program 2.12.

PROGRAM 2.12 Skipping Fields

```
5 PRINT "FIELD 1"," ","FIELD 3"," ","FIELD 5"
10 END

RUN
FIELD 1                         FIELD 3                         FIELD 5
```

The quoted blank for field skipping will work on all systems. ANSI BASIC will also permit field skipping without a quoted blank, using only the comma as a field spacer. For example:

5 PRINT "FIELD 1",,"FIELD 3",,"FIELD 5"

will produce the same result as line 5 of Program 2.12.

An additional feature of the comma is its use as a means of continuing output printing on one line even though two or more PRINT statements are used in a program. If a PRINT statement ends with a "dangling comma," the output will not advance to the next line. Instead, the output of the next PRINT statement will follow on the same line as the preceding output. This continuation is shown in Program 2.13.

PROGRAM 2.13 Commas at the End of a PRINT Statement

```
5 PRINT "GROSS WAGE",
10 PRINT "+ OVERTIME",
15 PRINT "= TOTAL WAGE",
20 PRINT "- TAXES",
25 PRINT "= NET WAGE"
99 END

RUN
GROSS WAGE      + OVERTIME      = TOTAL WAGE    - TAXES         = NET WAGE
```

Observe that the output from Program 2.13 is spaced in conformance with the five print field positions described earlier.

The Semicolon

The semicolon, when used in a PRINT statement between positive numerical data, will result in two blank spaces being placed between the printed output.* One blank is from the semicolon, the other represents the positive sign. If a semicolon is followed by a negative numeric, only one blank space will result. Using the semicolon instead of the comma enables output to be "packed" on a line. This packing can be seen in the output of Program 2.14. Line 25 of the program shows various numerical values separated by semicolons.

PROGRAM 2.14 Printing Packed Output Using the Semicolon

```
25 PRINT 1;2;3;4;5;6;7;8;9;10;100;2000;-888;12.6+83
99 END

RUN
 1  2  3  4  5  6  7  8  9  10  100  2000 -888  95.6
```

Program 2.15 shows a mixture of commas and semicolons in PRINT statements.

PROGRAM 2.15 Mixing Commas and Semicolons

```
5 PRINT 100/2;100/3,100/4;100/5
10 PRINT 100/2,100/3;100/4;100/5
99 END

RUN
 50  33.3333      25  20
 50              33.3333  25  20
```

When used with literals the semicolon does *not* provide extra spacing. The effect of a semicolon between literals is the same as using a hyphen in a word break at the end of a line. If the semicolon is at the end of a PRINT statement, the output paper will not advance. Program 2.16 shows the "dangling semicolon" at the end of line 10 with the resulting output. Program 2.17 shows what can happen to the output when the dangling semicolon is used between literals. Extra spacing is needed to make the output correct. Such spacing is supplied by using blanks within the quotes as shown in line 20 and 30 of Program 2.18.

*Not all systems follow these spacing patterns. On some, no space is inserted between numbers.

PROGRAM 2.16 Semicolon at the End of a PRINT Statement

```
10 PRINT "THERE ARE FIFTY STATES IN THE UNITED STATES OF A";
20 PRINT "MERICA."
99 END


RUN
THERE ARE FIFTY STATES IN THE UNITED STATES OF AMERICA.
```

PROGRAM 2.17 The Semicolon between Literals

```
10 PRINT "BETWEEN LITERALS";"THE SEMICOLON";
20 PRINT "DOES NOT PROVIDE SPACING."
99 END
RUN
BETWEEN LITERALSTHE SEMICOLONDOES NOT PROVIDE SPACING.
```

PROGRAM 2.18 The Semicolon between Literals with Spacing

```
10 PRINT "TO USE THE ; WITH LITERALS";
20 PRINT " YOU CAN PROVIDE";
30 PRINT " THE EXTRA SPACES NEEDED."
99 END


RUN
TO USE THE ; WITH LITERALS YOU CAN PROVIDE THE EXTRA SPACES NEEDED.
```

To understand the spacing that results when literals and numerics are separated by semicolons, study Program 2.19. A literal followed by either numerics or a computation, and separated by a semicolon, will be printed out with a single space after the literal if the numeric/computation is positive, and no space if negative. A numeric/computation before a literal, separated by a semicolon, will provide a single space between the printed output.

PROGRAM 2.19 The Semicolon between Literals and Numerics

```
10 PRINT "ENDING INVENTORY";200-15;"UNITS"
99 END


RUN
ENDING INVENTORY 185 UNITS
```

THE REM STATEMENT

Very often it is desired to provide statements within the written program that spell out in some detail the purpose of the program, as well as describe what various sections are supposed to do. These remark, or REM, statements are part of program documentation. This kind of documentation is useful to the programmer and to others who want to review and better understand the program.

Lines 5, 10, and 30 in Program 2.20 illustrate how comments are put into a program by using REM statements. The output is not affected by these statements, because they are ignored by the computer.

PROGRAM 2.20 REM Statements in a Program

```
5 REM THIS PROGRAM WAS WRITTEN BY B. BOSWORTH IN BASIC
10 REM IT ILLUSTRATES SOME ASPECTS OF PRINTING.
20 PRINT "SALES TAX IS";5;"% OF TOTAL"
30 REM COMPUTATIONAL PRINT IN LINE 40.
40 PRINT "TOTAL $";25+30+5.15
99 END


RUN
SALES TAX IS 5 % OF TOTAL
TOTAL $ 60.15
```

Program 2.21, using the information in Case 2.2, illustrates the many things that the PRINT statement can do.

CASE 2.2 The annual interest on corporate bonds is found as follows:

$$\text{Annual interest} = \text{par value} \times \text{annual interest rate}$$

An investor having the following bonds would use such a formula to compute the interest on each bond.

Total Par Value	Interest Rate
\$4000	6¼%
7000	7⅝
3000	6½
8000	8⅛

Program 2.21 calculates the interest for each bond in Case 2.2. Later on we will see that it is possible to solve problems like the above with less involved PRINT statements.

PROGRAM 2.21 Case 2.2, Computing Bond Interest with PRINT

```
5 REM PROGRAM TO COMPUTE BOND INTEREST
10 PRINT "    TOTAL","INTEREST"," ANNUAL"
15 PRINT "PAR VALUE"," RATE","INTEREST"
20 PRINT "---------------------------------------"
30 PRINT "$4000","6 1/4%","$";4000*.0625
40 PRINT "$7000","7 5/8%","$";7000*.07625
50 PRINT "$3000","6 1/2%","$";3000*.065
60 PRINT "$8000","8 1/8%","$";8000*.08125
90 END

RUN
  TOTAL          INTEREST        ANNUAL
PAR VALUE         RATE          INTEREST
---------------------------------------
$4000          6 1/4%          $ 250
$7000          7 5/8%          $ 533.75
$3000          6 1/2%          $ 195.
$8000          8 1/8%          $ 650
```

SUMMARY

A program in BASIC consists of statements. Each starts with a line number. Every BASIC program must have an END statement. It must have the highest line number in the program.

PRINT statements can generate alphabetic, numeric, and alphanumeric output. They can also perform computations. Output is printed from the left margin.

When directing the computer to perform computations, the following rules should be understood:

1. Higher order operations are done before lower order ones. The order of priority is (1) exponentiation, (2) multiplication and division, (3) addition and subtraction.
2. Expressions are evaluated from left to right.
3. Operations within parentheses are performed before those outside parentheses according to the order priority in rule 1.
4. With multiple parentheses, the order of evaluation starts with the innermost parentheses and proceeds outward.

Commas in a PRINT statement will typically generate output spacing in five fields of 15 character spaces each. A comma at the end of a PRINT statement will not advance the output to the next line if space is available on the current line. The next PRINT statement will use any available space and then continue to a new line if it is needed.

Semicolons in a PRINT statement leave:

1. One blank space if placed after a numeric and before a numeric or a quoted item.
2. No blank spaces if placed after a quoted item and before another quoted item or a numeric.

Remarks in the form of REM statements provide comments and descriptions (documentation) about a program. They can be placed anywhere in the program. They do not generate output.

EXERCISES

* 2.1 For the information listed, write a PRINT statement in BASIC that generates one line of output.
a. Earnings for 3rd Quarter
b. In field two, Division; in field four, Sales.
c. A heading with each item in a separate field; name, social security number, date of birth, number or dependents.

2.2 The following PRINT statements contain errors; correct them.
a. 10 PRINT "FINANCIAL REPORT
b. 20 "PRINT INVENTORY LEVEL"
c. 30 "JANUARY"
d. "40 PRINT CURRENT ASSETS"
e. PRINT "HELP"
f. PRINT 279, UNITS
g. 50 PRINT 10 + 62.5 =
h. 60 PRINT 20(485,000)

* 2.3 Convert these values from E format:
a. .528 $E-5$
b. .0153$E-5$
c. 4.68 $E6$
d. 3.41791$E-02$
e. 7531$E7$
f. $-1.23658E-02$

* 2.4 Write and run a program that will show your name, address, and course number.

2.5 Which of the following constants are acceptable in BASIC?
a. $-.00567$
b. $+8.1302$
c. 1,281.3
d. 2.61$-E3$
e. 161.00
f. +$28.56
g. $+28.56
h. -459176

2.6 Write the following expressions using BASIC notations:
a. $\frac{1}{2}bh$
b. $b^2 - 4ac$
c. $P(r + 1)^n$
d. t^{2n+2}
e. $6XY$
f. $X^2 + 2XY + Y^2$
g. $g - n + K$
h. $.80^5$
i. $-0.2X^3 + 10X$
j. $.35X \div 200$

* 2.7 Rewrite each of the following expressions in BASIC symbols and notation. Solve the expressions manually for the values $a = 5$, $b = 3$, $c = 4$, $d = 2$:

a. $\frac{b-2}{d+a}$ d. $a(b+1)^d$ g. $-abc^d$

b. $c^2 - \frac{b}{2+a}$ e. $\frac{2a}{b+d} - \frac{a-b}{d^2}$ h. $\frac{(-abc)^d}{5d}$

c. $\frac{b}{3} - ac$ f. $5^d - \frac{a}{-b+c}$

2.8 Use the digits in your social security number as data. Write and run a program that will:
a. print out the number.
b. sum up the digits of the number.
c. calculate the average of all the digits.
d. show the sum of all the digits squared.

2.9 Sales are \$5, \$10, and \$15. The tax rate is 5 percent. Write a program using the PRINT statement that when it runs has the output under the following heading:

Sales	Tax	Total

* 2.10 Redo *exercise 2.9* with "\$" signs in the output.

2.11 Redo *exercise 2.10* with the output in the following format:

Sales	\$	\$	\$
Tax	\$	\$	\$
Total	\$	\$	\$

2.12 The area of a triangle is found by using the expression ½ *bh*, where *b* is the base dimension and *h* is the height of the triangle. Write a program to find the area for each of the following triangles:

Base	Height
5	7
10.5	6.2
100	78

Your output should have labels for all the variables and the areas found.

2.13 To find the roots of an equation, $aX^2 + bX + c$, the quadratic formula can be used. That is,

$$X = \frac{-b \pm (b^2 - 4ac)^{1/2}}{2a}$$

Suppose $a = 2$, $b = 5$, and $c = 3$; write a program that uses this formula to get the roots of the equation with these values.

2.14 Redo *exercise 2.13* so that the output shows all values a, b, c, and X with labels.

* 2.15 Write a program using the computational PRINT to evaluate each of the following expressions, given that $a = 3$, $b = 6$, and $c = 3$:

a. $a + \frac{b}{c}$ c. $\frac{(a + b)^2}{c}$

b. $\frac{a + b}{c}$ d. $a^2 + \frac{b}{c}$

2.16 Redo *exercise 2.15* so that the output shows each of the expressions that were evaluated, the values used, and the final answer.

2.17 Many marketing promotions consist of computerized letters sent through the mail. Write a program that generates the following letter:

Today's Date

Dear Student:

Stop by the computer lab for a demonstration of the timesharing equipment being used. Before coming, please read the chapters in in the text that I have assigned. Looking forward to seeing you in the lab.

____

Your Instructor

2.18 Revise *exercise 2.12* to include REM statements describing the program.

2.19 In accounting, one measure of a company's financial condition is the current ratio. This ratio is computed as current assets divided by current liabilities. Below are several years of data for the GIGO Computer Company, Inc.:

	1978	1979	1980
Current assets	$370,000	$400,000	$450,000
Current liabilities	160,000	100,000	150,000

Write a program that will output this data as well as the current ratio for each year. Have the current ratio appear on a line below the current liabilities for each of the years shown.

2.20 Redo *exercise 2.19* so that output follows this format:

Year	Assets	Current Liabilities	Ratio
1978			
1979			
1980			

2.21 A firm estimates that 5 years from now it will need $2 million to purchase some new equipment. To accumulate this sum, the firm decides to set aside an amount each year. The firm can earn 9 percent compounded annually on their cash. To find the amount that must be deposited at the end of each of the 5 years to accumulate the $2 million, the following formula is used:

$$A = F\left[\frac{r}{(1 + r)^n - 1}\right]$$

where A is the amount to be deposited at the end of n years, with the annual interest rate of r, and F is the future sum needed. Write a program that will find A. Include REM statements in your program. In addition to A, have the output show F, r, and n.

chapter 3

READ/DATA, RESTORE, and INPUT

Chapter 2 showed how the PRINT statement can be used to generate specific output based on numeric data that is placed in PRINT statements. Only limited amounts of data can be placed into a program using the PRINT statement. To enter larger amounts of data into a program the READ/DATA statements can be used. In this chapter, we will see how numerical data can be entered into a BASIC program and assigned to variables by means of the READ/DATA and INPUT statements.

BASIC VARIABLES

A *variable* represents a value that is not fixed. In the compound interest formula shown earlier, the components P, r, and n represent factors that can change and thus are variables. For compound interest we may want to find the value of A for numerous sets of variables P, r, and n. For example,

P	r	n
$1000	5%	5 years
2000	6	10
4000	8	12

In BASIC any single alphabetic letter from *A* to *Z*, or any alphabetic letter followed by a numeric value from 0 (zero) to 9, may be used to specify a variable. This gives a total of 286 possibilities for variable names: 26 single letters, plus 10 times 26 combinations of *A*0 to *A*9, . . . , *Z*0 to *Z*9. Some examples of acceptable variable names are:

A	*B*	*X*	*Z*3	*B*2
*C*9	*F*1	*D*5	*X*7	*M*8

Some unacceptable variable names are:

5*X*	. . . alphabetic character must be first
*A*22	. . . only a single numeric is allowed
JOE	. . . only a single alphabetic is allowed
B−	. . . either a single alphabetic or an alphabetic followed by a numeric is permitted

Program 3.1 shows how the compound interest for many sets of variables can be found. The above values for *P, r,* and *n* are used.

PROGRAM 3.1 Finding Compound Interest Using Variables

```
10 READ P,R,N
20 DATA 1000,.05,5,2000,.06,10
30 DATA 4000,.08,12
40 LET A = P*(1.0 + R)↑N
50 PRINT A
60 GO TO 10
70 END
```

Note that the variables in BASIC, as well as the words in each line of Program 3.1, are capitalized. This is because most computer systems will print only with uppercase letters. Therefore, throughout this book all BASIC programs and examples will be in uppercase letters. When you write a BASIC program, all letters should be capitalized.

THE READ AND DATA STATEMENTS

The general forms for the READ and DATA statements follow:

line # READ variable name list
line # DATA data list

Each variable name except the last in the READ statement is followed by a comma. No punctuation is required at the end of the READ statement. The DATA statement has items separated by commas and, like the READ statement, requires no ending punctuation.

Program 3.2 illustrates the READ/DATA statements. The READ A, B in line 10 will cause the value in line 15 to be assigned to the variables *A* and *B*, respectively. Variable *A* will take on the value 5, and variable *B* will take on the value 10.

PROGRAM 3.2 READ/DATA Statements

```
5 REM THIS PROGRAM ADDS TWO NUMBERS
10 READ A,B
15 DATA 5,10
40 PRINT "A=";A;"B=";B,"SUM=";A+B
99 END


RUN
A= 5 B= 10         SUM= 15
```

The variable names and items in READ/DATA statements have to be matched on a sequential one-for-one basis. Thus if we have three values, we could write three variable names:

10 READ X, Y, Z
20 DATA 10, −6, 5.2

X is set equal to 10, *Y* is set equal to −6, and *Z* is set equal to 5.2. If there was additional data in line 20, say

20 DATA 10, −6, 5.2, 16, 38

the values 16 and 38 would not be read, since only three variables are specified in line 10. If the data was

20 DATA 10, −6

the program execution would terminate, since the data set has only two items while the READ requests values for three variables. An "OUT OF DATA LINE 10" message would appear as output.* Program 3.3 illustrates what happens when the program has excess data or insufficient data.

PROGRAM 3.3 Excess Data and Insufficient Data

Excess Data

```
5 PRINT "X","Y","Z"
10 READ X,Y,Z
15 DATA 10,-6,5.2,16,38
20 PRINT X,Y,Z
99 END


RUN
X              Y              Z
 10            -6              5.2
```

Insufficient Data

```
5 PRINT "X","Y","Z"
10 READ X,Y,Z
15 DATA 10,-6
20 PRINT X,Y,Z
99 END


RUN
X              Y              Z

OUT OF DATA- LN #  10
```

*This output is not true of all systems. Check your system manual to see what the output would be.

Program 3.4 shows various READ/DATA statement arrangements. Since the computer matches variables and data on a sequential one-for-one basis, breaking up the READ and DATA statements as shown in Programs 3.4b, 3.4c, and 3.4d does not change the output.

PROGRAM 3.4 READ/DATA Statement Arrangements

(a)
```
10 READ A,B,C
15 DATA 5, -7, 9
20 PRINT A,B,C
40 END

RUN
 5             -7             9
```

(b)
```
5 READ A
10 READ B
20 READ C
30 DATA 5, -7, 9
35 PRINT A,B,C
40 END

RUN
 5             -7             9
```

(c)
```
10 READ A,B
15 DATA 5, -7
20 READ C
25 DATA 9
30 PRINT A,B,C
40 END

RUN
 5             -7             9
```

(d)
```
10 READ A,B,C
20 DATA 5,-7
30 DATA 9
35 PRINT A,B,C
40 END

RUN
 5             -7             9
```

As seen in Program 3.4, the DATA statement can be placed either before or after the READ statement, as long as it is before the END statement. This point is made in Program 3.5. The output for Program 3.5a–d is the same, regardless of where the DATA statement is located. If the data list is to be changed, it is easier to have the data in statements just before the END statement (Program 3.5c).

PROGRAM 3.5 Positions of the DATA Statement

(a)
```
5 REM DATA BEFORE READ
10 DATA 15,6,7
20 READ A,A1,A2
30 PRINT A,A1,A2
40 END

RUN
 15            6              7
```

(b)
```
5 REM DATA IMMEDIATELY AFTER READ
20 READ A,A1,A2
25 DATA 15,6,7
30 PRINT A,A1,A2
40 END

RUN
 15            6              7
```

(c)
```
5 REM DATA JUST BEFORE THE END
20 READ A,A1,A2
30 PRINT A,A1,A2
35 DATA 15,6,7
40 END

RUN
 15            6              7
```

(d)
```
5 REM DATA BEFORE AND AFTER READ
10 DATA 15
15 READ A,A1,A2
20 DATA 6
30 PRINT A,A1,A2
35 DATA 7
40 END

RUN
 15            6              7
```

Printing a variable before a value has been assigned to it can on some systems result in an error message such as "UNDEFINED VARIABLE IN LINE #." On some systems undefined variables are assigned a value of zero. Program 3.6 illustrates the printing of an undefined variable, A, in line 10.

PROGRAM 3.6 Printing an Undefined Variable

```
5 DATA 331
10 PRINT A
15 READ A
40 END

RUN
 0
```

Since the computer retains only the current value of a variable, a PRINT statement with a variable in it will result in output for the current value of the variable. Program 3.7 illustrates this point. Line 10 of the program reads variable A twice, first assigning $A = 7$, and then $A = 3$. When line 20 (the PRINT statement) is executed, the value of A that is printed out is 3, as shown by the output.

PROGRAM 3.7 Printing the Current Value

```
10 READ A,B,C,A
20 PRINT A;B;C;A
30 DATA 7,9,6,3
40 END

RUN
 3  9  6  3
```

In the previous chapter, numerical data in *E* form were introduced. Such data in *E* form can be assigned to variables in the same way ordinary data values are. Program 3.8 illustrates this point. Line 10 of the program reads values that are in the *E* form from the data list in line 20. Line 30 will print out the value in *E* form if it exceeds six character spaces; otherwise the output result is an ordinary numerical value.

PROGRAM 3.8 Data in *E* Form

```
10 READ A,B,C,D
20 DATA 1E 5, 4.56E-2,  2.5E 8, .65E 4
30 PRINT A,B,C,D
40 END

RUN
 100000         .0456           2.5E 8          6500
```

The use of the READ/DATA statements in a programming application is shown in Program 3.9. This program is based on Case 3.1.

CASE 3.1 Total profit is found by subtracting total cost from total revenue. Total revenue is found by multiplying revenue per unit (price) times the number of units sold; and total cost is obtained by multiplying the cost of each unit sold times the number of units sold. Symbolically, we can write $T = P \times U - C \times U$.

Program 3.9 obtains the total revenue, total cost, and total profit if the selling price per unit is $10, cost per unit is $6.50, and 225 units are sold.

PROGRAM 3.9 Case 3.1, Finding Total Profit, READ/DATA Statements

```
5 REM PROGRAM TO FIND TOTAL PROFITS.  TOTAL PROFITS = TOTAL REVENUE -
1Ø REM TOTAL COST.  WHERE P=PRICE PER UNIT, C=COST PER UNIT,
15 REM AND U=# UNITS SOLD AND BOUGHT
3Ø READ P,C,U
4Ø DATA 1Ø,6.5Ø,225
65 PRINT
68 PRINT
7Ø PRINT "TOTAL PROFIT REPORT"
75 PRINT
8Ø PRINT "NUMBER OF UNITS SOLD";U
85 PRINT "PRICE PER UNIT";P,"COST PER UNIT";C
9Ø PRINT "TOTAL REVENUE";P*U
92 PRINT "LESS TOTAL COST";C*U
95 PRINT "-----------------------------------"
1ØØ PRINT "TOTAL PROFIT";P*U-C*U
199 END


RUN


TOTAL PROFIT REPORT

NUMBER OF UNITS SOLD 225
PRICE PER UNIT 1Ø                 COST PER UNIT 6.5
TOTAL REVENUE 225Ø
LESS TOTAL COST 1462.5
-----------------------------------
TOTAL PROFIT 787.5
```

Program 3.9 demonstrates one advantage of using READ/DATA statements. Specifically, when the program is generalized so that it can be used over and over again—with different sets of data each time—only the data lines have to be changed. If computational PRINT statements were used instead of the READ/DATA statement, such a program would be impractical as well as troublesome to change each time new data had to be used.

THE RESTORE STATEMENT

There are times when it is necessary to reread data previously read in a program. Data once read cannot be read again unless the DATA lines are repeated or a RESTORE statement is used. The RESTORE statement has the form

line # RESTORE

This statement causes the data initially read from storage to be replaced in storage. Program 3.10 shows a simple program using the RESTORE. The data was initially read in and corresponds to the variables *A*, *B*, and *C*. The RESTORE in line 20 restores the data beginning with the first data value in the first data statement, line 10. A partial RESTORE from a point in the data list *after* the first data value is not possible on most computers. Line 25 causes the data 1, 2, 3 to be assigned to the variables *X*, *Y*, and *Z*, respectively.

PROGRAM 3.10 RESTORE Statement

```
1  PRINT "A","B","C"
5  READ A,B,C
10 DATA 1
12 DATA 2,3
15 PRINT A,B,C
16 PRINT
20 RESTORE
22 PRINT "X","Y","Z"
25 READ X,Y,Z
30 PRINT X,Y,Z
99 END

RUN
A              B              C
 1              2              3

X              Y              Z
 1              2              3
```

If the RESTORE was not inserted at line 20, the READ statement at line 25 could not be executed, since no data would be available to read.

In the case that follows, the RESTORE is used to assign a single set of data to a variable list other than the one initially read.

CASE 3.2 A linear equation in two variables is a straight line when plotted on graph paper. Such equations have wide application in business in the areas of price theory, break-even analysis, linear programming, etc. Symbolically linear equations are presented in two general forms

1. $y = mx + b$ where m is the slope, b is a constant, and x is a variable.
2. $y = a + bx$ where b is the slope, a is a constant, and x is a variable.

To show that both forms would produce the same answer for y, we substitute the values of 30, 100, and 20 for the variable x, the constant term, and the slope, respectively.

Program 3.11 computes the value of y for both forms of the linear equation in Case 3.2. Note that the first READ in line 10 assigns 100 to A, 20 to B, and 30 to X. The RESTORE in line 40 makes the data list in line 20 available for the next READ. Line 50, READ B, M only, uses the constant value ($B = 100$) and the slope ($M = 20$). The value for X does not have to be assigned again, since there is to be no change to this variable.

PROGRAM 3.11 Case 3.2, Linear Equations

```
10 READ A,B,X
20 DATA 100,20,30
30 PRINT "Y = A + B*X ="; A+B*X
40 RESTORE
50 READ B,M
60 PRINT "Y = M*X + B ="; M*X+B
90 END

RUN
Y = A + B*X = 700
Y = M*X + B = 700
```

THE INPUT STATEMENT

One of the major advantages of using a terminal is the ability to carry out a "conversation" with the computer via the program being run. Such "conversational programming" permits direct and almost immediate response from the computer. Real time systems, such as airlines reservation systems, use this kind of interactive programming.

To write a program where a dialogue between the terminal user and the computer takes place, the READ/DATA statements are replaced by an INPUT statement. This statement has the form

line # INPUT variable list

A simple program using INPUT is shown in Program 3.12.

PROGRAM 3.12 INPUT Statement

```
10 INPUT A,B
20 PRINT "SUM OF";A;"AND";B;"IS";A+B
99 END

RUN
 ?5,10
SUM OF 5 AND 10 IS 15
```

When the INPUT statement is executed by the computer, a "?" mark appears as the initial output, as shown in Program 3.12. The programmer or program user must then type in the values for A and B. In this case, 5 and 10 are typed in, separated by a comma, and without any ending punctuation.

Note that inputting of data is similar to the placement of data in a DATA statement.

On some systems if the program user fails to type in all of the data as needed to conform to the INPUT statement, an error message will appear, indicating more data is needed. This is shown in Figure 3.1. Figure 3.2 shows what happens when too much data is typed. An error message "INCORRECT FORMAT–RETYPE" has occurred, because the data input does not conform to the variable list in line 10 of Program 3.12. Once the data is typed in and conforms to the variable list, the execution of the program continues as though no error was made.

```
RUN
 ?5

INCORRECT FORMAT - RETYPE--
 ?5,10
SUM OF 5 AND 10 IS 15
```

FIGURE 3.1 Insufficient Data Inputted to Program 3.12

```
RUN
 ?5,10,7

INCORRECT FORMAT - RETYPE--
 ?5,10
SUM OF 5 AND 10 IS 15
```

FIGURE 3.2 Excess Data Inputted to Program 3.12

Since application programs are often used by people other than the programmers who write them, an INPUT statement in a program should be preceded by some statements that will explain to the user the format of the data to be inputted. Otherwise, the "?" could be meaningless to the program user when it appears. Thus the programmer should write additional PRINT statements as shown in Program 3.13, which is a conversational version of Program 3.9.

PROGRAM 3.13 Case 3.1, Finding Total Profit, INPUT Statement

```
5 REM PROGRAM TO FIND TOTAL PROFITS.  TOTAL PROFITS = TOTAL REVENUE -
10 REM TOTAL COST.  WHERE P=PRICE PER UNIT, C=COST PER UNIT,
15 REM AND U=# UNITS SOLD AND BOUGHT.
25 PRINT "TO GENERATE OUTPUT FROM THE TOTAL PROFIT PROGRAM"
30 PRINT "WHEN THE ? APPEARS TYPE AFTER IT THE FOLLOWING ITEMS"
35 PRINT "EACH SEPARATED BY A COMMA:  PRICE PER UNIT, COST PER UNIT,"
38 PRINT "NUMBER OF UNITS SOLD."
39 INPUT P,C,U
65 PRINT
68 PRINT
70 PRINT "TOTAL PROFIT REPORT"
75 PRINT
80 PRINT "NUMBER OF UNITS SOLD";U
85 PRINT "PRICE PER UNIT";P,"COST PER UNIT";C
90 PRINT "TOTAL REVENUE";P*U
92 PRINT "LESS TOTAL COST";C*U
95 PRINT "-----------------------------------"
100 PRINT "TOTAL PROFIT";P*U-C*U
199 END
```

PROGRAM 3.13 continued

```
RUN
TO GENERATE OUTPUT FROM THE TOTAL PROFIT PROGRAM
WHEN THE ? APPEARS TYPE AFTER IT THE FOLLOWING ITEMS
EACH SEPARATED BY A COMMA:  PRICE PER UNIT, COST PER UNIT,
NUMBER OF UNITS SOLD.
 ?10,6.50,225


TOTAL PROFIT REPORT

NUMBER OF UNITS SOLD 225
PRICE PER UNIT 10                COST PER UNIT 6.5
TOTAL REVENUE 2250
LESS TOTAL COST 1462.5
-----------------------------------
TOTAL PROFIT 787.5
```

There is no limit to the number of INPUT statements that can be placed in a program. Multiple INPUTs are possible as illustrated by lines 15 and 25 in Program 3.14, which is based on Case 3.3.

CASE 3.3 As one part of controlling and analyzing its inventory system, the ABC Company has a program that is run each week. As input data this program takes the inventory level at the end of the previous week, as well as the number of units sold each day of the current week. As output the program generates for each day of the week, the beginning inventory, the number of units sold, and the ending inventory; it also shows the total number of units sold during the entire week.

PROGRAM 3.14 Case 3.3, Inventory Analysis, Multiple INPUTs

```
10 PRINT "WHAT IS BEGINNING INVENTORY?"
15 INPUT I
20 PRINT "WHAT WERE SALES FOR EACH DAY OF THE WEEK?"
25 INPUT M,T,W,T1,F
30 PRINT
35 PRINT "BEG. INV.";I;"UNITS"
40 PRINT
45 PRINT "                     DAILY SALES"
50 PRINT "                     ----------- "
55 PRINT "MON.","TUES.","WED.","THUR.","FRI."
60 PRINT M,T,W,T1,F
65 PRINT
70 PRINT "NUMBER OF UNITS SOLD THIS WEEK";M+T+W+T1+F
75 PRINT "ENDING INVENTORY";I-(M+T+W+T1+F)
99 END


RUN
WHAT IS BEGINNING INVENTORY?
 ?150
WHAT WERE SALES FOR EACH DAY OF THE WEEK?
 ?20,30,15,25,10

BEG. INV. 150 UNITS
```

PROGRAM 3.14 continued

```
                    DAILY SALES
                    -----------
 MON.            TUES.           WED.            THUR.           FRI.
 20              30              15              25              10

NUMBER OF UNITS SOLD THIS WEEK 100
ENDING INVENTORY 50
```

A program can have both READ/DATA and INPUT statements in it. The conversational part of the program will be based on the variable list of the INPUT statements. Other data that is required for the program can be entered by the READ/DATA statements.

Program 3.15 shows a program that converts miles to kilometers. The conversion factor is 1.609 kilometers to a mile. This constant is entered into the program by the READ in line 10. The INPUT statement is used to enter the number of miles to be converted to kilometers, since that will change each time. The READ/DATA are used for the constant factor.

PROGRAM 3.15 A Program with Both READ/DATA and INPUT Statements

```
10 READ K
20 DATA 1.609
30 INPUT M
35 PRINT
40 PRINT M;"MILES IS EQUIVALENT TO";K*M;"KILOMETERS"
50 END

RUN
 ?2000

 2000 MILES IS EQUIVALENT TO 3218 KILOMETERS
```

Another example of a program containing both READ/DATA and INPUT statements is Program 3.16 based on Case 3.4.

CASE 3.4 An individual retirement account (IRA) permits an annual contribution of up to $2000 a year. The total accumulation for such an account is calculated by the formula

$$F = A\left[\frac{(1 + R)^N - 1}{R}\right]$$

where F is the total, A is the amount paid into the account each year for N years, and R is the rate of interest.

If $1500 a year is put into an IRA at 7.5 percent compounded annually for 10 years, what is the total accumulation?

Treating R as a constant and A and N as variables to be entered by an INPUT statement, Program 3.16 supplies the answer. The flowchart for this program is shown in Figure 3.3.

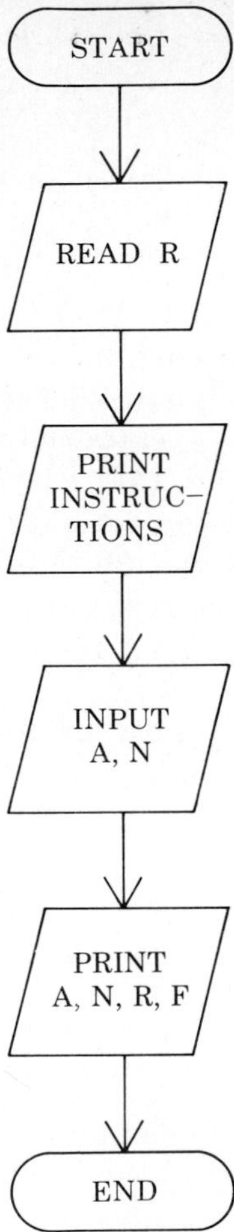

FIGURE 3.3 Flowchart for Case 3.4, IRA Account Program 3.16

Note that the output for Program 3.16 shows two sets of results. The second set was obtained by running the program again with a different set of inputs for A and N. Thus, results for different sets of contributions and years can be calculated by running the program over again.

Also observe the dangling semicolon at the end of line 80. This symbol causes the INPUT question mark to appear on the same line as the output of the PRINT statement.

PROGRAM 3.16 Case 3.4, Finding the Accumulation in an IRA Account with READ/DATA and INPUT Statements

```
10 READ R
20 DATA .075
30 PRINT "AFTER THE QUESTION MARK APPEARS TYPE THE"
40 PRINT "ANNUAL CONTRIBUTION, AND THE NUMBER OF YEARS IT"
50 PRINT "WILL BE PAID INTO THE IRA ACCOUNT."
60 PRINT
70 PRINT "WHAT IS THE ANNUAL CONTRIBUTION, AND HOW MANY YEARS"
80 PRINT "WILL IT BE PAID IN";
90 INPUT A,N
100 PRINT
110 PRINT"A YEARLY CONTRIBUTION OF $";A;"FOR";N;"YEARS"
120 PRINT"COMPOUNDED AT 7.5% EACH YEAR, GENERATES A TOTAL"
130 PRINT"IRA ACCOUNT OF $";A*(((1.0 + R)↑N - 1.0)/R)
140 END


RUN
AFTER THE QUESTION MARK APPEARS TYPE THE
ANNUAL CONTRIBUTION, AND THE NUMBER OF YEARS IT
WILL BE PAID INTO THE IRA ACCOUNT.

WHAT IS THE ANNUAL CONTRIBUTION, AND HOW MANY YEARS
WILL IT BE PAID IN ?1500,10

A YEARLY CONTRIBUTION OF $ 1500 FOR 10 YEARS
COMPOUNDED AT 7.5% EACH YEAR, GENERATES A TOTAL
IRA ACCOUNT OF $ 21220.6



RUN
AFTER THE QUESTION MARK APPEARS TYPE THE
ANNUAL CONTRIBUTION, AND THE NUMBER OF YEARS IT
WILL BE PAID INTO THE IRA ACCOUNT.

WHAT IS THE ANNUAL CONTRIBUTION, AND HOW MANY YEARS
WILL IT BE PAID IN ?1000,15

A YEARLY CONTRIBUTION OF $ 1000 FOR 15 YEARS
COMPOUNDED AT 7.5% EACH YEAR, GENERATES A TOTAL
IRA ACCOUNT OF $ 26118.4
```

SUMMARY

Possible variable names are the 26 letters of the alphabet and each letter followed by a single numeric, zero to nine—for a total of 286 variable names. Data can be entered into a program by using either the READ statement or the INPUT statement, or both.

When using the READ/DATA statements, there must be enough data to agree with the variable list in the READ. Too little data will result in an error message.

A RESTORE statement can be used so that the DATA statements of a program can be reread.

Interactive or conversational programs use the INPUT statement. When data is typed in response to an input statement, it must be typed in exact conformance with the variable format. Too much or too little data may result in an error message.

EXERCISES

* 3.1 Which of the following are unacceptable BASIC variables and why?

a. $X11$	c. $-M5$	e. PI	g. $K9$
b. I3	d. $C.2$	f. N	h. $D + 8$

3.2 Use appropriate variables and notation to write a BASIC expression that will give you net pay, which is gross pay less a deduction equal to 22 percent of gross pay.

* 3.3 In inventory analysis we attempt to find what is called the *economic order quantity.* This quantity can be calculated using the following formula:

$$\sqrt{\frac{2 \times \text{annual required units} \times \text{cost per order}}{\text{Cost per unit of item} \times \text{percent carrying cost}}}$$

Rewrite this expression with symbols and notation acceptable to BASIC. It is helpful to note that the square root of a number is equal to that number raised to the one-half power.

3.4 The Cobb-Douglas production function often encountered in macroeconomics has the form

$$\text{Output} = A \times L^{\alpha} \times K^{1-\alpha}$$

where A is technical progress, L is the employed labor force, K is the stock of capital for production, α (alpha) is the fraction of total output earned by labor, and $1 - \alpha$ is the fraction of total output earned by capital. Write the function as an expression in BASIC. Remember that α is not an acceptable BASIC symbol.

* 3.5 What output will result from the following program?

```
10 DATA 60,4,20
20 READ A, B, C
30 PRINT A+B+C/B
40 PRINT (A/B)*C+B
99 END
```

3.6 What output will result from each of the following programs?

a.
```
5 READ A
10 PRINT A;
15 DATA -32
20 READ A
25 PRINT A
30 DATA 7
99 END
```

b.
```
5 READ A,A
10 PRINT A,A
20 PRINT A;
25 PRINT A
30 DATA -32,7
99 END
```

c.
```
5 READ G,E,O,R,G,E
10 DATA 1,2,3,4,5,6
20 PRINT G;E;O;R;G;E
99 END
```

3.7 Write programs using READ/DATA statements for the following Chapter 2 *exercises:*

* a. 2.9 b. 2.12 c. 2.13 d. 2.19

3.8 Real estate brokers are often compensated on a straight commission basis. Their total earnings are computed this way:

$$\begin{pmatrix}\text{value of real estate}\\\text{property sold}\end{pmatrix} \times \begin{pmatrix}\text{commission}\\\text{rate \%}\end{pmatrix} = \begin{pmatrix}\text{commission}\\\text{on sale}\end{pmatrix}$$

If there is a 6 percent commission rate on all property less than \$100,000 sold, write a program that computes the commissions for the following salespersons on each of the properties they sold:

Person	Value of Property Sold
A. Smith	\$40,000
	62,500
	47,500
J. Jenkins	76,250
	49,500
	57,500

3.9 The United Computer Company pays its salespersons a monthly salary of \$1000 plus 1½ percent commission for equipment sold during the month. The table below shows the sales figures by person for last month.

Salesperson	Amount Sold
1	\$13,500
2	21,000
3	9,600
4	24,400

a. Write a program that will produce a table containing the above information plus an additional column that shows the total salary plus commission on sales. Have the sales, percent, and salary in one DATA line.

b. Why is it practical to have the salary and percent as part of your DATA line instead of using these values in a computational PRINT?
c. When would it be practical to have two DATA lines, one for sales and one for salary and percent?

3.10 The ABC Company has four divisions selling various products. Management wants to know what percent of total sales volume is generated by each division. Below are the gross sales figures by division for the last year.

Division	Sales (million $)
1	2.85
2	7.62
3	3.57
4	2.81

Write a program that reads in the sales data and generates as output a table that (1) shows the above with total sales and with a third column headed "% OF TOTAL", and (2) shows the percent for each division. The last column will sum to 100.0.

3.11 For the program below what will the output look like?

```
10 READ A, B, C
20 DATA 2, 4, 6
30 PRINT (A+B)/C,
40 RESTORE
50 READ B, A, C
60 PRINT (A+B)/C,
70 RESTORE
80 READ C,A,B
90 PRINT (A+B)/C,
100 RESTORE
110 READ C,B,A
120 PRINT (A+B)/C,
130 RESTORE
140 READ A,C,B
150 PRINT (A+B)/C,
199 END
```

3.12 What will the following program print when it is run?

```
10 DATA 1,2
15 READ A,B,C
20 DATA 6,7,8,9
25 READ D,E
30 RESTORE
35 PRINT A,B,C,D,E
40 READ C,A,D
45 PRINT A,B,C,D,E
50 END
```

3.13 Below are a set of investments that are to be increased by the same three interest rates, first by 7 percent, then by 7½ percent, and then by 8¼ percent. Write a program that will increase this set of investments by these three rates.

One year investments: $3,000; $10,000; $12,500; $17,000

3.14 Do *exercise 3.13,* making use of the INPUT statement.

* 3.15 Do *exercise 3.9,* making use of an INPUT statement for the sales, the salary, and the commission's percent.

3.16 The ABC Company (see *exercise 3.10*) anticipates that, for this year and the next 2 years, sales in each division will grow above last year's sales by the following percentage growth rates:

	Last Year-1	This Year-2	Next Year-3	Year After-4
Percent	100.0	108.0	114.2	121.3

Write a program that will generate for each of the divisions the expected sales for the years involved. Your output should have the following headings:

Three Year Sales Forecast—ABC Company

Division	Year 1	Year 2	Year 3	Year 4
1				
2				
3				
4				

Put both the sales and the percents in DATA lines.

3.17 Using the Cobb-Douglas production function shown in *exercise* 3.4, if A is 15, L is 500, K is 250, and α is .5, write a program that reads in this data and computes output. The program should also print out all of the components that went into the function.

3.18 A balance sheet in accounting is divided into two parts. On the left are the "assets" and on the right are the "liabilities and capital," Assets consist of current plus fixed assets. Suppose the XYZ Company has current assets of $45,000, fixed assets of $78,000, current liabilities of $32,000, and capital of $91,000; write a program that reads in this data and prepares a balance sheet with a heading and labels for all the items mentioned, including totals for both parts.

3.19 Write a program having a single DATA statement,

100 DATA 2,4,6,8,10

Assign the following numbers to the designated variables:

Variable:	*A*	*B*	*C*	*D*	*E*	*F*	*G*	*X*
Number:	2	4	6	8	2	6	8	4

(*Hint*: Use the RESTORE statement.)

* 3.20 There is a mathematic property that states: for a set of data the sum of the deviations about its mean is equal to zero; or $\Sigma\ (X_i - U) = 0$, where Σ is the sum of, X_i is each data value, and U is the average or mean of all the X_i. For the following data, write a program that illustrates this property. (*Hint*: First compute the mean, then INPUT the mean.)

$$5,\ -3,\ 7,\ 8,\ -2$$

3.21 In statistics there is a measure of variation called the *standard deviation*, which has the formula:

$$\sigma = \sqrt{\frac{\Sigma(X_i - U)^2}{N}}$$

where N is number of data values. Write a program to find the standard deviation for the data in *exercise 3.20. Note:* $\sqrt{X} = X^{1/2}$. See hint in *exercise 3.20.*

3.22 Suppose in **Program 3.14** the PRINT statements in lines 10 and 20 ended with semicolons after the quotes. How would that affect the program? If you are not sure, first try this program:

```
10 PRINT "TYPE A AND B VALUES AFTER THE ? MARK";
20 INPUT A, B
30 PRINT "A + B = "; A + B
99 END
```

3.23 Revise **Program 3.13** treating price (P) and cost (C) as constants entered by READ/DATA statements.

3.24 What would **Program 3.14** print if the variables in lines 25 and 60 were changed to M,T,W,T,F?

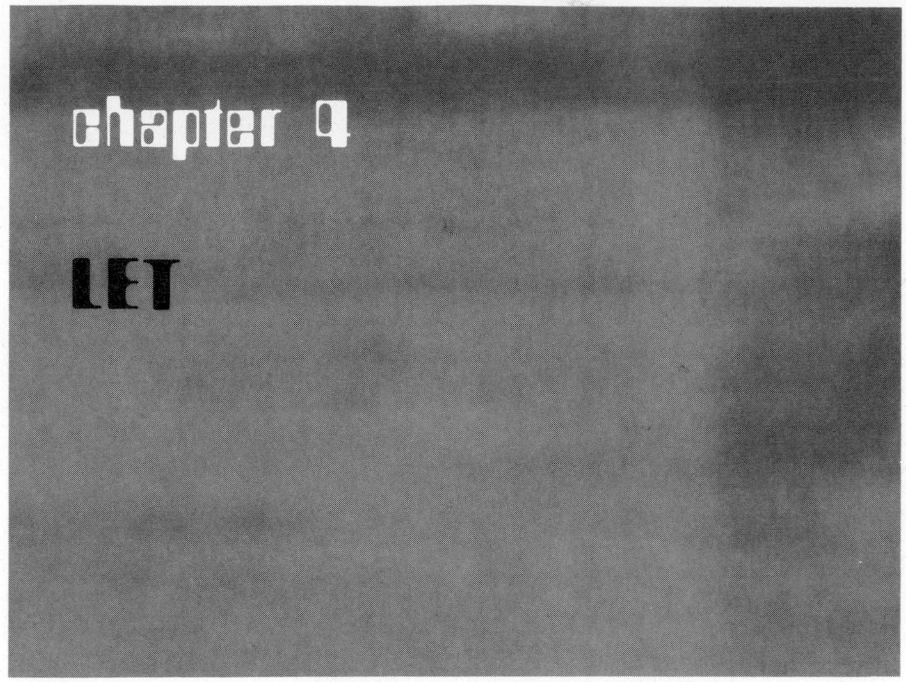

THE LET STATEMENT

In the previous chapter, we studied how to assign values to variables with the READ/DATA and INPUT statements. Another way in which we can assign values to variables is with the LET statement. The LET statement is also used to evaluate expressions. The form of the LET statement is

$$\text{line \# LET \{variable\}} = \left\{\begin{array}{l}\text{constant}\\ \text{variable}\\ \text{expression}\end{array}\right\}$$

The LET statement evaluates the expression on the right side of the equal sign and assigns that value to the variable on the left side of the equal sign. An expression here means any variable or constant or a valid combination of variables, constants, and operators (+, −, *, /, and ↑).

Some examples of the LET statement are given below:

1. 100 LET N = 5
2. 100 LET Y = A*X↑2 + B*X + C
3. 100 LET A = B
4. 100 LET B = A
5. 100 LET J = J + 1

Example 1 assigns the value of 5 to variable N, even if N had some other value before the execution of line 100.

Example 2 evaluates the expression $A*X\uparrow 2 + B*X + C$ and assigns the value of that expression to the variable Y. The variables A, B, C, and X must have been assigned values before the execution of line 100. Again the previous value of variable Y, if any, would be replaced by the value of the expression.

In example 3 the value of variable B is assigned to variable A. That is, if variable A had the value 2 and variable B had the value 3, after line 100 is executed both variables have the value of 3.

Example 4 differs from example 3 in that the value of variable A is assigned to variable B. Thus if variable A had the value 2 and variable B had the value 3, after line 100 in this example both variables would have the value of 2.

Example 5 requires that variable J have been defined previously. It takes the old value of variable J, adds 1 to that value, and assigns that increased value to the variable J. So if variable J had the value of 10 before line 100, then after line 100 is executed variable J has the value of 11.

Note that the symbol "=" in the BASIC language does not mean *equal.* Example 5 clearly demonstrates this, since J is never equal to $J + 1$. It means, rather, "assign the value on the right to the variable on the left."

Below are some examples of invalid LET statements.

1. 100 LET 5 = N
2. 100 LET A*X↑2 + B*X + C = Y
3. 100 LET J + 1 = J

These examples are all invalid, since the left side of the "=" can contain a single variable only.

Thus while $A = B + C$ is the same as $B + C = A$ in mathematics, in the BASIC language

LET A = B + C

is a valid statement, but

LET B + C = A

is invalid. Program 4.1 illustrates the LET statement.

PROGRAM 4.1 The LET Statement

```
10 READ A,B,C
15 LET X=A+B+C
20 PRINT X,X↑2,X↑3
25 DATA 1,2,3
30 END

RUN
 6             36            216
```

Note that in Program 4.1 it would have been possible to omit line 15 and replace line 20 with Figure 4.1.

```
20 PRINT A + B + C, (A+B+C) ↑2, (A+B+C) ↑ 3
```

FIGURE 4.1 PRINT without Using LET in Program 4.1

One advantage of Program 4.1 is that it avoids the lengthy statement in Figure 4.1. Another advantage is that the statement in Figure 4.1 requires the computer to add A+B+C three times. The computer does not remember the sum of *A, B,* and *C* unless it is assigned to a variable. Thus Program 4.1 requires less computations than a program having the statement in Figure 4.1.

Another application of the LET statement arises when lengthy computations are required. Suppose we wish to compute the value of

$$\frac{A^2 + B^2}{C(B - A)} \div \frac{(D - A)B}{C^2 - D^2}$$

Figure 4.2 shows us how. An easier way is illustrated in Figure 4.3.

```
10 PRINT ((A ↑ 2 + B ↑ 2)/(C*(B − A)))/(((D − A)*B)/(C ↑ 2 − D ↑ 2))
```

FIGURE 4.2 Lengthy Computations without Using LET

```
10 LET X1 = A ↑ 2 + B ↑ 2
15 LET X2 = C*(B−A)
20 LET X3 = (D−A)*B
25 LET X4 = C ↑ 2 − D ↑ 2
30 PRINT (X1/X2)/(X3/X4)
```

FIGURE 4.3 Lengthy Computations Using LET

Programs with statements like those in Figure 4.3 are much less prone to error than programs with statements like the one in Figure 4.2.

Program 4.2 has no practical application, but it does illustrate some of the ramifications of the LET statement.

PROGRAM 4.2 Several LET Statements

```
10 READ A, B, C, D
20 LET C=A
30 LET A=B+C
40 LET D=A+D
50 LET B=A
60 PRINT A, B, C, D
70 DATA 1, 2, 3, 4
80 END

RUN
 3             3             1             7
```

The variables changed as follows:

Line	A	B	C	D
10	1	2	3	4
20	1	2	1	4
30	3	2	1	4
40	3	2	1	7
50	3	3	1	7

Note that the order in which the statements are executed makes a considerable difference in the final output. Consider Program 4.3; this program consists of the identical statements of Program 4.2 but the output is completely different.

PROGRAM 4.3 The Order of the LET Statements

```
10 READ A,B,C,D
20 LET B=A
30 LET A=A+C
40 LET C=A
50 LET D=A+D
60 PRINT A,B,C,D
70 DATA 1,2,3,4
80 END

RUN
 4              1              4              8
```

If we have the statement

10 LET X = A + 1

and A has not been given a value previously, an error message may be printed such as "UNDEFINED VARIABLE ACCESSED ON LINE 10" referring to variable A. Some systems, though, will automatically assign the value zero to any undefined variable. Applications of LET statements are given in Cases 4.1 and 4.2.

CASE 4.1 One method of measuring inventory management is by finding the merchandise inventory turnover ratio and comparing it to the ratio of prior years or with similar industry measures. This ratio can be computed by taking the cost of goods sold and dividing by the average inventory. First, average inventory must be obtained. It is determined by taking the sum of the beginning and ending inventory and dividing by 2. The ratio can be found this way:

1. $\text{Average inventory} = \dfrac{\text{beginning inventory} + \text{ending inventory}}{2}$

2. $\text{Merchandise inventory turnover ratio} = \dfrac{\text{cost of goods sold}}{\text{average inventory}}$

If over a period of time your business has sold $480,000 worth of goods, and beginning period inventory was $40,000 and ending period inventory was $20,000, what is the inventory turnover at cost?

Program 4.4 shows how the merchandise inventory turnover ratio can be obtained using only LET statements. These statements are found in lines 15–50.

Program 4.5 also calculates the merchandise inventory turnover ratio, but this program uses READ/DATA statements to place the data into the program rather than LET statements as in Program 4.4.

PROGRAM 4.4 Case 4.1, Merchandise Inventory Turnover, Using LET Statements

```
5 REM PROGRAM TO CALCULATE MERCHANDISE
10 REM INVENTORY TURNOVER AT COST
15 LET C=480000
20 LET B=40000
25 LET E=20000
30 LET I=B+E
40 LET A=I/2
50 LET T=C/A
60 PRINT "COST OF GOODS SOLD $";C
70 PRINT "BEG. INVENTORY $";B
80 PRINT "END. INVENTORY $";E
90 PRINT "AVERAGE INVENTORY $";A
100 PRINT
110 PRINT "MERCHANDISE INVENTORY TURNOVER AT COST $";T
199 END


RUN
COST OF GOODS SOLD $ 480000
BEG. INVENTORY $ 40000
END. INVENTORY $ 20000
AVERAGE INVENTORY $ 30000

MERCHANDISE INVENTORY TURNOVER AT COST $ 16
```

PROGRAM 4.5 Case 4.1, Merchandise Inventory Turnover, Using READ/DATA Statements

```
5 REM PROGRAM TO CALCULATE MERCHANDISE
10 REM INVENTORY TURNOVER AT COST
20 READ C,B,E
25 DATA 480000,40000,20000
30 LET I=B+E
40 LET A=I/2
50 LET T=C/A
60 PRINT "COST OF GOODS SOLD $";C
70 PRINT "BEG. INVENTORY $";B
80 PRINT "END. INVENTORY $";E
90 PRINT "AVERAGE INVENTORY $";A
100 PRINT
110 PRINT "MERCHANDISE INVENTORY TURNOVER AT COST $";T
199 END


RUN
COST OF GOODS SOLD $ 480000
BEG. INVENTORY $ 40000
END. INVENTORY $ 20000
AVERAGE INVENTORY $ 30000

MERCHANDISE INVENTORY TURNOVER AT COST $ 16
```

An illustration of both LET and INPUT statements is found in Program 4.6, which is based on Case 4.2.

CASE 4.2 One method of determining the depreciation of an item is by the straight line approach. In this approach, annual depreciation is found by dividing the cost of the item (less any salvage) by the estimated years of life of the item. This can be stated in the following way:

$$\frac{\text{Cost} - \text{salvage value}}{\text{Estimated years of life}} = \text{depreciation per year}$$

Suppose at the start of the year the XYZ Construction Company purchases a piece of equipment that costs $36,000. The useful life of this type of equipment is three years. At the end of that time, the resale or salvage value is $1200. It is desired to calculate the annual depreciation for the equipment.

Program 4.6 computes the annual depreciation. This "conversational" program uses an INPUT statement in line 20 to request the required values for the program. Line 25 calculates cost less salvage, and line 30 finds the depreciation. If another depreciation result is needed, we can type RUN again and the program will start over.

The flowchart for Program 4.6 is shown in Figure 4.4. Note the numbers placed in the upper right-hand corner of the flowchart symbols. These numbers correspond to the line numbers of the program and provide a means of cross-reference between flowchart and program.

PROGRAM 4.6 Case 4.2, Depreciation, Using LET and INPUT Statements

```
1 REM CONVERSATIONAL PROGRAM FOR STRAIGHT LINE
5 REM DEPRECIATION DETERMINATION
10 PRINT "****STRAIGHT LINE DEPRECIATION DETERMINATION****"
12 PRINT
15 PRINT "AFTER ONE ? MARK, TYPE IN THE FOLLOWING ITEMS EACH"
16 PRINT "SEPARATED BY A , :  COST, SALVAGE VALUE (TYPE 0 IF"
17 PRINT "NONE),EST. YEARS OF LIFE"
18 PRINT
20 INPUT C,V,L
25 LET T=C-V
30 LET D=T/L
35 PRINT
40 PRINT "WITH A COST OF $";C;", A SALVAGE VALUE OF $";V;
50 PRINT " AND A USEFUL LIFE OF";L;"YEARS"
60 PRINT "THE ANNUAL DEPRECIATION FOR THIS ITEM IS $";D
99 END

RUN
****STRAIGHT LINE DEPRECIATION DETERMINATION****

AFTER ONE ? MARK, TYPE IN THE FOLLOWING ITEMS EACH
SEPARATED BY A , :  COST, SALVAGE VALUE (TYPE 0 IF
NONE),EST. YEARS OF LIFE

 ?36000,1200,3

WITH A COST OF $ 36000 , A SALVAGE VALUE OF $ 1200  AND A USEFUL LIFE OF
 3 YEARS
THE ANNUAL DEPRECIATION FOR THIS ITEM IS $ 11600
```

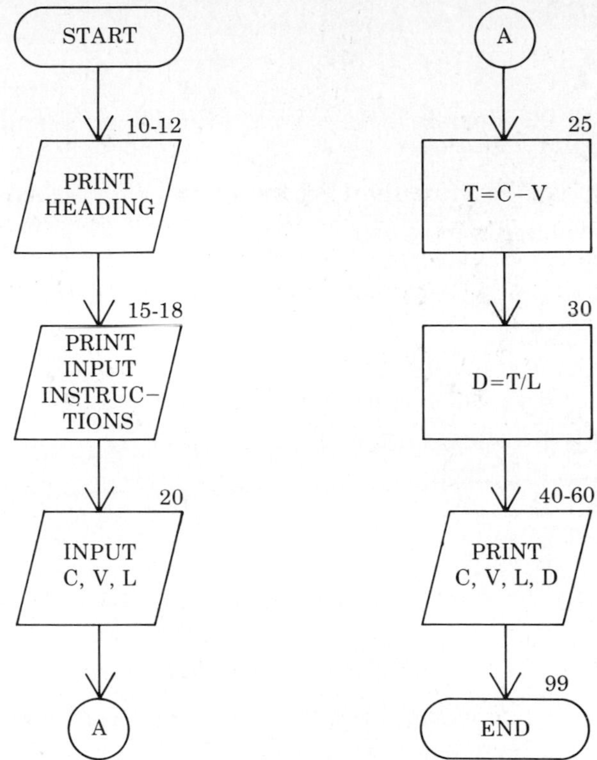

FIGURE 4.4 Flowchart for Program 4.6, Case 4.2, Depreciation, Using LET and INPUT Statements

SUMMARY

The LET statement, like the READ and INPUT statements, can be used to assign constant values to variables. In addition, the LET statement can be used to evaluate expressions and assign the values of those expressions to variables.

EXERCISES

* 4.1 Show what the following program will print when it is run:

```
10 READ A,B,C,D
15 DATA 1,2
20 LET X = A + B
25 LET B = X + A
30 LET A = X↑B/C * A − 5
35 DATA 4,5,6
40 PRINT A,B,C,X
45 END
```

* 4.2 What will the program in *exercise 4.1* print if lines 25 and 30 are interchanged?

4.3 Compare and contrast the LET statement with READ/DATA.

4.4 Correct the following program:

```
10 READ A + B
20 LET 5 = C
30 PRINT X
40 LET A + B + C = X
50 DATA 12, 16, 9, 3, 8, 10
```

4.5

```
20 LET I = P*(1 + R) ↑ N
30 LET P = 2000
40 LET R = .085
50 LET N = 6
60 PRINT P, R, N, I
90 END
```

What results will this program produce? Can you suggest any revisions?

4.6 Trace the values of the variables A, B, C, and D for **Program 4.3** as was done in the text for **Program 4.2.**

4.7 Using READ/DATA and LET, redo *exercises 2.21* where:

$$A = F\left[\frac{r}{(1 + r)^n - 1}\right]$$

4.8 Using READ/DATA and LET, redo *exercises 3.17* for the Cobb-Douglas production function:

$$\text{OUTPUT} = AL^{\alpha}K^{1-\alpha}$$

4.9 For **Case 3.4,** the individual retirement account, write and run a program using READ/DATA and LET where:

$$F = A\left[\frac{(1 + R)^N - 1}{R}\right]$$

4.10 Write a program that reads in values for A, B, C, and D and then calculates

$$Y = \frac{(A + B)\uparrow 2}{C\uparrow 2 + D\uparrow 2} \div \frac{1/D + 1/B}{C\uparrow A - B}$$

Use LET statements to evaluate each of the numerators and denominators. The data to be used is 1, 2, 3, 4.

* 4.11 Rewrite **Program 3.9** using LET statements to evaluate total revenue, total cost, and total profit. Assign the variable *T*1 to total revenue, *T*2 to total cost, and *T* to total profit.

4.12 Rewrite **Program 3.14** using LET statements to evaluate the number of units sold this week using variable *N*, and the ending inventory using variable *E*.

4.13 Write a program to READ an employee's number, the number of hours that he worked, and his hourly rate, and prepare a table showing his number, his salary (number of hours × hourly rate), his federal tax (20 percent of his salary), his social security tax (.05478 × his salary), and his net salary (i.e., gross salary − all deductions). Use the LET statement. Data for the program is: number, 3542; hours worked, 37; and rate, 4.50.

4.14 Write a program to read into variables *D*1, *D*2, *D*3, and *D*4 the amounts sold by the four divisions of a company and print the following table with the given DATA:

Division	Amount Sold	% of Total
1	150	–
2	275	–
3	70	–
4	100	–

Hint: Use a LET statement to compute the total of all four divisions.

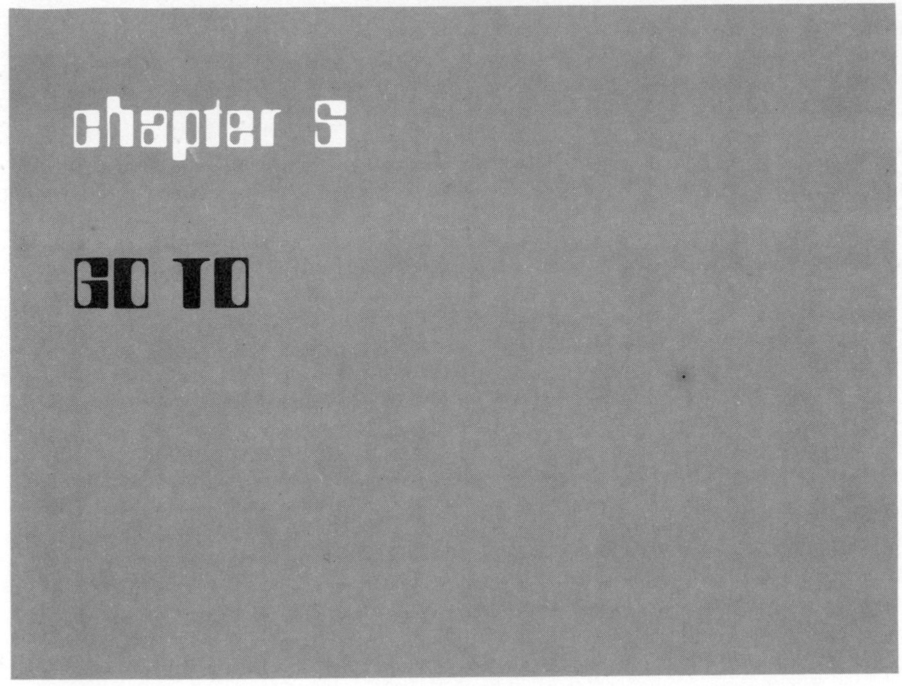

If the only capabilities of computers were to carry out statements like PRINT, READ/DATA, LET, and INPUT, the importance of computers would be similar to the importance of electronic calculators. The branching statements introduced in this chapter and Chapters 6 and 7 give computers their immense power.

In all of the programs in the previous chapters, the statements were executed sequentially; that is, the first statement to be executed was the first statement in the program, the second statement executed was the second statement in the program, and so on, until the END statement was encountered. Branching statements change this normal sequence of statement execution. There are two types of branching statements. The type discussed in this chapter is the unconditional branch—the GO TO statement.

THE GO TO STATEMENT

Consider Program 5.1, which presents an example of how the GO TO statement changes the normal sequence of the execution of the statements.

PROGRAM 5.1 GO TO Statement

```
10 READ X
15 PRINT X,X↑2,X↑3
20 GO TO 10
25 DATA 2, 4, 5, 10, 8, -3
30 END

RUN
 2             4             8
 4             16            64
 5             25            125
 10            100           1000
 8             64            512
-3             9            -27

OUT OF DATA- LN #  10
```

In line 10 the READ X assigns the number 2 to the variable X. The PRINT statement on line 15 then prints the numbers 2, 4, and 8. The GO TO 10 on line 20 tells the computer to execute line 10 again. This time, the READ X assigns the number 4 to variable X since the first number in the DATA statement, the number 2, was already read. The program then prints the current values of X, X^2, and X^3; namely, 4, 16, and 64. When the GO TO 10 is encountered a second time, it again sends the computer looping back to line 10 to read another value of X. This procedure continues until there are no more numbers in the DATA statement that can be read. When the computer is told to read a number from the DATA statement and all of the numbers in the DATA statement have already been read, the computer prints "OUT OF DATA" in the line that tries to do the reading. The above program is an example of what is called a *loop*. See the flowchart in Figure 5.1.

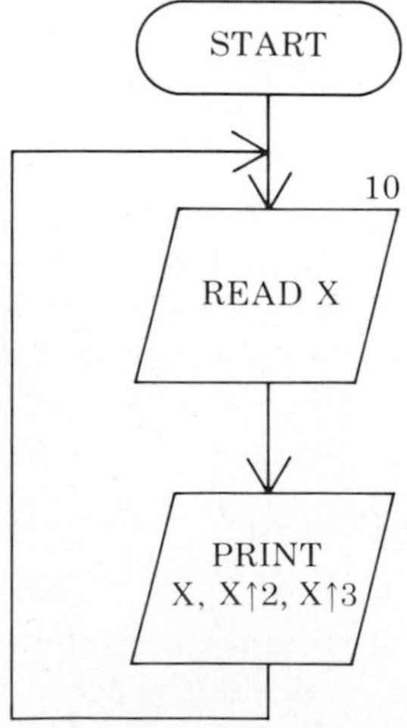

FIGURE 5.1 Flowchart of Program 5.1

Thus the GO TO statement changes the normal sequence of the execution of the statements. It tells the computer what is the next statement to be executed. Program 5.1 will work for as many numbers as there are in the DATA statement(s). We are beginning to see the power of the computer.

The form of the GO TO statement is

line #1 GO TO line #2

When line 1 is encountered, the next statement to be executed will be line 2. Line 2 may be greater than line 1, in which case we wish to skip some statements; or, as in Program 5.1, line 2 may be less than line 1, in which case we want to repeat a number of statements.

We need never have statements like

```
100 GO TO 101
101
```

Statement 100 accomplishes nothing, since the next statement to be executed would be 101 anyway.

Program 5.2 has no practical importance other than illustrating the GO TO statement. The statements are executed in the following order: 10, 15, 45, 50, 35, 40, 55, 60, 20, 30, and 99, resulting in the printing of the statement EVERY GOOD PERSON DOES FINE.

PROGRAM 5.2 Several GO TO Statements

```
10 PRINT "EVERY";
15 GO TO 45
20 PRINT " FINE";
30 GO TO 99
35 PRINT " PERSON";
40 GO TO 55
45 PRINT " GOOD";
50 GO TO 35
55 PRINT " DOES";
60 GO TO 20
99 END

RUN
EVERY GOOD PERSON DOES FINE
```

Case 5.1 shows a program that uses a GO TO loop sequence of operation.

CASE 5.1 Because of increased labor and raw materials costs, the Global Manufacturing Company has decided to revise its prices on the items listed below. The new price for each item is to be 6.6 percent above the current price.

Item Number	Current Price	Item Number	Current Price
218	$ 200	406	$ 179
233	1,456	407	1,000
345	545	557	267
367	248	679	470
401	225	887	359

Program 5.3, using a GO TO loop, generates a revised price list for Case 5.1.

PROGRAM 5.3 Case 5.1, Revising Price List

```
5 REM PROGRAM TO UPDATE PRICE LIST
10 PRINT "ITEM","CURRENT","REVISED"
11 PRINT "NUMBER","PRICE","PRICE"
15 READ I,P
20 LET R=P*1.066
30 PRINT I,"$";P,"$";R
40 GO TO 15
50 DATA 218,200,233,1456,345,545,367,248,401,225,406,179
55 DATA 407,1000,557,267,679,470,887,359
90 END


RUN
ITEM              CURRENT           REVISED
NUMBER            PRICE             PRICE
 218              $ 200             $ 213.2
 233              $ 1456            $ 1552.1
 345              $ 545             $ 580.97
 367              $ 248             $ 264.368
 401              $ 225             $ 239.85
 406              $ 179             $ 190.814
 407              $ 1000            $ 1066
 557              $ 267             $ 284.622
 679              $ 470             $ 501.02
 887              $ 359             $ 382.694

OUT OF DATA- LN #   15
```

COUNTING AND ACCUMULATING

Program 5.4 illustrates how the LET statement can be used as either a counter of items or as an accumulator of values. Variable *C* in the program, at line 18, is being used to count the number of times the program cycles through the GO TO loop. Each time line 18 is executed, a constant value of 1 is added to the prior value of *C*. Line 5 gives an initial value of Ø to variable *C*. This defining of a variable is often referred to as *initialization*.

PROGRAM 5.4 A Counter and an Accumulator

```
5 LET C=0
10 LET S=0
12 PRINT "C","X","S"
15 READ X
18 LET C=C+1
20 LET S=S+X
25 PRINT C,X,S
30 GO TO 15
35 DATA 7,3,5,6
99 END


RUN
C                X                S
 1                7                7
 2                3                10
 3                5                15
 4                6                21

OUT OF DATA- LN #   15
```

Variable S is used in Program 5.4 to accumulate the sum (hence the variable name S) of the values in the DATA statement. The purpose of line 10 is to initialize the variable S to Ø so that it can be used to accumulate the values of variable X in line 20 later on. More about initialization will be discussed later in this chapter.

When line 15 is executed the first time, the variable X is assigned the value 7. In line 20, variable S, which was Ø because of line 10, becomes 7 since $0 + 7 = 7$. Line 25 prints the values of X and S, which are both 7, along with C, the counter, which is 1.

The GO TO 15 on line 30 causes the next value of X to be changed to 3 from 7, since the second entry in the DATA statement is 3. Line 20 now changes the value of S from 7 to 10 since $7 + 3 = 10$. Note that S did not become zero again since line 10 was only executed the first time. Line 25 then prints the current values of C, X, and S which are now 2, 3, and 10. This program will continue until all of the numbers in the DATA statement have been read. When GO TO 15 is then encountered, the computer attempts to read another value for X from the DATA statement and, since there is no data, the computer says "OUT OF DATA," as it did in Program 5.1. Figure 5.2 is a flowchart of Program 5.4.

Program 5.5 is another illustration of the GO TO statement.

PROGRAM 5.5 An Infinite Loop

```
1Ø LET X=1
15 PRINT X,X↑2,X↑3,X↑.5,1/X
2Ø LET X=X+1
25 GO TO 15
99 END


RUN
1             1             1             1             1
2             4             8             1.41421       .5
3             9             27            1.73205       .333333
4             16            64            2             .25
5             25            125           2.236Ø7       .2
6
```

The execution of Program 5.5 will not stop unless the "plug is pulled out" (actually, you should never pull out the plug), or the computer reaches a number that is too large. Each system has its own method for branching out of an infinite closed loop, as in Program 5.5. On many systems you must type the letter S followed with a carriage return.

Line 10 initializes, that is, assigns initially to the variable X the number 1. Line 15 then prints the value of 1, 1^2, and 1^3, $\sqrt{1}$, and 1/1. In line 20, the variable X is increased by 1 so that it now assumes the value 2. Line 25 returns the execution to line 15 where 2, 2^2, 2^3, $\sqrt{2}$, and 1/2 are printed. X is then increased by 1 to 3 and the process is repeated. Note that the data is generated in this program and hence the program will never run "OUT OF DATA" as Program 5.1 did. Thus, with a program of only five statements,

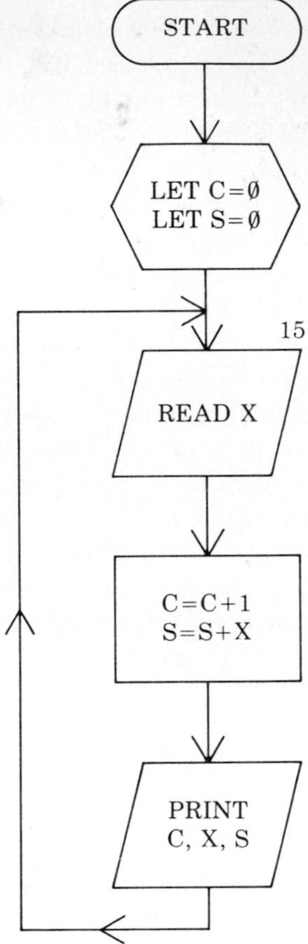

FIGURE 5.2 Program 5.4 Flowchart

we can get, theoretically, an infinite amount of information; namely, the squares, cubes, square roots, and reciprocals of all of the positive integers. With this program we see the real power of the computer. We can tell the computer to repeat a series of statements an infinite number of times. The computer, unlike people, does not get tired.

Program 5.6, which is based on Case 5.2, provides another illustration of the GO TO statement.

CASE 5.2 To calculate simple interest, the following formula is used:

$$\text{Interest} = \text{Principal} \times \text{Rate} \times \text{Time}$$

where the interest is the amount charged for the loan, the principal is the amount borrowed, the rate is the annual percentage charge, and the time is the fractional part of a year.

Given the following amounts that have been borrowed, the above formula could be used to determine the interest on each loan.

Loan	Principal	Rate	Time
1	$1,200.00	7.00%	7 months
2	850.00	9.50	6
3	11,250.00	9.25	9
4	8,566.50	11.75	4
5	2,500.00	10.50	8
6	925.75	8.25	5

Program 5.6 shows how the interest for the above loans can be calculated. A counter is used in this program (line 65) rather than including the loan number with the data. Note that in line 50 the interest rate is converted into decimal form by dividing by 100, and that the time, T, is divided by 12 to obtain the fractional part of the year.

PROGRAM 5.6 Case 5.2, Calculating Interest on Loans

```
5 REM PROGRAM TO FIND INTEREST ON LOANS
10 LET L=1
20 PRINT "LOAN","PRINCIPAL","RATE-%","TIME","INTEREST"
25 PRINT
30 READ P,R,T
50 LET I=P*(R/100)*(T/12)
60 PRINT L,"$";P,R,T;"MOS.","$";I
65 LET L=L+1
70 GO TO 30
90 DATA 1200,7,7,850,9.5,6,11250,9.25,9,8566.50,11.75,4
95 DATA 2500,10.5,8,925.75,8.25,5
99 END
```

```
RUN
LOAN            PRINCIPAL       RATE-%          TIME            INTEREST

 1              $ 1200          7                7 MOS.         $ 49.
 2              $ 850           9.5              6 MOS.         $ 40.375
 3              $ 11250         9.25             9 MOS.         $ 780.469
 4              $ 8566.5        11.75            4 MOS.         $ 335.521
 5              $ 2500          10.5             8 MOS.         $ 175.
 6              $ 925.75        8.25             5 MOS.         $ 31.8227

OUT OF DATA- LN #  30
```

SUMMARY

The GO TO statement transfers control unconditionally to the statement indicated by the specified line number, instead of to the next statement in sequence. The GO TO statement causes the computer to repeat a number of steps or to skip them.

EXERCISES

* 5.1 What would **Program 5.1** do if line 20 was changed to
  a. 20 GO TO 15?
  b. 20 GO TO 30?

5.2 What would **Program 5.1** do if a RESTORE statement was added on
  a. line 5 ?
  b. line 12?
  c. line 17?
  d. line 22?
  e. line 27?

5.3 What would **Program 5.2** do if all of the GO TO statements in lines 15, 30, 40, 50, and 60 were removed?

5.4 What would **Program 5.2** do if line 30 was removed?

5.5 a. What is wrong with the following statement?
  100 GO TO 100
  b. What would happen if this statement was the first statement in a program?

5.6 What would **Program 5.4** do if
  a. line 35 was changed to 35 DATA 1,2,3,4,5,6?
  * b. line 30 was changed to 30 GO TO 10?
  c. line 30 was changed to 30 GO TO 20?
  d. line 30 was changed to 30 GO TO 25?
  * e. line 30 was changed to 30 GO TO 99?
  f. line 20 was changed to 20 LET X = X + S?
  g. line 20 was changed to 20 LET S = S + X↑2?
  h. a line 40 was added that read 40 DATA −4, −9, −8, − 1?
  * i. line 30 was eliminated?
  * j. line 20 was eliminated?
  k. a RESTORE statement was added on line 16?

5.7 What would **Program 5.5** do if
  a. line 10 was changed to 10 LET X = 5?
  b. line 20 was changed to 20 LET X = X + 2?
  c. line 25 was changed to 25 GO TO 10?
  d. line 25 was changed to 25 GO TO 20?

5.8 What changes are necessary to change **Program 5.5** so that the output prints the results for
  a. only the even numbers. (*Hint:* Lines 10 and 20 must be changed.)
  b. only the odd numbers.
  c. the numbers 5, 10, 15, 20, ...

* 5.9 Using the concept of the counter and the GO TO statement, write the program for *exercise 3.9.*

5.10 Using the GO TO statement, do *exercise 3.16.*

5.11 The current ratio is an accounting measure of a company's financial condition. This ratio is found by dividing current assets by current liabilities. Write and run a program producing a completed table as shown below. Your program should have a GO TO and READ loop.

Year	Current Assets	Current Liabilities	Current Ratio
1978	$500,000	$400,000	–
1979	$160,000	$120,000	–
1980	$950,000	$320,000	–

5.12 A large retail establishment uses a wage payment plan of straight salary, $300.00 per week, plus a commission of 1 percent on the amount of merchandise each employee sells. For the information given below, write and run a program that completes the table shown computing commissions and total earnings. Your program should have a GO TO and READ loop.

Employee Number	Regular Salary	Amount Sold	Com-mission	Total Earnings
1015	300.00	500.00	–	–
1068	300.00	580.00	–	–
1135	300.00	485.00	–	–
1359	300.00	610.50	–	–

5.13 Using the data given below, write and run the program required for *exercise 4.13.* Use a GO TO and READ loop.

Number	Hours Worked	Rate
3542	37	4.50
2876	35	5.25
4356	39	4.75
3987	34	4.00

5.14 For the data given below, write and run a program to find the percent increase for each month shown. That is, (second year/first year)*100 for each month using a GO TO and READ loop.

	Month		
Units sold:	1	2	3
First year	400	450	440
Second year	500	575	600
% Increase	–	–	–

5.15 Using a GO TO and READ loop and the data given below, find the total accumulation for six IRA accounts (see **Case 3.4**). Use the formula:

$$F = A\left[\frac{(1 + R)^N - 1}{R}\right]$$

Data: R is $8\frac{1}{2}$ percent; N is 10, 15, and 20 years; A is \$1,000 and \$1,500.

chapter 6

IF/THEN, Computed GO TO, and STOP

THE IF/THEN STATEMENT

Whereas the GO TO statement branches unconditionally, that is, no matter what, the IF/THEN statement will branch only if a particular condition is true. Otherwise, it will not branch but will execute the next statement in the sequence. That is, it will only branch conditionally.

The form of the IF/THEN statement is

line #1 IF{expression 1}relation{expression 2}THEN line #2

The kinds of relationships available on the computer are

Symbol	Example	Meaning
$<$	$A < B$	A is less than B
$<=$	$X <= 5$	X is less than or equal to 5
$>$	$A + B > C$	$A + B$ is greater than C
$>=$	$Y >= P + 5$	Y is greater than or equal to $P + 5$
$=$	$N = 10$	N is equal to 10
$<>$	$K <> L + M$	K is not equal to $L + M$

An example of an IF/THEN statement is

50 IF N = 10 THEN 80
60

Statement 50 says, test if the variable *N* is equal to the number 10. If it is, then execute line 80 next. If the variable *N* is not equal to the number 10, then execute the next statement in sequence (the one following this IF), which is 60 in this example.

PROGRAM 6.1 The IF/THEN Statement

```
10 REM   THIS PROGRAM READS TWO NUMBERS AND PRINTS
15 REM   THE LARGER OF THE TWO
20 READ A, B
25 IF A>B THEN 40
30 PRINT B
35 GO TO 99
40 PRINT A
45 DATA 7, 3
99 END


RUN
 7
```

Program 6.1 assigns the number 7 to variable *A* and the number 3 to variable *B* in line 20. Then *A* is compared to *B* by line 25. Since *A* is greater than *B*, the next statement to be executed is line 40, which prints the value of *A*, which is 7. If the DATA statement in line 45 was 45 DATA 4, 12, variable *A* would be assigned the value 4, and variable *B* would be 12. Now when line 25 is encountered, the condition $A > B$ is not true, so line 40 is not executed next; instead line 30 is executed next. In line 30, the value of the variable *B*, which is 12, is printed. The GO TO 99 in line 35 prevents the variable *A* from being printed when *B* is the larger number.

Note that in the flowchart in Figure 6.1 the diamond-shaped box has two lines coming from it. The one to the right with a YES over it points to the instruction that should be executed if the relation $A > B$ is true. That is, if *A* is greater than *B* then PRINT A. If the relation is false, that is if *A* is less than *B* or equal to *B*, the line below the diamond box indicates that the next statement to be executed is PRINT B. Program 6.2, based on 6.1, illustrates the use of the IF/THEN statement.

CASE 6.1 A school would like to print a list of the student numbers of all students who have at least a 3.0 cumulative grade index. Each student number is followed by the corresponding grade index in the DATA statement.

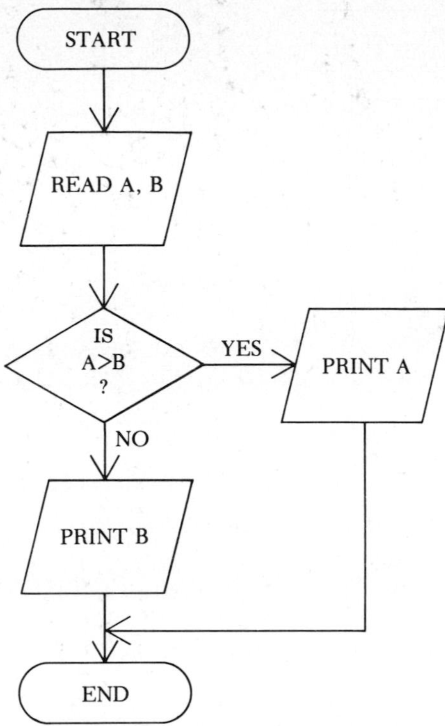

FIGURE 6.1 Flowchart for Program 6.1

PROGRAM 6.2 Case 6.1, Students Honor List

```
5 READ N,G
1Ø IF G>=3.Ø THEN 2Ø
15 GO TO 5
2Ø PRINT N
25 GO TO 5
26 DATA 1234,3.5,9376,2.9,1763,3.Ø,1357,2.3
3Ø END

RUN
 1234
 1763

OUT OF DATA- LN #    5
```

A flowchart for the above program is shown in Figure 6.2.

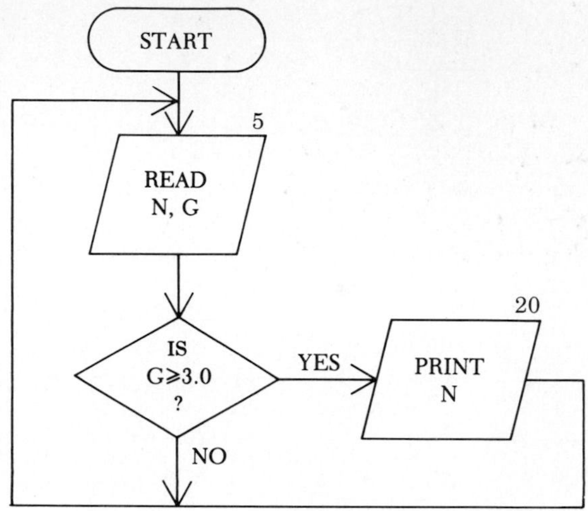

FIGURE 6.2 Flowchart for Program 6.2

Program 6.3 is another illustration of the IF/THEN statement.

PROGRAM 6.3 Summing Numbers and Their Squares

```
10 REM THIS PROGRAM READS 5 NUMBERS FROM THE DATA STATEMENT
20 REM AND PRINTS THE NUMBERS, THE SQUARES OF THE NUMBERS,
30 REM AND THE SUMS OF THE NUMBERS AND THEIR SQUARES.
40 LET S=Ø
45 LET S2=Ø
50 LET N=1
55 READ X
60 LET S=S+X
65 LET S2=S2+X↑2
70 PRINT X,X↑2
75 IF N=5 THEN 90
80 LET N=N+1
85 GO TO 55
90 PRINT "---","---"
95 PRINT S,S2
100 DATA 7,2,3,4,1
999 END
```

```
RUN
 7              49
 2              4
 3              9
 4              16
 1              1
---             ---
 17             79
```

Variables S and $S2$ will accumulate the sum of the numbers and the sum of the squares of the numbers, respectively. These sums are initialized to zero, in lines 40 and 45. Variable N is used as a counter to count the number of data values that have been read in. N is initialized to 1 before the first number is read in. Lines 60 and 65 accumulate the sum and the sum of the squares of the numbers, and line 70 prints the number and its square. In line 75, we test if $N = 5$. That is, we see if we are finished processing all five numbers. If N is not 5, we proceed to line 80 where 1 is added to the variable N. Then we go back to line 55 to read the next number from the DATA statement. We repeat this process until all five numbers have been read, at which time N is equal to 5 and control is transferred to line 90.

Program 6.3 is a typical illustration of a program designed to do something a fixed number of times. The flowchart of this program appears in Figure 6.3.

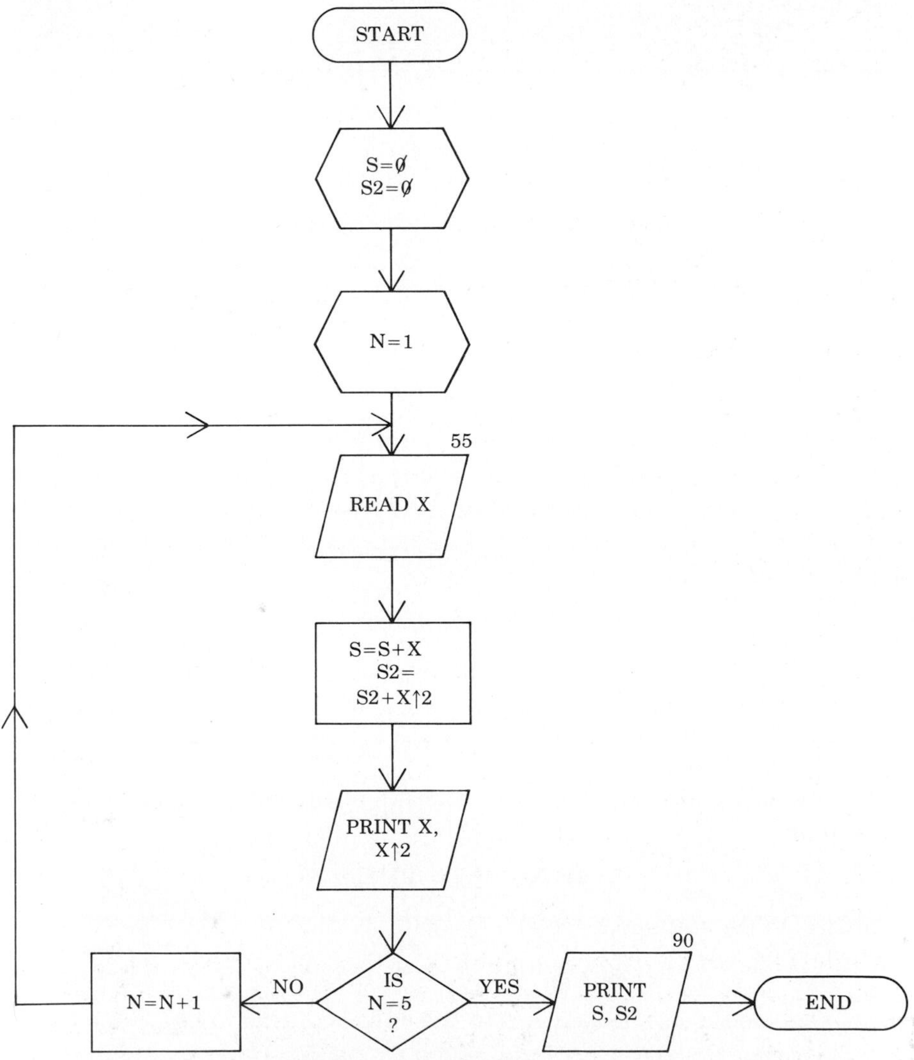

FIGURE 6.3 Flowchart for Program 6.3

Sometimes, we may not know exactly how many times we are to perform an operation but we want to keep performing it until we have read all of the data. This is illustrated in Program 6.4.

PROGRAM 6.4 Testing DATA to End Program

```
1Ø REM THIS PROGRAM ACCOMPLISHES THE
15 REM SAME THING AS PROGRAM 6.3 EXCEPT
25 REM THE DECISION TO END IS MADE DIFFERENTLY
4Ø LET S=Ø
45 LET S2=Ø
5Ø READ X
55 IF X=999 THEN 8Ø
6Ø LET S=S+X
65 LET S2=S2+X↑2
7Ø PRINT X,X↑2
75 GO TO 5Ø
8Ø PRINT "---","---"
85 PRINT S,S2
9Ø DATA 7,2,3,4,1,999
999 END
```

```
RUN
 7              49
 2              4
 3              9
 4              16
 1              1
---             ---
 17             79
```

Note that Program 6.4 has the same output as Program 6.3. Program 6.3 will work for any five numbers in the DATA statement. Program 6.4 will work for all numbers in the DATA statement up to the number 999. Thus, if line 90 were changed to

90 DATA 7, 2, 3, 999, 4, 1

the numbers 4 and 1 would not be read by the program, since as soon as the 999 were encountered the totals would be printed. Similarly, if there were 50 numbers followed by a 999 in the DATA statement, all 50 numbers would be processed.

Any number can be used to signal the end of the DATA. Thus, if line 55 were changed to

55 IF X = 1000 THEN 80

and the DATA statement were

90 DATA 7, 2, 3, 4, 1, 1000

the output would also be identical to the output of Programs 6.3 and 6.4.

Case 6.2 shows an application of the IF/THEN and GO TO statements.

CASE 6.2 The ABC Company computes salesperson's monthly earnings on the following basis: monthly earnings are 20 percent of total sales; plus a bonus of 12½ percent of any amount sold in excess of $5000. There are nine salespersons in the company and last month their sales were as follows:

Person	Monthly Sales
1	$4,000
2	6,250
3	4,750
4	4,800
5	7,125
6	6,050
7	8,300
8	3,500
9	9,625

Program 6.5 shows how earnings and bonuses can be found. Note that the program ends when the number −9999 is encountered in the DATA statement. In this case, we could not use the number 999 to signal the end of the DATA as was done in Program 6.4 since it is possible for a salesperson to sell exactly $999 worth of merchandise, which would cause the program to end prematurely. A flowchart for Program 6.5 appears in Figure 6.4.

PROGRAM 6.5 Case 6.3, Calculation of Bonuses

```
5 LET P=0
8 READ E
11 IF E=-9999 THEN 99
12 DATA 4000,6250,4750,4300,7125,6050,3300,3500,9625,-9999
13 LET P=P+1
14 REM TEST FOR BONUS
15 IF E>5000 THEN 50
20 LET E1=.20*E
30 PRINT "PERSON";P,"NO BONUS THIS MONTH","EARNINGS $";E1
37 PRINT
40 GO TO 8
45 REM COMPUTATION OF BONUS
50 LET B=.125*(E-5000)
60 LET E1=.20*E+B
70 PRINT "PERSON";P,"BONUS    $";B,"EARNINGS $";E1
72 PRINT
80 GO TO 8
99 END
```

PROGRAM 6.5 continued

```
RUN
PERSON 1        NO BONUS THIS MONTH               EARNINGS $ 300

PERSON 2        BONUS      $ 156.25               EARNINGS $ 1406.25

PERSON 3        NO BONUS THIS MONTH               EARNINGS $ 950

PERSON 4        NO BONUS THIS MONTH               EARNINGS $ 960

PERSON 5        BONUS      $ 265.625              EARNINGS $ 1690.63

PERSON 6        BONUS      $ 131.25               EARNINGS $ 1341.25

PERSON 7        BONUS      $ 412.5                EARNINGS $ 2072.5

PERSON 8        NO BONUS THIS MONTH               EARNINGS $ 700

PERSON 9        BONUS      $ 578.125              EARNINGS $ 2503.13
```

Case 6.3 shows how several IF/THEN statements can be combined to perform involved decisions.

CASE 6.3 The ACME Company wishes to print a list of the employee numbers of all employees who are eligible for retirement. In order to be eligible for retirement, any one of the following conditions must be satisfied:

1. The employee must be at least 65 years old.
2. The employee must have worked at least 30 years with the company.
3. The employee must be over 60 years old and have worked at least 25 years with the company.
4. The employee must be over 55 years old and have worked at least 20 years and have a salary of at least $30,000 per year (early retirement for executives).

We will now write a program that will read an employee's number, age, years employed with the company, and salary. We will then determine if he or she is eligible for retirement. If so, we will print his or her number. If not, we will go on to the next employee. We will continue until we have processed the data for all of the employees. The DATA for the last employee is followed by zeros to signal the program to end. Note that we also need zeros (or any number) for the variables *A*, *Y*, and *S* since the READ on line 10 reads all four variables.

The variables that we will use in this program will be:

Variable	Explanation
N	Employee number
A	Employee's age
Y	Years employed with the company
S	Employee's salary

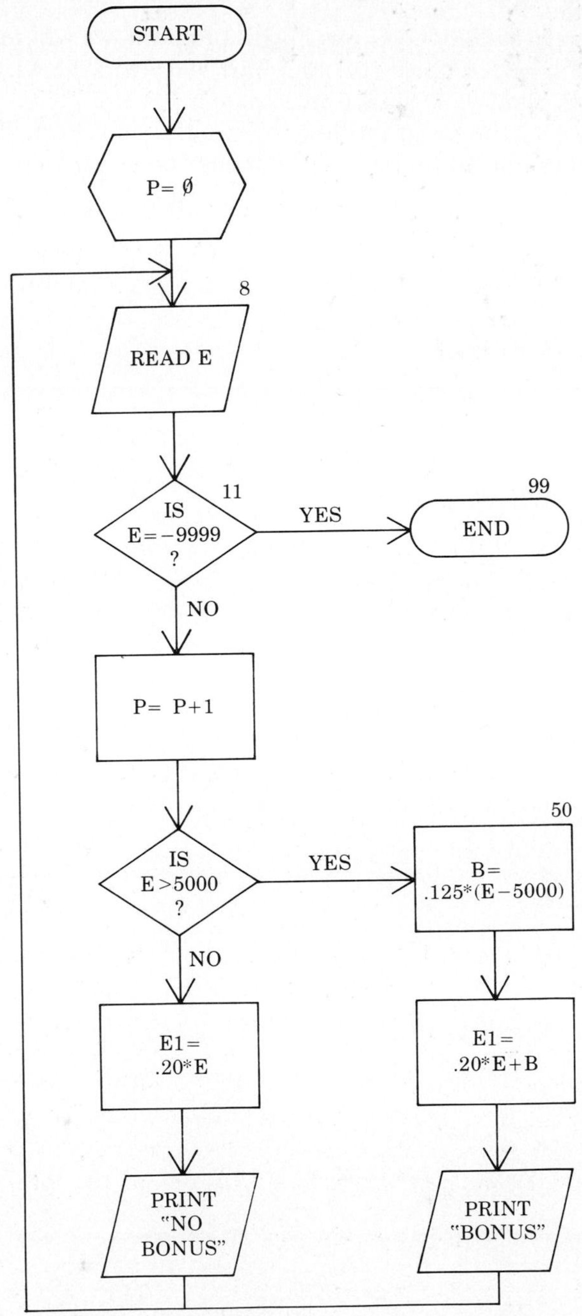

FIGURE 6.4 Flowchart for Case 6.2, Bonus Program 6.5

Since there are many decisions in this program, we will first draw a flowchart. See Figure 6.5. Once the flowchart is drawn, the writing of the program follows readily, as shown in Program 6.6.

Note the way the program flow follows the flowchart. We first read *N*, *A*, *Y*, and *S* in line 10 (note the 10 outside the upper right-hand corner of

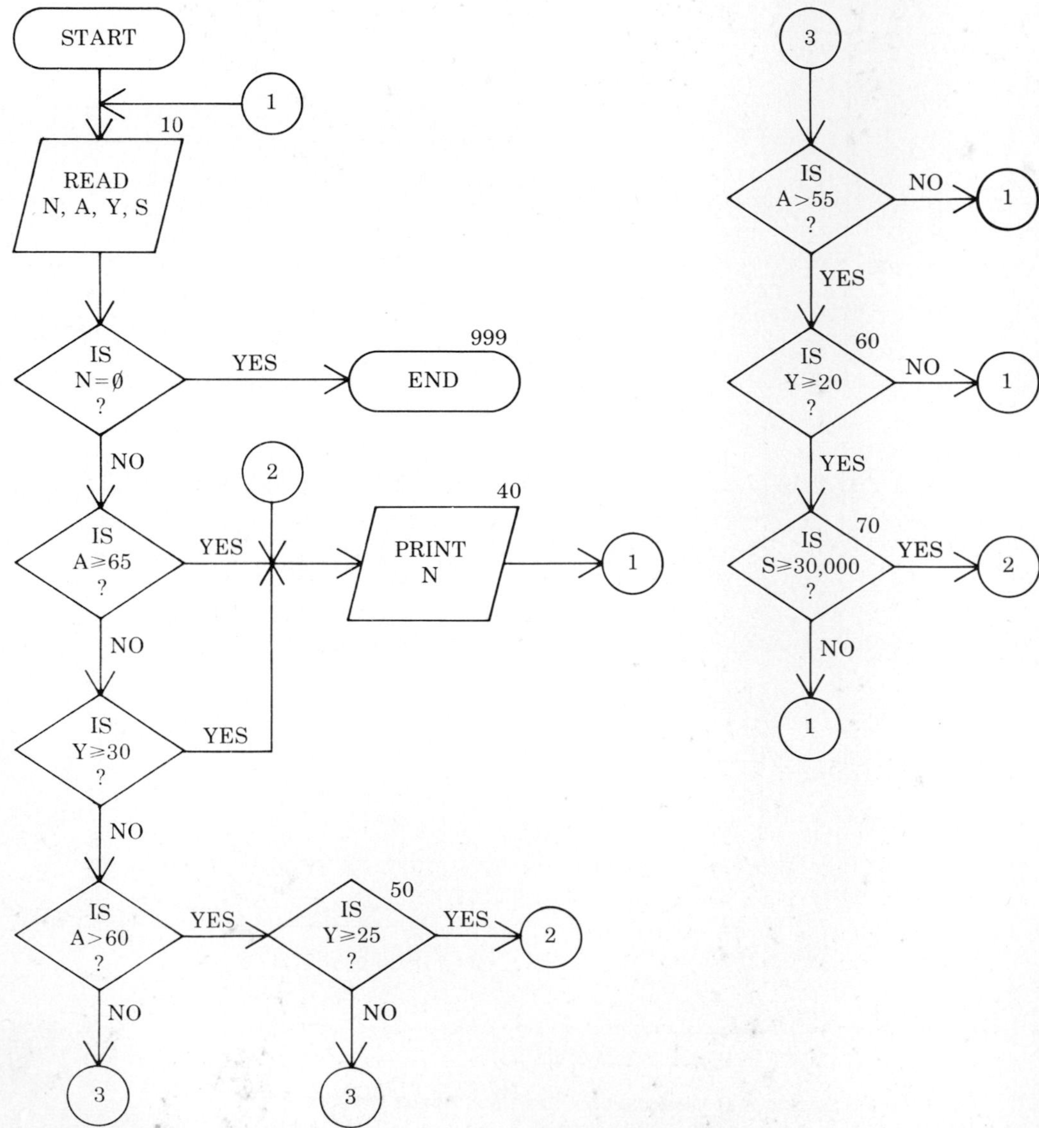

FIGURE 6.5 Flowchart for Program 6.6

PROGRAM 6.6 Case 6.3, Eligibility for Retirement

```
10 READ N,A,Y,S
12 IF N=0 THEN 999
15 IF A>=65 THEN 40
20 IF Y>=30 THEN 40
25 IF A>60 THEN 50
30  IF A>55 THEN 60
35 GO TO 10
40 PRINT N
45 GO TO 10
50 IF Y>=25 THEN 40
55 GO TO 30
60 IF Y>=20 THEN 70
65 GO TO 10
70 IF S>=30000 THEN 40
75 GO TO 10
80 DATA 1234,40,5,12500,1235,61,25,15000
85 DATA 1236,56,21,30000,1237,71,15,18000
90 DATA 1238,62,19,41000,1239,59,30,11000
95 DATA 1240,20,10,10000,1241,56,22,29000
100 DATA 1242,57,18,31000,1243,62,24,35000
101 DATA 0,0,0,0
999 END

RUN
 1235
 1236
 1237
 1239
 1243
```

the READ N,A,Y,S box). Then we test if $N = 0$, in which case there is a branch to the end. Then we test if $A >= 65$. If this condition is true, we then GO TO 40 which is the PRINT statement. If this condition is false, we then test if $Y >= 30$, and so on. Observe that there are four statements that say GO TO 10, and note also that there are four arrows pointing to a 1 in the circles, which refers to the READ N,A,Y,S corresponding to line 10.

PROCESSING CONTROLS

The IF/THEN statement has a wide use in programs that incorporate *processing controls*. These controls are written into programs to ensure that abnormal or undesirable actions do not occur during processing. We will examine three control applications.

Counting of records is a very common method of process control. In order to be sure that all documents or records that are to be entered are in fact entered, the computer is programmed to count each document in a batch of documents processed. An initial "batch total" is compared to the number of documents entered to determine if any records or documents were missed during processing. An illustration of the control process, *counting of records*, is shown by Case 6.4.

CASE 6.4 A large insurance company has much of its claims data entered from forms through cathode-ray tube (CRT) terminals. Terminal operators are given batches of up to 25 documents to be processed. An operator has to enter two items from each document. These data values ultimately become part of a total for each of the items. Along with the batch of documents, the operator also receives a document count to be entered before processing starts.

Program 6.7 shows how document counts can be incorporated into a program. Before data items are entered for processing, the operator must respond to 35 INPUT B, with the number of documents in the batch to be processed. Line 50 INPUT A,A1 requests the required data items from each document. A test is performed in line 55 to determine if the operator has finished processing the batch of documents. Line 60, LET T = T + 1, is the counter of the records processed. This count is compared with the initial number of documents value, *B*, entered earlier. If *B* does not equal *T* (line 80), then either too few or too many documents have been processed. Too few will produce the printed message shown by the first output. This result occurs because the test in line 90, IF $B < T$ then 105, is *not* true. When this test is true, it means that too many documents have been processed; that is, an operator may have entered the same data more than once. As a result, a message as shown in the second output is printed out. If all counts are equal, $B = T$, processing continues to completion, producing the third output shown.

PROGRAM 6.7 Case 6.4 Insurance Forms, Document Count

```
10 REM PROCESSING CONTROLS,  DOCUMENT COUNT
15 LET T= 0
20 LET S1 = 0
25 LET S2 = 0
30 PRINT "HOW MANY DOCUMENTS IN THE BATCH";
35 INPUT B
40 PRINT "AFTER THE BATCH IS COMPLETED TYPE -99,-99"
45 PRINT "ENTER FIRST ITEM, SECOND ITEM";
50 INPUT A,A1
55 IF A = -99 THEN 80
60 LET T= T+1
65 LET S1= S1+A
70 LET S2= S2+A1
75 GO TO 45
80 IF B = T THEN 115
85 PRINT "BATCH CONTROL TOTAL";B;" DOES NOT EQUAL NUMBER OF ENTRIES";T
90 IF B<T THEN 105
95 PRINT "CHECK FOR";B-T;"SKIPPED DOCUMENT(S)."
100 STOP
105 PRINT T-B;"TOO MANY DOCUMENTS HAVE BEEN ENTERED, PLEASE CHECK."
110 STOP
115 PRINT "BATCH CONTROL TOTAL";B;" EQUALS THE NUMBER DOCUMENTS ENTERED.

120 PRINT
125 PRINT"ITEM 1 TOTAL IS";S1;" ITEM 2 TOTAL IS";S2
130 END
```

PROGRAM 6.7 continued

```
RUN
HOW MANY DOCUMENTS IN THE BATCH ?2
AFTER THE BATCH IS COMPLETED TYPE -99,-99
ENTER FIRST ITEM, SECOND ITEM ?3,4
ENTER FIRST ITEM, SECOND ITEM ?4,6
ENTER FIRST ITEM, SECOND ITEM ?3,5
ENTER FIRST ITEM, SECOND ITEM ?-99,-99
BATCH CONTROL TOTAL 2  DOES NOT EQUAL NUMBER OF ENTRIES 3
 1 TOO MANY DOCUMENTS HAVE BEEN ENTERED, PLEASE CHECK.

RUN
HOW MANY DOCUMENTS IN THE BATCH ?5
AFTER THE BATCH IS COMPLETED TYPE -99,-99
ENTER FIRST ITEM, SECOND ITEM ?4,7
ENTER FIRST ITEM, SECOND ITEM ?5,6
ENTER FIRST ITEM, SECOND ITEM ?3,5
ENTER FIRST ITEM, SECOND ITEM ?-99,-99
BATCH CONTROL TOTAL 5  DOES NOT EQUAL NUMBER OF ENTRIES 3
CHECK FOR 2 SKIPPED DOCUMENT(S).

RUN
HOW MANY DOCUMENTS IN THE BATCH ?3
AFTER THE BATCH IS COMPLETED TYPE -99,-99
ENTER FIRST ITEM, SECOND ITEM ?3,4
ENTER FIRST ITEM, SECOND ITEM ?4,5
ENTER FIRST ITEM, SECOND ITEM ?4,7
ENTER FIRST ITEM, SECOND ITEM ?-99,-99
BATCH CONTROL TOTAL 3  EQUALS THE NUMBER DOCUMENTS ENTERED.

ITEM 1 TOTAL IS 11  ITEM 2 TOTAL IS 16
```

Sequence checking is another form of processing control. It can be used to ensure that documents containing input data are processed in the correct sequence. In many processing operations the original source document has a preprinted sequential document number. Such document numbers are useful in that they provide a means of accounting for all source documents. The numbers provide a means of identifying specific documents if some error or a customer complaint arises.

An illustration of sequence checking as a program control is given in Case 6.5.

CASE 6.5 The Central General Hospital keeps track of drug prescriptions written each week for out-patients of the hospital by requiring the use of multiple-copy prescription pads with sequence numbers. One copy goes to the patient, the other copy is kept for record keeping and internal controls. Each week the hospital copies are processed to count the number of narcotic and non-narcotic prescriptions written over the period. The source documents are sequenced by number. A missing number suggests that either the document was skipped, the document number was entered incorrectly, or a document is missing. Whatever the case, a message is generated, indicating that some action is necessary.

Program 6.8 illustrates the idea of sequence control for Case 6.5. The program assumes that data is entered in data lines by sequence number (S), and a code number (C) of either 0 for a non-narcotic prescription or 1 for a narcotic prescription. Although other information may also be entered—for example, patient name, date, type of drug, and so on—for our case only the two items mentioned above will be used.

PROGRAM 6.8 Case 6.5 Central General Hospital, Sequence Checking

```
15 LET T1=0
20 LET T2=0
25 LET M=0
30 PRINT "NUMBER","NARC. OR NON-NARC."
35 READ N
40 REM X REPRESENTS THE FIRST SEQUENCE NUMBER
45 LET X=N
50 RESTORE
55 READ N,C
60 REM TEST FOR END OF DATA
65 IF N=- 99 THEN 155
70 REM TEST FOR DOCUMENT AND SEQUENCE NUMBER
75 IF N<>X THEN 110
80 PRINT N,C
85 LET X=N+1
90 REM T1-COUNT DOCUMENTS
95 LET T1=T1+1
100 IF C=1 THEN 135
105 GOTO 55
110 PRINT "* NOTE- THERE ARE";N-X;"DOCUMENTS MISSING*"
115 REM M-COUNT MISSING DOCUMENTS
120 LET M=M+(N-X)
125 GOTO 80
130 REM T2-COUNT NARCOTICS
135 LET T2=T2+1
140 GO TO 55
145 DATA 1245,0,1246,1,1243,1,1249,0,1252,1
150 DATA -99,-99
155 PRINT
160 PRINT "TOTALS:";T1;"DOCUMENTS"
165 PRINT "NARCOTIC";T2;"OTHER";T1-T2
170 PRINT "MISSING" ;M
175 END


RUN
NUMBER          NARC. OR NON-NARC.
 1245             0
 1246             1
* NOTE- THERE ARE 1 DOCUMENTS MISSING*
 1243             1
 1249             0
* NOTE- THERE ARE 2 DOCUMENTS MISSING*
 1252             1

TOTALS: 5 DOCUMENTS
NARCOTIC 3 OTHER 2
MISSING 3
```

Reasonableness tests are a third type of processing control that can be included in programs. Such tests are used to determine if something unusual, unlikely, or logically inconsistent has occurred. For example, petty cash disbursements should not exceed $100.00. Or the number of units of a certain item shipped are usually in a range of 1000-2000 units.

In a situation where a *reasonableness test* fails, the program will cause some type of "unreasonable" information report to be printed out. Such an output report can be reviewed to determine if a data entry error has been made, some illegal processing is being attempted (a computer embezzlement scheme), or whatever. There is an increasing awareness of the possibilities of computer crime and computer fraud. One purpose of processing controls is to prevent such activities.

CASE 6.6 A large manufacturing company has hundreds of employees who are paid weekly, based on an hourly rate and the number of hours worked. As one part of a large payroll program, there are several reasonableness tests on weekly pay before a check is issued. The tests that this program segment performs are: (1) is gross wage above $625, based on the premise that there is a 40-hour week; the maximum hourly wage at this time is $10 per hour; and there is overtime pay at "time and a-half," but it is never more than 15 hours per week; (2) is overtime over 15 hours per week; (3) is the hourly pay more than $10 per hour.

Program 6.9 shows how the reasonableness tests of Case 6.6 can be carried out. Line 55 tests to see if the overtime hours exceed 15. If they do, a NOTE is printed out, indicating that some action should be taken to see why excess overtime is being reported. Maybe there is a data entry error. Maybe this was an exceptional case of overtime, etc. Line 70 tests to see if wages exceeded a limit of $625, and line 75 tests to see if the hourly rate is above $10. If either or both tests are true, a NOTE is printed out, indicating that either wages are in excess of the limit, the wage rate is too high, or both items are unreasonable and have to be looked at.

PROGRAM 6.9 Case 6.6 Employee Payroll, Reasonableness Tests

```
15 READ N,R,H
2Ø      IF H>4Ø THEN 4Ø
25 LET W=R*H
3Ø PRINT "EMPLOYEE";N;"GROSS WAGE=$";W;
35 GO TO 7Ø
4Ø LET T= H-4Ø
45 LET W= R*4Ø+(1.5*(R*T))
5Ø PRINT "EMPLOYEE";N;"GROSS WAGE=$";W;
55       IF T>15 THEN 65
6Ø GO TO 7Ø
65 PRINT "NOTE-EXCESS OVERTIME ";
7Ø       IF W>625 THEN 9Ø
75       IF R>1Ø THEN 9Ø
8Ø PRINT
85 GO TO 15
9Ø PRINT "NOTE-EXCESS WAGES/RATE"
95 GO TO 15
1ØØ DATA 1,6,45,2,15,52,3,2Ø,3Ø
1Ø5 DATA 4,5,56,5,1Ø,39
11Ø DATA 6,3,43,7,12,51
115 DATA 3,15,6Ø
12Ø END
```

```
RUN
EMPLOYEE 1 GROSS WAGE=$ 235
EMPLOYEE 2 GROSS WAGE=$ 370 NOTE-EXCESS WAGES/RATE
EMPLOYEE 3 GROSS WAGE=$ 600 NOTE-EXCESS WAGES/RATE
EMPLOYEE 4 GROSS WAGE=$ 320 NOTE-EXCESS OVERTIME
EMPLOYEE 5 GROSS WAGE=$ 390
EMPLOYEE 6 GROSS WAGE=$ 416
EMPLOYEE 7 GROSS WAGE=$ 673 NOTE-EXCESS WAGES/RATE
EMPLOYEE 3 GROSS WAGE=$ 1050 NOTE-EXCESS OVERTIME NOTE-EXCESS WAGES/RATE
```

THE COMPUTED GO TO STATEMENT

Whereas the GO TO statement branches unconditionally to the statement indicated by the line number, the computed GO TO will branch to any one of several statements depending on the value of a particular variable or expression. For example, the statement:

100 ON X GO TO 50, 200, 75, 30

will branch to line 50 if $X = 1$, to line 200 if $X = 2$, to line 75 if $X = 3$, and to line 30 if $X = 4$. If X has any value less than 1, or 5 or more, an error message may be printed. If X has a fractional part, it is truncated. An illustration of the computed GO TO statement appears in Program 6.10. Note that if $X = 3.6$, the program transfers control to line 50 where "THREE" is printed. It does not round X to the nearest integer. Also note that when $X = 5$, the error message "ON −5 LN # 15" was printed.

PROGRAM 6.10 Computed GO TO Statement

```
10 READ X
15 ON X GO TO 30,20,50,40
20 PRINT X;"TWO"
25 GO TO 10
30 PRINT X;"ONE"
35 GO TO 10
40 PRINT X;"FOUR"
45 GO TO 10
50 PRINT X;"THREE"
55 GO TO 10
60 DATA 1,2,3,4,1.5,4.8,3.6,2.2,5
99 END
```

```
RUN
 1 ONE
 2 TWO
 3 THREE
 4 FOUR
 1.5 ONE
 4.8 FOUR
 3.6 THREE
 2.2 TWO

ON- 5  LN #  15
```

Program 6.11, based on Case 6.7, illustrates an application of the computed GO TO statement.

CASE 6.7 A certain state will take the following actions against the owners of motor vehicles who have at least one outstanding parking violation.

No. of Violations	Action
1 or 2	Send polite warning letter
3	Send strong letter
4	Send to collection agency
5 or more	Revoke registration

Program 6.11 reads the licenses and number of unpaid parking violations of all registrations with at least one unpaid ticket and prints a list of the licenses with the appropriate action to be taken.

PROGRAM 6.11 Case 6.7, Parking Violations, Computed GO TO Statement

```
5 PRINT "LICENSE","ACTION"
10 READ L,N
15 IFL=-99 THEN 99
20 IF N<=5 THEN 30
25 LET N=5
30 ON N GO TO 35,35,45,55,65
35 PRINT L,"POLITE WARNING"
40 GO TO 10
45 PRINT L,"STRONG LETTER"
50 GO TO 10
55 PRINT L,"COLLECTION AGENCY"
60 GO TO 10
65 PRINT L,"REVOKE REGISTRATION"
70 GO TO 10
72 DATA 30903,2,49943,1,93760,3,20939,3
75 DATA 17603,2,33344,1,45655,1,93739,5,77777,6,37676,4,36476,3,-99,0
99 END

RUN

LICENSE          ACTION
 30903           POLITE WARNING
 49943           POLITE WARNING
 93760           REVOKE REGISTRATION
 20939           STRONG LETTER
 17603           POLITE WARNING
 33344           POLITE WARNING
 45655           POLITE WARNING
 93739           REVOKE REGISTRATION
 77777           REVOKE REGISTRATION
 37676           COLLECTION AGENCY
 36476           STRONG LETTER
```

THE STOP STATEMENT

The STOP statement does just what its name implies—it stops the program. If the END statement is on line 999, a STOP statement anywhere in the program is the same as a GO TO 999. The STOP statement differs from the END statement in that there can be several STOP statements anywhere in the program but there can be only one END statement and it must be the very last statement in the program. An example of the STOP statement is in line 35 in Program 6.12. Instead of 35 STOP we could have had 35 GO TO 99, which would have done the same thing, and is identical to Program 6.1.

PROGRAM 6.12 The STOP Statement

```
10 REM SAME PROGRAM AS 6.1
15 REM BUT USES THE STOP STATEMENT
20 READ A,B
25 IF A>B THEN 40
30 PRINT B
35 STOP
40 PRINT A
45 DATA 7,3
99 END

RUN
 7
```

Program 6.13 prints the smallest of three numbers. It shows that there can be more than one STOP statement in a program. Note the STOP statements in lines 30, 50, and 60. Note also that the STOP statement in 60 is not necessary. Figure 6.6 shows the flowchart for Program 6.13.

PROGRAM 6.13 Several STOP Statements

```
10 READ A,B,C
15 IF A<B THEN 35
20 IF B<C THEN 55
25 PRINT C
30 STOP
35 IF A<C THEN 45
40 GO TO 25
45 PRINT A
50 STOP
55 PRINT B
60 STOP
65 DATA 15,56,35
70 END

RUN
 15
```

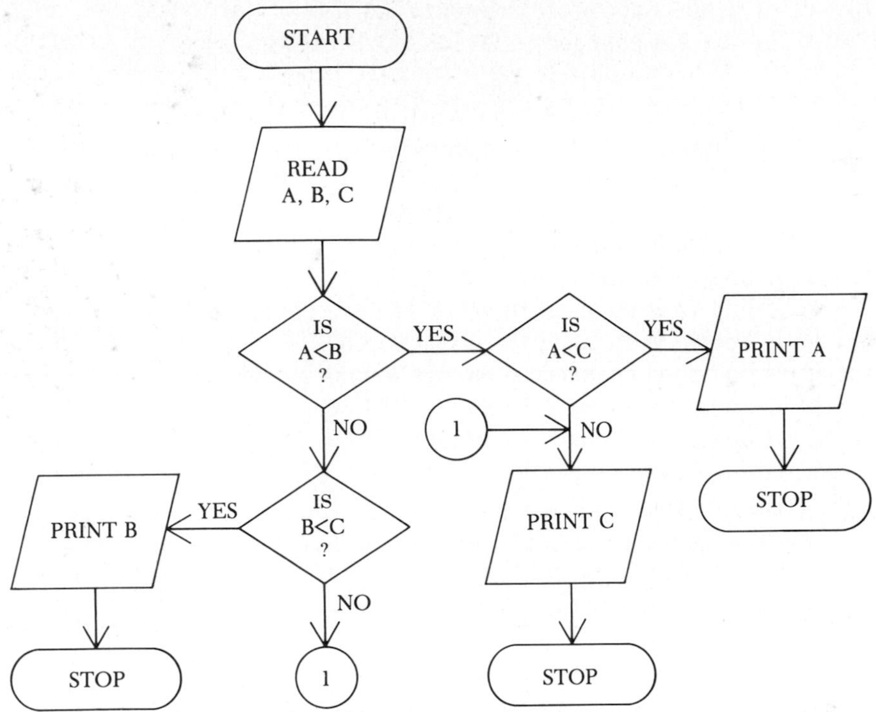

FIGURE 6.6 Flowchart for Program 6.13

SUMMARY

The IF/THEN statement transfers control to the statement indicated by the line number only if a certain condition is true. If the condition is not true, the statement following the IF/THEN statement is executed next. The relations that can be used in expressing conditions that can be tested are >, >=, <, <=, =, and <>.

The computed GO TO statement allows control to be transferred to any one of several statements based on the current value of a particular variable. The STOP statement stops the program execution, just as a GO TO to the END statement does.

EXERCISES

6.1 What is wrong with the following statement?

```
50 IF A>B THEN 50
```

* 6.2 What would happen to **Program 6.1** if
a. line 20 was changed to 20 READ B, A?
b. line 35 was omitted?

6.3 What will **Program 6.3** do when each of the following changes is made? (Each part of this exercise is independent of the others.)
a. If line 75 is changed to 75 IF N <> 5 THEN 90
b. If line 75 is changed to 75 IF N < =5 THEN 90
c. If line 75 is changed to 75 IF N <> 5 THEN 80
d. If line 75 is changed to 75 IF N >= 5 THEN 90
e. If line 75 is changed to 75 IF N > 5 THEN 90
f. If line 85 is changed to 85 GO TO 50
g. If line 85 is changed to 85 GO TO 60
h. If line 85 is changed to 85 GO TO 65
i. If line 85 is changed to 85 GO TO 70
j. If line 80 is changed to 80 LET N = N + 2

6.4 What will **Program 6.4** do when each of the following changes is made? (Each part of this exercise is independent of the others.)
a. line 75 is changed to 75 GO TO 40
b. line 75 is changed to 75 GO TO 45
c. line 75 is changed to 75 GO TO 55
d. line 55 is changed to 55 IF X = 999 THEN 999

6.5 What would **Program 6.3** do if line 75 was changed to line 58?

* 6.6 What would **Program 6.4** do if line 55 was changed to line 72?

6.7 Rewrite **Program 6.2** so that only the numbers of those students whose index is less than 3.0 will be printed. The program should print an appropriate heading.

6.8 Write a program to print the sum of the odd numbers between 7 and 33.

6.9 Write a program to read three numbers and print the largest of the three.

6.10 Write a program to read three numbers and print the median (e.g., the median of 8, 12, 2 is 8).

6.11 Write a program to read numbers until 999 is encountered. Then have the computer print the average of the numbers.

6.12 Write a program to read 10 numbers that are grades in a programming examination. Have the computer print the average passing grade, the average failing grade, and the class average. Grades of 60 or above are considered passing. The data values to be used are: 60, 59, 40, 88, 98, 75, 90, 72, 82, and 77.

6.13 Modify **Program 6.5** so that the sum of all of the bonuses and the sum of all of the earnings are printed. The output should look like this:

PERSON	BONUS	EARNINGS
1	0	800
2	156.25	1406.25
:	:	:
:	:	:
9	578.125	2503.13
TOTALS	XXXX.XX	XXXXX.XX

6.14 Rewrite **Program 6.6** to test for the following conditions for retirement:

1. Age must be at least 62, or
2. Age must be at least 60 and the years employed must be at least 20, or
3. Years employed must be at least 25, or
4. Age must be at least 58 and years employed must be at least 20 and salary must be at least $25,000.

6.15 Write a program that reads in a product number, quantity ordered, and unit price, and have the computer print a table with the following heading:

PRODUCT NO. PRICE QUANTITY DISCOUNT AMOUNT

A discount of 10 percent is given on all orders of at least 100 items. The amount is equal to price times quantity less discount. There is no discount on orders of fewer than 100 items. Use the following data:

Product Number	Price	Quantity
101	$2	250
210	6	95
330	3	110

6.16 Write a program that reads in four numbers and prints one of the following messages as appropriate:

"All of the numbers are equal to each other"

or

"Not all of the numbers are equal to each other"

6.17 Write a program that will compute federal and state tax deductions, based on the gross wages given below, and also the net wage after all taxes have been deducted.

Federal Deduction		State Deduction	
Gross Wage	%	Gross Wage	
Less than or equal $200	15	Less than or equal $200	2
Greater than $200 but less than $301	20	Greater than $200	3
Greater than $300	22		

Have a heading that looks like this:

```
GROSS   FEDERAL   STATE      TOTAL       NET
WAGE      TAX      TAX    DEDUCTIONS    WAGE
```

Use these data values: 200, 350, 300, 250, 100, 500.

6.18 The following table shows the first quarter sales of the EXACT Company, by division. Sales are in thousands of dollars.

Division	January	February	March
1	$1,000	$ 750	$ 750
2	1,200	800	1,000
3	1,200	500	1,200
4	500	1,050	950

Write a program that outputs this table with total sales for each month at the bottom of each column.

6.19 Revise **Program 6.6** so that the output will have a heading:

```
EL. EMP.   AGE   YRS. EMPL.   SALARY
```

with all the relevant data following.

6.20 Revise **Program 6.6** so that the READ/DATA statements are replaced by an INPUT statement.

6.21 The bank your company uses for checking has the following method for checking account charges each month:

a. If the end of the month balance is $400 or more, there is no charge for the month regardless of the number of checks written.
b. If the end of the month balance is less than $400, there is a 25¢ per check charge for checks written during the month.

These charges are deducted from the balance in the account. There is already a $500 starting balance from the previous month to be carried over to month one.

Using the monthly data given below, write a program that generates output as follows:

Month	Checks Written	Ending Balance	Monthly Charges
1	xxxx	xxxxx	xxxx
2	xxxx	xxxxx	xxxx
.			
.			
.			
5	xxxx	xxxxx	xxxx

Data:

Month	Amount of Each Check Written	Deposits
1	$25, 500, 300, 75, 20, 10, 1500, 200, 700	$300, 200, 1000, 1500
2	$575, 500, 75, 725, 50, 65, 300, 55, 15	$750, 1200, 800
3	$30, 1200, 45, 55, 700, 1500, 400	$500, 1800, 1200
4	$1075, 125, 350, 60, 1440, 560, 200, 50	$1500, 1000, 1600
5	$75, 1025, 750, 35, 25, 165, 450, 565, 20	$1250, 1700, 1300

* 6.22 Many airlines have computerized reservation systems for their flights. As reservations are taken, the number of seats available begins to decline. It is important to be forewarned when the number of seats on a particular flight get low so as to prevent overbooking.

Suppose Goodflight Airlines has three daily flights as follows:

Flight No.	No. Seats Available at This Hour
381	25
402	15
283	30

In the last 4 hours the following number of reservations have been made for each of these flights:

Hour	No. Seats Reserved per Flight		
	381	402	283
1	5	7	0
2	7	1	2
3	5	3	3
4	5	2	5

Assume that at the end of every hour these figures are fed into the computer by a clerk to get an update on the seats available. If for any flight the number of seats is 10 or less, a warning for that flight is printed out on the computer terminal. Your job is to write and run a conversational program that a nonprogramming clerk will run so that at the end of each hour the current seating status for each flight is obtained. Your program should ulilize the above information and be neatly structured with fully labeled output in your own format.

* 6.23 Write a program that will read 10 persons' application numbers, annual salary, rent, years employed at same job, and years living at same address. Have the computer print the application numbers of people who are eligible for a credit card. To be eligible, one must have a salary of over $25,000 per year, or have an annual salary of over $20,000 and pay a rent of less than one-quarter of a month's salary, or have an annual salary of over $15,000 and be living at the same address for more than 5 years, or have an annual salary of at least $10,000 and be living at the same address for at least 5 years and be employed at the same job for at least 3 years. All other applications are rejected. Before writing this program, draw a flowchart of the logic required.

Use the following data:

Application Number	Salary	Rent	Years Employed	Years Residing
605	$21,000	$560	4	5
610	18,000	500	10	14
614	35,000	750	2	10
656	11,000	280	20	19
678	15,500	400	6	2
692	8,000	200	10	11
694	32,000	850	3	3
697	12,500	375	4	6
698	40,000	950	15	8
700	20,000	395	5	5

6.24 To **Program 6.5** add the following processing controls:

a. A counter to check that data for all nine employees has been processed.

b. A reasonableness test that produces an asterisk (*) at the end of the output for each employee earning more than $2000.

6.25 To **Program 6.11** add a reasonableness test to prevent the data entry of a license number greater than 99999, a five-digit maximum.

6.26 Revise **Program 6.6** to perform a sequence check on the employee number.

6.27 What will the following program print when it is run?

```
10 LET I = 1
15 ON I GO TO 40, 20, 30
20 PRINT "IS",
25 GO TO 45
30 PRINT "EASY"
35 GO TO 45
40 PRINT "PROGRAMMING",
45 LET I = I + 1
50 IF I < = 3 THEN 15
55 END
```

6.28 Modify the program in *exercise 6.27* to have it print "IS PROGRAMMING EASY." Change only line 15.

6.29 If we replaced line 55 in the program in *exercise 6.27* with

55 STOP

what would the computer print?

6.30 What would be printed if line 15 of the program in *exercise 6.27* was changed to
a. 15 ON I+1 GO TO 40,20,30?
b. 15 ON 2*I GO TO 40,20,30?
c. 15 ON 3*I GO TO 40,20,30?

6.31 What will **Program 6.10** do if line 15 is changed to:
a) 15 ON X GO TO 30,20,50,40,99?
b) 15 ON X GO TO 30,20,50,40,10?
c) 15 ON X GO TO 30,20,50,40,20?

6.32 Write a program that will read 10 account numbers, each followed by the number of months that no payment has been made. Have the computer print the account number followed by the appropriate action for each as given in the following table:

No. of Months	Action
0	none
1	gentle reminder
2 or 3	strong reminder
4 or more	lawyer's letter

Test your program using the following data:

Account Number	Months	Account Number	Months
2370	2	2182	3
3542	3	1352	5
2372	0	1519	1
8282	1	2315	2
3838	4	1820	0

6.33 Write a program that reads in an employee's number, the number of his or her dependents, the number of hours that he or she worked during the week, the hourly rate that applies, and a code number of 0, 1, or 2 to indicate that the employee carries no insurance, personal insurance only, or family insurance, respectively.

Have the computer calculate the employee's wages. This should be number of hours × the hourly rate if the number of hours worked is 40 hours or less. If the number of hours worked is greater than 40, the employee should receive 1½ times the hourly rate for the additional hours above 40. The taxes deducted from the wages should be according to the following table:

Number of Dependents	Percent Deducted
0	28
1	26
2	24
3	22
4	20
5	18
6	16
7 or more	14

The insurance deducted should be according to the following table:

Code	Meaning	Amount Deducted
0	No insurance	$ 0
1	Insurance for self only	5
2	Insurance for family	10

Have the following table prepared:

Employee Number	Gross Wages	Tax Deducted	Insurance Deducted	Net Pay
Totals	_____	_____	_____	_____

Prepare the DATA statement for 10 employees and execute the program.

```
920 DATA 6044,0,37,3.50,1,4411,2,42,3.75,2
930 DATA 7158,1,40,4.10,2,1142,0,47,4.50,1
940 DATA 6482,8,45,2.80,2,1231,4,50,2.50,1
950 DATA 7111,2,40,3.00,1,1421,5,42,2.60,2
960 DATA 8421,7,38,4.25,2,1333,0,41,2.80,0
```

Use the computed GO TO statement to determine the tax rate and the amount of insurance to be deducted.

* 6.34 Why will **Program 6.6** work more efficiently if line 55 is omitted?

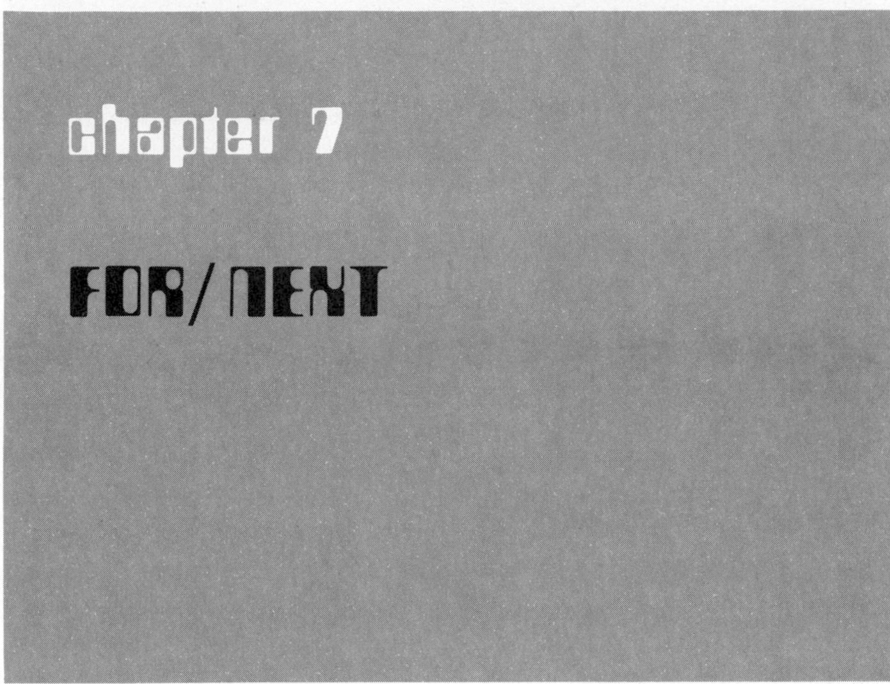

THE FOR AND NEXT STATEMENTS

Any time we wish to perform an operation or several operations a fixed number of times, the FOR/NEXT statements can be used. For example, in Program 6.3 we wanted to read five numbers from the DATA statement and add them and their squares. That program logic could have been set up much more easily with the FOR/NEXT statements. This will be done in Program 7.3. To introduce the FOR/NEXT statements, let us write a program that prints the numbers from 1 through 10, first using the IF statement.

PROGRAM 7.1 Printing the Numbers 1 through 10 Using IF/THEN

```
10 LET N=1
15 PRINT N;
20 IF N>=10 THEN 35
25 LET N=N+1
30 GO TO 15
35 END

RUN
 1  2  3  4  5  6  7  8  9  10
```

We will now rewrite the program using the FOR/NEXT statements.

PROGRAM 7.2 Printing the Numbers 1 through 10 Using FOR/NEXT

```
10 FOR N=1 TO 10
15 PRINT N;
20 NEXT N
25 END


RUN
 1  2  3  4  5  6  7  8  9  10
```

The FOR statement in line 10 initializes the variable *N* to 1. Line 15 then prints the number 1. The NEXT statement in line 20 compares the current value of the variable *N* (the number 1) to the upper limit mentioned in the FOR statement, namely, the number 10. If the variable *N* is less than 10, it will be incremented by 1, and execution will continue with the line following the FOR statement. Thus, the number 2 will be printed by line 15. This will continue until the variable *N* is finally equal to 10, at which time execution will continue with the statement following the NEXT statement, which in this case is the END statement.

Suppose we wished to have the computer print all the odd numbers between 1 and 10. To alter Program 7.1, we would replace line 25 with

25 LET N = N + 2

That is, we would like to have the variable *N* incremented by 2 rather than 1. This change can also be accomplished with the FOR/NEXT statements by replacing line 10 in Program 7.2 with

10 FOR N = 1 TO 10 STEP 2

That is, if we wish the index variable *N* to be changed by any number other than the number 1, we can add the word STEP at the end of the FOR statement and specify by how much we would like the index variable to be changed. Note that Program 7.1 would stop printing with the number 11, while Program 7.2 would stop printing with the number 9. The difference in logic is that Program 7.1 increments *N* by 2, prints *N*, and then tests *N* to see if it is greater than 10, whereas Program 7.2 increments *N* by 2, then tests to see if *N* is greater than 10, and then prints *N*. Some examples of FOR statements follow:

1. 100 FOR K = 2 TO 8
2. 100 FOR R = 1 TO M STEP .5
3. 100 FOR L = S TO Q STEP Z
4. 100 FOR J = A+B TO C+D−E/3 STEP F*G+8.7
5. 100 FOR P = 10 TO −7 STEP −2

There is less variety possible with the NEXT statement. Some examples are NEXT K, NEXT R, etc.

The generalized form of the FOR statement is

$$\text{line \# FOR \{variable\}} = \left\{\begin{matrix}\text{constant}\\ \text{variable}\\ \text{expression}\end{matrix}\right\} \text{TO} \left\{\begin{matrix}\text{constant}\\ \text{variable}\\ \text{expression}\end{matrix}\right\} \text{STEP} \left\{\begin{matrix}\text{constant}\\ \text{variable}\\ \text{expression}\end{matrix}\right\}$$

The word FOR must be followed by some variable. This variable need not have been previously given a value. If that variable had some value previously, its previous value would be lost.

Following the = sign and the word TO must be some constant, variable, or expression. The variable, as well as any variables in the expression, must have been previously given values.

The STEP is optional and may be omitted if you wish to increment the index variable by the number 1. Note that it is possible to have a STEP of a fraction as in example 2 above, and to have a negative STEP as in example 5 above. Whenever the STEP is negative, the starting value should be greater than the finishing value. The looping in that case will continue until the value of the index variable becomes less than or equal to the finishing value.

The form of the NEXT statement is

line # NEXT variable

For each FOR statement in a program there must exist one and only one NEXT statement using the same variable.

We will now rewrite Program 6.3 using the FOR/NEXT statements but omitting all of the REM statements. Note that the output in Program 7.3 is identical to that of Program 6.3, which is shown again below.

PROGRAM 6.3 Summing Numbers and Their Squares

```
10 REM THIS PROGRAM READS 5 NUMBERS FROM THE DATA STATEMENT
20 REM AND PRINTS THE NUMBERS, THE SQUARES OF THE NUMBERS,
30 REM AND THE SUMS OF THE NUMBERS AND THEIR SQUARES.
40 LET S=0
45 LET S2=0
50 LET N=1
55 READ X
60 LET S=S+X
65 LET S2=S2+X↑2
70 PRINT X,X↑2
75 IF N=5 THEN 90
80 LET N=N+1
85 GO TO 55
90 PRINT "---","---"
95 PRINT S,S2
100 DATA 7,2,3,4,1
999 END
```

PROGRAM 6.3 continued

```
RUN
 7              49
 2              4
 3              9
 4              16
 1              1
---            ---
 17             79
```

PROGRAM 7.3 Rewriting Program 6.3 Using the FOR/NEXT Statement

```
10 LET S=0
15 LET S2=0
20 FOR N=1 TO 5
25 READ X
30 LET S=S+X
35 LET S2=S2+X↑2
40 PRINT X,X↑2
45 NEXT N
50 PRINT"---","---"
55 PRINT S,S2
100 DATA 7,2,3,4,1
999 END
```

```
RUN
 7              49
 2              4
 3              9
 4              16
 1              1
---            ---
 17             79
```

The FOR/NEXT statements permit a process to be repeated as many times as specified in the FOR statement. In the case that follows, three different sets of data are processed within a single program using the FOR and NEXT statements.

CASE 7.1 A fast-food chain has three geographic regions, each with a different number of stores in it. A program provides a report of the monthly sales for each region by producing a total and average sales per store. Last month's sales were:

Region	Store Sales (in thousands of $)					
1	40	20	50	60		
2	50	40	55	35	70	65
3	35	46	25			

Program 7.4 produces the results desired. The FOR/NEXT loop (lines 10 through 70) is set to repeat the accumulation processes for each set of data. Each data set ends with a −99 value to trigger the IF/THEN in line 35, which transfers control to line 60. When the third data set is completed,

the program execution ends. Note that there is no "OUT OF DATA" message, because the program logic ensures that after all the data has been read, control will pass to line 70 and then finally to line 90. A flowchart in Figure 7.1 provides the logic of Program 7.4.

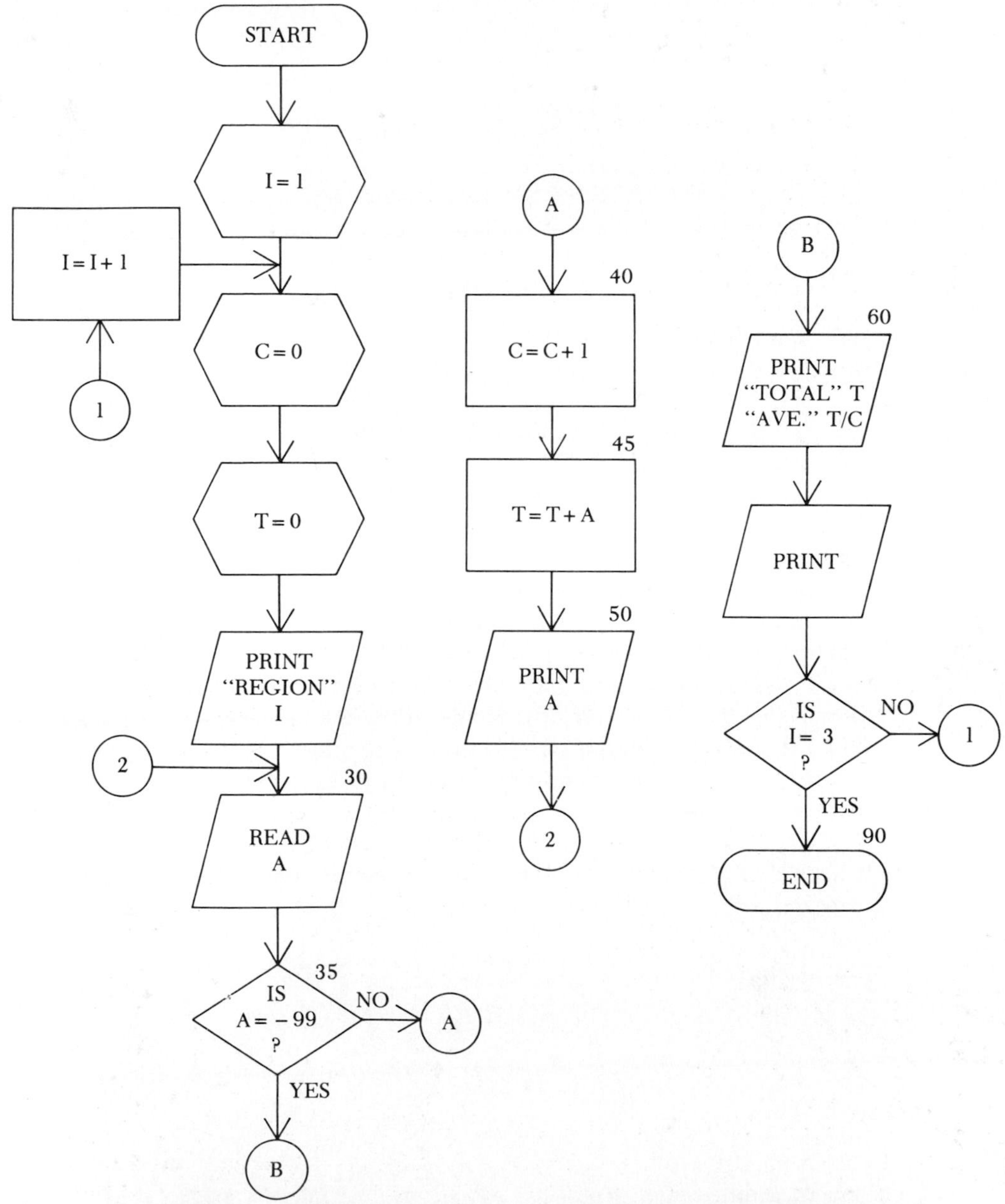

FIGURE 7.1 Flowchart for Program 7.4, Case 7.1, Food-Chain Sales Analysis

PROGRAM 7.4 Case 7.1, Food Chain Sales Analysis Program

```
10 FOR I= 1 TO 3
15 LET C= 0
20 LET T= 0
25 PRINT "REGION";I;
30 READ A
35 IF A= -99 THEN 60
40 LET C= C+1
45 LET T= T+A
50 PRINT A;
55 GO TO 30
60 PRINT " TOTAL";T;" AVERAGE";T/C
65 PRINT
70 NEXT I
75 DATA 40,20,50,60,-99
80 DATA 50,40,55,35,70,65,-99
85 DATA 35,46,25,-99
90 END

RUN
REGION 1  40  20  50  60  TOTAL 170  AVERAGE 42.5

REGION 2  50  40  55  35  70  65  TOTAL 315  AVERAGE 52.5

REGION 3  35  46  25  TOTAL 106  AVERAGE 35.3333
```

Another illustration of the FOR/NEXT statements is found in Program 7.5, which is based on Case 7.2. This case describes a situation in which the FOR/NEXT loop should never be completed.

CASE 7.2 Suppose we have 10 product numbers, each followed by the amount in inventory of that product in DATA statements. A salesperson will input a product number and we want the computer to print the amount of that product in inventory. If the salesperson inputs an incorrect product number (i.e., one that is not listed in the DATA statements), we will inform him or her of this and allow the salesperson to try again. When the salesperson has completed asking questions, he or she can type in a zero for the product number, signaling the computer that the data entry is completed.

A flowchart that helps to plan out the program for this case is shown in Figure 7.2.

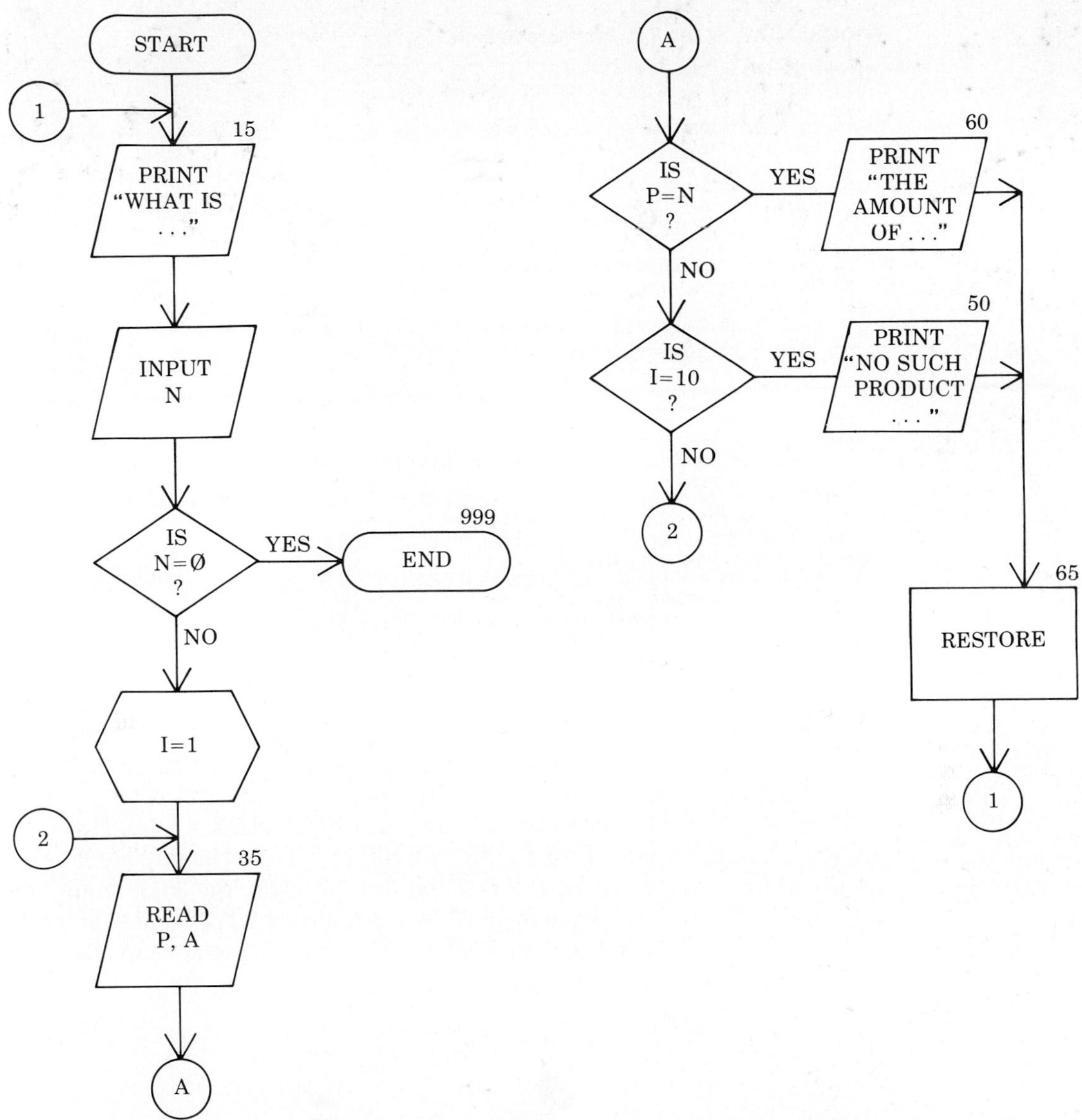

FIGURE 7.2 Flowchart for Program 7.5, Case 7.2, Inventory Search

PROGRAM 7.5 Case 7.2, Inventory Search

```
10 REM INVENTORY PROGRAM
15 PRINT "WHAT IS THE PRODUCT NUMBER";
20 INPUT N
25 IF N=0 THEN 999
30 FOR I=1 TO 10
35 READ P,A
40 IF P=N THEN 60
45 NEXT I
50 PRINT "NO SUCH PRODUCT NUMBER AS";N;"TRY AGAIN"
55 GO TO 65
60 PRINT " THE AMOUNT OF PRODUCT";P;"IN INVENTORY IS";A
65 RESTORE
70 GO TO 15
75 DATA 1234,100,2345,150,1345,50,1432,75,3214,25,4321,10
80 DATA 3241,250,2233,80,1144,200,3311,500
999 END

RUN
WHAT IS THE PRODUCT NUMBER ?2345
 THE AMOUNT OF PRODUCT 2345 IN INVENTORY IS 150
WHAT IS THE PRODUCT NUMBER ?3311
 THE AMOUNT OF PRODUCT 3311 IN INVENTORY IS 500
WHAT IS THE PRODUCT NUMBER ?2233
 THE AMOUNT OF PRODUCT 2233 IN INVENTORY IS 80
WHAT IS THE PRODUCT NUMBER ?1122
NO SUCH PRODUCT NUMBER AS 1122 TRY AGAIN
WHAT IS THE PRODUCT NUMBER ?1144
 THE AMOUNT OF PRODUCT 1144 IN INVENTORY IS 200
WHAT IS THE PRODUCT NUMBER ?0
```

Note that in Program 7.5 we do not wish to complete the FOR/NEXT loop 10 times. If the program does complete the loop without branching out from it, this would mean that we have not found a product number in the DATA statements that matches the one that was INPUT.

Thus we see that we can branch out of a FOR/NEXT loop. However, we should never branch into a FOR/NEXT loop from the outside. For example, if we would have a GO TO 35 on line 17 or on line 55, it would immediately cause an error message to be printed out.* We can branch to a statement in a FOR/NEXT loop from some other statement in the same loop without any difficulty. (See, for example, Program 7.8.)

CONCEPTS OF STRUCTURE

We have waited to discuss *structured programming* concepts until now because it is at this point in the text that you have developed a capability to do such programming in BASIC.

*On some systems it may be possible to branch into a FOR/NEXT loop from the outside.

As with all concepts, *structured programming* is not simply defined*. In fact, such languages as BASIC and FORTRAN lack features that are essential for a "true" structured programming approach. We will examine the ideas of structured programming as they can best be used within the BASIC language presented in this text.

The philosophy of structured programming is to develop programs in such a way so that coding is more easily accomplished. Program clarity and understandability are regarded as essential. People besides the originator of a program should be able to read the program and know how and what it does. Programs developed according to structured concepts can be modified easily at a later date.

One aspect of structured programming is the avoidance of logic that is "tricky" or overly involved. We will point out various control structures that can be used to develop understandable programs that avoid overly complex and unnecessary logic. In addition, we will illustrate how program clarity can be improved by using *indentation* of statements.

Logical Structures

One of the main concepts of structured programming is the idea that programs can be created by using only three basic control structures. These structures will be described first in general and then as they relate to the BASIC language.

Figure 7.3 illustrates these three basic control structures. These logical structures are: (a) simple sequence, (b) selection sequence, and (c) repetition sequence.

a. The simple sequence is a structure that follows a sequential execution of statements. The program goes from one line to the next without a transfer or branch.
b. The selection sequence is exemplified by a comparison or test. In this logical sequence, the computer performs a test to determine whether a condition is "true" or "false". The result of the test is the execution of one of two statements. This structure is also called "IF THEN ELSE" and is written without blanks, as IFTHENELSE. That is, *if* the condition is true, *then* execute the statement indicated, or *else* execute the other statement.

---

*Suggested readings on this topic include: Bohl, Marilyn, *Tools for Structured Design* (Chicago: Science Research Associates, 1978) or Hughes, Joan K. and Jay I. Michtom, *A Structured Approach to Programming* (Englewood Cliffs, N.J.: Prentice-Hall, 1977).

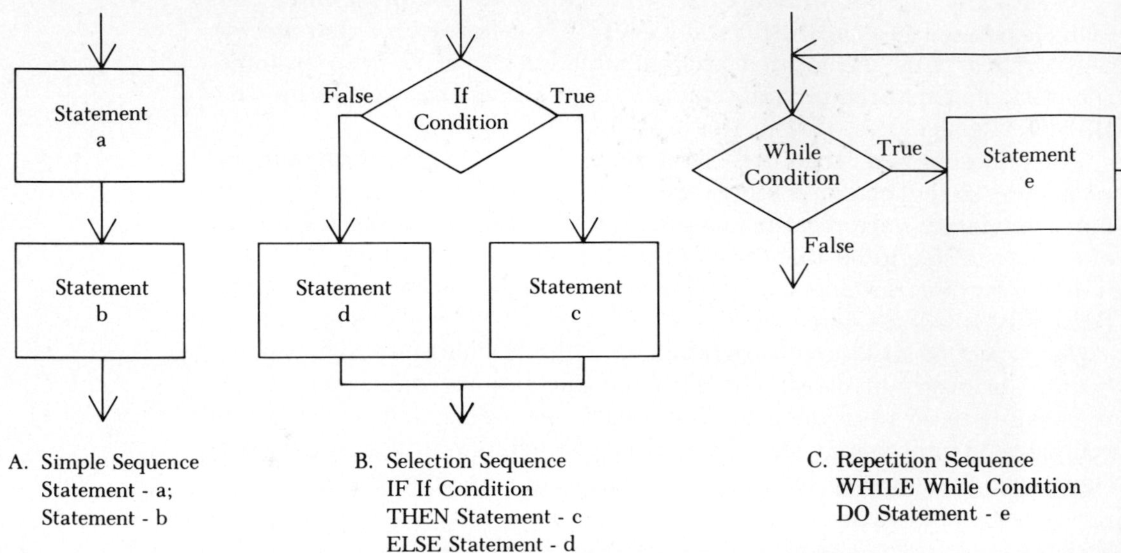

A. Simple Sequence
Statement - a;
Statement - b

B. Selection Sequence
IF If Condition
THEN Statement - c
ELSE Statement - d

C. Repetition Sequence
WHILE While Condition
DO Statement - e

FIGURE 7.3 Three Basic Control Structures

c. The repetition sequence provides for loops. A sequence of statements will be executed or repeated a specified number of times until a certain condition is met. This structure is called a DOWHILE; that is, *do* the statements *while* the condition is true.

These three structures should be sufficient to write any program. Several other structures have been proposed to provide improved programming convenience. Two of these structures are the DOUNTIL and CASE. Figure 7.4 illustrates these.

a. The DOUNTIL structure is similar to the DOWHILE in providing a loop capability. Whereas the DOWHILE would test the condition *before* processing the statement, the DOUNTIL will test the condition *after* the statement. This means the statement will be executed at least once. The loop will be repeated until the condition is true.
b. The CASE structure is an extension of the IFTHENELSE structure (Figure 7.3b.). It is useful when there are several alternatives and only one is to be executed on the basis of the test condition.

In examining these control structures, you will find that there is only one entrance and one exit from the structure. This is significant, in that programs written with these structures will have distinct blocks of statements, or *modules*, that can easily be followed by anyone looking at a program listing. In addition, such modules improve the testing and debugging of the program by making it easier to locate the error.

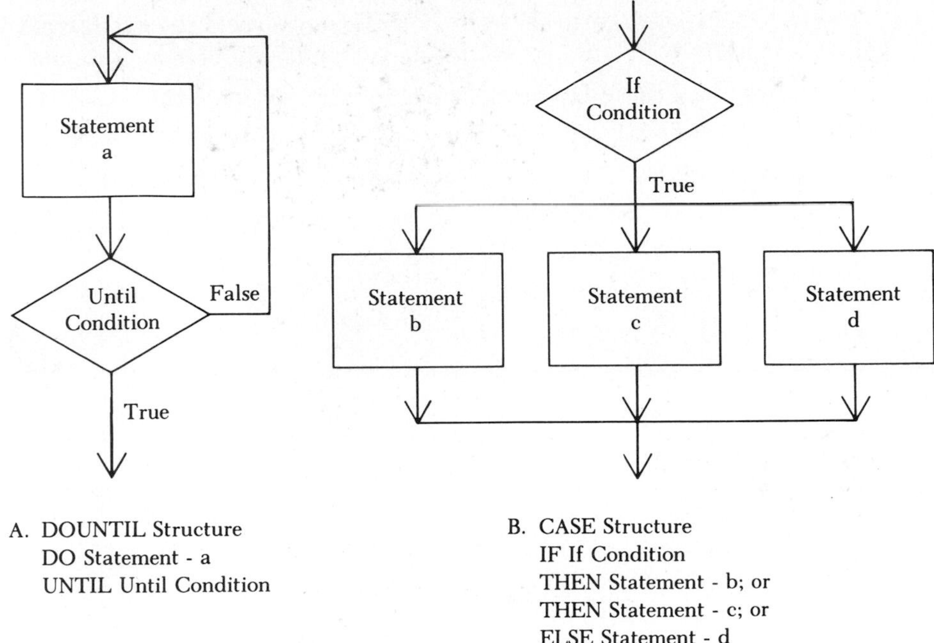

A. DOUNTIL Structure
DO Statement - a
UNTIL Until Condition

B. CASE Structure
IF If Condition
THEN Statement - b; or
THEN Statement - c; or
ELSE Statement - d

FIGURE 7.4 DOUNTIL and CASE Structures

Logical Structures and BASIC

The capability of writing BASIC programs using the control structures described above depends on the dialect of the language available to the programmer. In general, using the statements already available allows you to write BASIC programs by using the various structures outlined. The following illustrations provide examples of this capability. The one exception is the selection sequence IFTHENELSE. ANSI Basic contains only the IFTHEN sequence. But many computers do have the IFTHENELSE sequence. This is something you can find out by checking the manual for your system.

Constructing a simple sequence usually involves a data entry process such as READ/DATA or INPUT, followed by computations using LET, and finally processing the output with PRINT. Such a sequence is shown in Figure 7.5, using Program 4.6.

A selection sequence can be structured using IF/THEN statements, as shown in Figure 7.6, using Program 6.1.

A repetition sequence that follows a DOWHILE structure can be developed using IF/THEN statements to cause a loop. This process is shown in Figure 7.7.

The DOUNTIL structure has as its BASIC counterpart the FOR/NEXT loop. The DOUNTIL can also be developed using IF/THEN statements. Figure 7.8, using Programs A and B, illustrates the DOUNTIL.

PROGRAM 4.6 Case 4.2, Depreciation, Using LET and INPUT Statements

```
1 REM CONVERSATIONAL PROGRAM FOR STRAIGHT LINE
5 REM DEPRECIATION DETERMINATION
10 PRINT "****STRAIGHT LINE DEPRECIATION DETERMINATION****"
12 PRINT
15 PRINT "AFTER ONE ? MARK, TYPE IN THE FOLLOWING ITEMS EACH"
16 PRINT "SEPARATED BY A , :   COST, SALVAGE VALUE (TYPE 0 IF"
17 PRINT "NONE),EST. YEARS OF LIFE"
18 PRINT
20 INPUT C,V,L
25 LET T=C-V
30 LET D=T/L
35 PRINT
40 PRINT "WITH A COST OF $";C;", A SALVAGE VALUE OF $";V;
50 PRINT " AND A USEFUL LIFE OF";L;"YEARS"
60 PRINT "THE ANNUAL DEPRECIATION FOR THIS ITEM IS $";D
99 END

RUN
****STRAIGHT LINE DEPRECIATION DETERMINATION****

AFTER ONE ? MARK, TYPE IN THE FOLLOWING ITEMS EACH
SEPARATED BY A , :   COST, SALVAGE VALUE (TYPE 0 IF
NONE),EST. YEARS OF LIFE

 ?36000,1200,3

WITH A COST OF $ 36000 , A SALVAGE VALUE OF $ 1200  AND A USEFUL LIFE OF
 3 YEARS
THE ANNUAL DEPRECIATION FOR THIS ITEM IS $ 11600
```

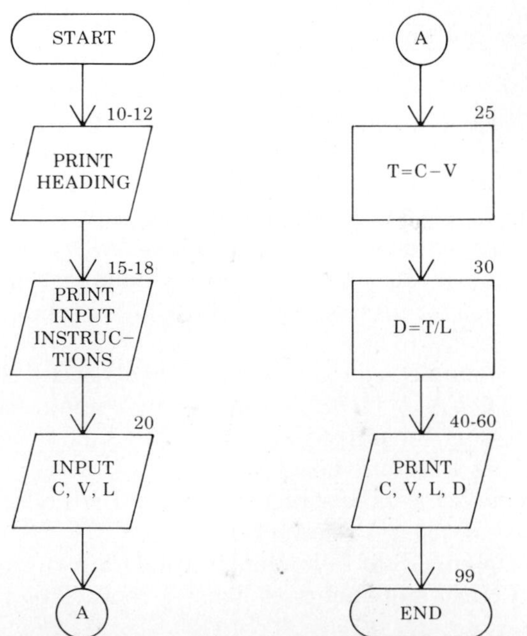

FIGURE 7.5 Simple Sequence Structure, Program 4.6 and Flowchart

PROGRAM 6.1

```
10 REM   THIS PROGRAM READS TWO NUMBERS AND PRINTS
15 REM   THE LARGER OF THE TWO
20 READ A, B
25 IF A>B THEN 40
30 PRINT B
35 GO TO 99
40 PRINT A
45 DATA 7, 3
99 END

RUN
 7
```

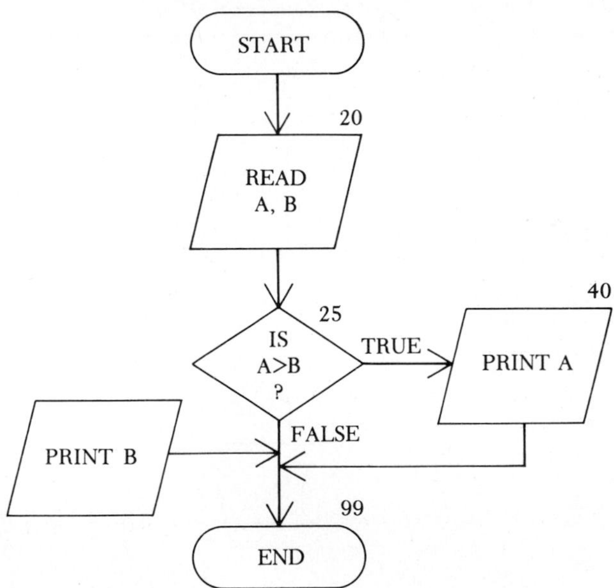

FIGURE 7.6 Selection Sequence, Program 6.1 and Flowchart

```
5 REM DOWHILE STRUCTURE
10 READ B
20 IF B <> -99 THEN 30
25 STOP
30 LET C = B*1.15
40 PRINT B,C
50 GOTO 10
60 DATA 12,17,10,15,19,18,-99
99 END
```

FIGURE 7.7 Program, Repetition Sequence, DOWHILE

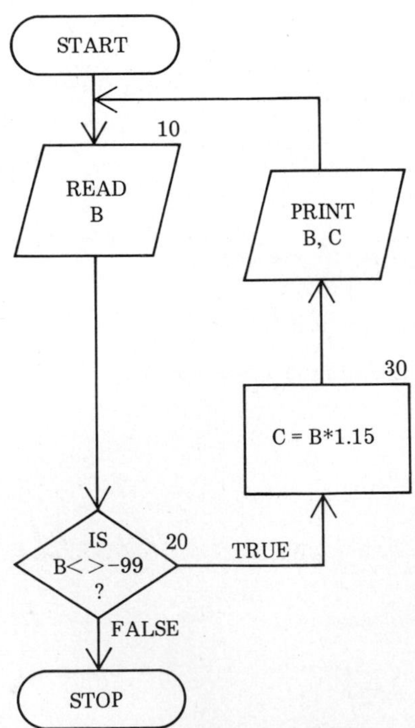

FIGURE 7.7 Repetition Sequence, DOWHILE Structure

PROGRAM A

```
5 REM DOUNTIL STRUCTURE
10 LET N=0
15 LET N=N+1
20 PRINT N;
25 IF N>=10 THEN 35
30 GOTO 15
35 END

RUN
  1  2  3  4  5  6  7  8  9  10
```

PROGRAM B

```
5 REM DOUNTIL STRUCTURE
10 FOR N=1 TO 10
15 PRINT N;
20 NEXT N
25  END

RUN
  1  2  3  4  5  6  7  8  9  10
```

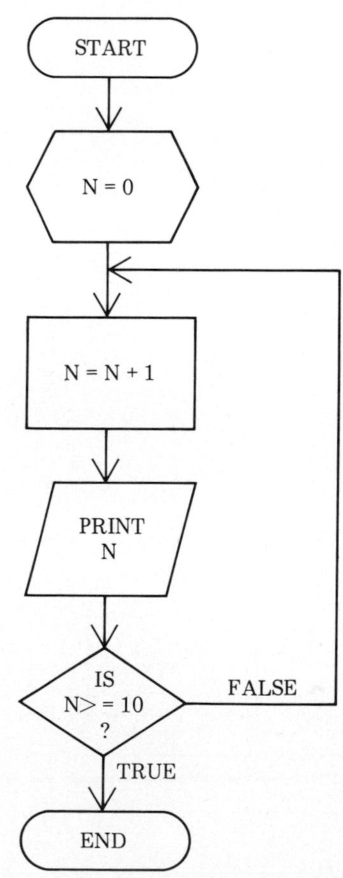

FIGURE 7.8 DOUNTIL Structure, Programs A and B with Flowchart

The CASE structure in BASIC would be implemented by using the computed GO TO statement. This statement is used when there are more than two possible alternatives, and only one can be executed on the basis of a test condition. Figure 7.9, using Program 6.10, illustrates the CASE structure.

PROGRAM 6.10

```
10 READ X
15 ON X GO TO 30,20,50,40
20 PRINT X;"TWO"
25 GO TO 10
30 PRINT X;"ONE"
35 GO TO 10
40 PRINT X;"FOUR"
45 GO TO 10
50 PRINT X;"THREE"
55 GO TO 10
60 DATA 1,2,3,4,1.5,4.8,3.6,2.2,5
99 END
```

```
RUN
 1 ONE
 2 TWO
 3 THREE
 4 FOUR
 1.5 ONE
 4.8 FOUR
 3.6 THREE
 2.2 TWO

ON- 5  LN #  15
```

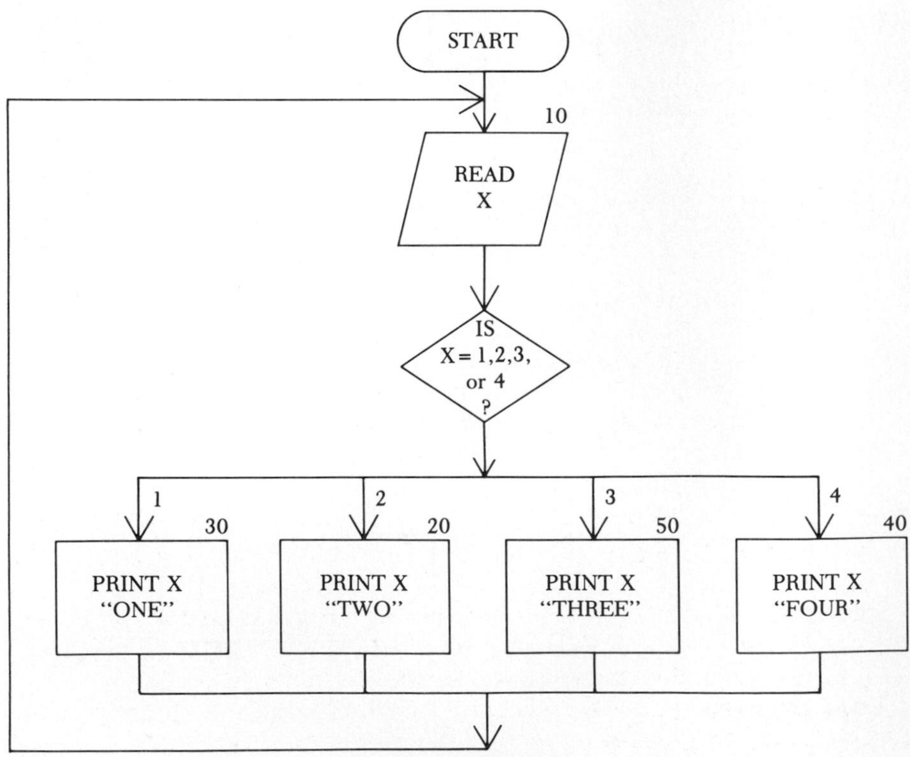

FIGURE 7.9 CASE Structure, Program 6.10 and Flowchart

Program Clarity

To make programs more readable, we can use the idea of *indentation.* This involves typing the program so that significant statements are indented from the line number toward the right side of the program. By using indentation it is possible to set off some of the logical structures described above. This will improve the readability of the program. It will not affect any of the program processes as carried out by the computer.

There are no specific rules for the indentation of BASIC statements. It is suggested that whenever a program has many selection processes, the relevant statements be indented. An example of such indentation is found in Chapter 6, Program 6.9.

When a program uses FOR/NEXT loops structures, it can be made more readable by indenting each loop and its contents. Such indentation is illustrated by Programs 7.6 through 7.12.

NESTED LOOPS

Consider Program 7.6.

PROGRAM 7.6 Nested Loops

```
10 FOR I=1 TO 3
15      FOR J=1 TO 5
20      PRINT I;J,
25      NEXT J
30 NEXT I
35 END

RUN
 1  1            1  2            1  3            1  4            1  5
 2  1            2  2            2  3            2  4            2  5
 3  1            3  2            3  3            3  4            3  5
```

Whenever we have one FOR/NEXT loop (lines 15–25) contained entirely within another FOR/NEXT loop (lines 10–30), these loops are called *nested loops.*

The inner loop (lines 15–25) is indented slightly to improve the readability of the program and to give the program a structured look. However, the program would work just as well without this indentation.

Note that in Program 7.6 the variable *J* goes from 1 to 5 each time variable *I* assumes a value. Note also that the NEXT J statement comes *before* the NEXT I statement. It must, because the FOR J = 1 TO 5 statement is *after* the FOR I = 1 TO 3 statement.

The output further aids in understanding how the nested loops are working. First the outer loop FOR statement in line 10 is executed. The value of I = 1 is fixed. This can be seen in the first row of output. The inner loop FOR statement in line 15 is executed and varies *J* from 1 to 5, while *I* is fixed at 1. Again look at the first line of output. Line 20, the PRINT statement, generates the fixed value of the outer loop and the varying values of the inner loop. Each row of output follows a similar pattern. The row value from the outer loop is fixed, while the column value derived from the inner loop changes.

Nested loop operations can also be seen in Programs 7.7 and 7.8. Program 7.7 prints a 5 × 5 multiplication table.

PROGRAM 7.7 A 5 × 5 Multiplication Table

```
10 FOR I=1 TO 5
15      FOR J=1 TO 5
20      PRINT I*J,
25      NEXT J
30 NEXT I
35 END

RUN
 1             2             3             4             5
 2             4             6             8             10
 3             6             9             12            15
 4             8             12            16            20
 5             10            15            20            25
```

Program 7.8 prints a 10 × 10 table of zeros with ones along the major diagonal.

PROGRAM 7.8 Branching in a FOR/NEXT Loop

```
10 FOR I=1 TO 10
15      FOR J=1 TO 10
20      LET X=0
25      IF I<>J THEN 35
30      LET X=1
35      PRINT X;
40      NEXT J
45 PRINT
50 NEXT I
55 END

RUN
 1  0  0  0  0  0  0  0  0  0
 0  1  0  0  0  0  0  0  0  0
 0  0  1  0  0  0  0  0  0  0
 0  0  0  1  0  0  0  0  0  0
 0  0  0  0  1  0  0  0  0  0
 0  0  0  0  0  1  0  0  0  0
 0  0  0  0  0  0  1  0  0  0
 0  0  0  0  0  0  0  1  0  0
 0  0  0  0  0  0  0  0  1  0
 0  0  0  0  0  0  0  0  0  1
```

The kind of table created by Program 7.8 is called the *identity matrix.* We will return to that and other matrices in Chapter 13. Program 7.8 illustrates the fact that we can branch from one part of a FOR/NEXT loop to another part of the same loop without difficulty because of line 25. Observe that the PRINT statement on line 45 is necessary to go to the next line after each line is complete.

Case 7.3 gives an application of nested FOR/NEXT loops.

CASE 7.3 Each year the planning department for a large corporation prepares a 3-year projection, by division, of sales, Presently, they are assuming a 12 percent growth rate compounded annually. The sales figures for this year by division are:

Division	Sales (million $)
1	$5.25
2	6.10
3	4.75
4	8.70
5	6.75
6	3.30

Program 7.9 generates a table with the required projections. This table is derived by the nested FOR/NEXT loops in the program. The outer loop (lines 25, 100) represents each of the six divisions. The inner loop (lines 40, 80) supplies the value for the variable *Y*, which is found in the compounding formula in line 60. Note the placement of line 33 between the FOR statements. Because of this PRINT statement, the division numbers are outputted as part of the table.

PROGRAM 7.9 Case 7.3, Sales Projections, Nested FOR/NEXT Statements

```
2 REM GROWTH PROJECTION PROGRAM
5 PRINT " ","DIVISIONS SALES PROJECTIONS - MILLIONS $"
1Ø PRINT " ","CURRENT","        PROJECTION YEARS"
15 PRINT "DIVISION","YEAR",1,2,3
2Ø LET R=.12
22 REM OUTER LOOP FOR EACH DIVISION
25 FOR D=1 TO 6
3Ø READ S
33 PRINT D,S,
35     REM INNER LOOP FOR PROJECTED SALES
4Ø     FOR Y=1 TO 3
6Ø     LET P=S*(1+R)↑Y
7Ø     PRINT "$";P,
8Ø     NEXT Y
9Ø PRINT
1ØØ NEXT D
11Ø PRINT "    PROJECTION TABLE PREPARED BY PLANNING DEPARTMENT"
12Ø DATA 5.25,6.1,4.75,8.7,6.75,3.3
19Ø END
```

PROGRAM 7.9 continued

```
RUN
                 DIVISIONS SALES PROJECTIONS - MILLIONS $
                 CURRENT             PROJECTION YEARS
DIVISION         YEAR               1                   2                   3
 1                5.25            $ 5.88              $ 6.5856            $ 7.37587

 2                6.1             $ 6.832             $ 7.65184           $ 8.57006

 3                4.75            $ 5.32              $ 5.9584            $ 6.67341

 4                8.7             $ 9.744             $ 10.9133           $ 12.2229

 5                6.75            $ 7.56              $ 8.4672            $ 9.48326

 6                3.3             $ 3.696             $ 4.13952           $ 4.63626

    PROJECTION TABLE PREPARED BY PLANNING DEPARTMENT
```

A flowchart showing the logic of Program 7.9 is shown in Figure 7.10.

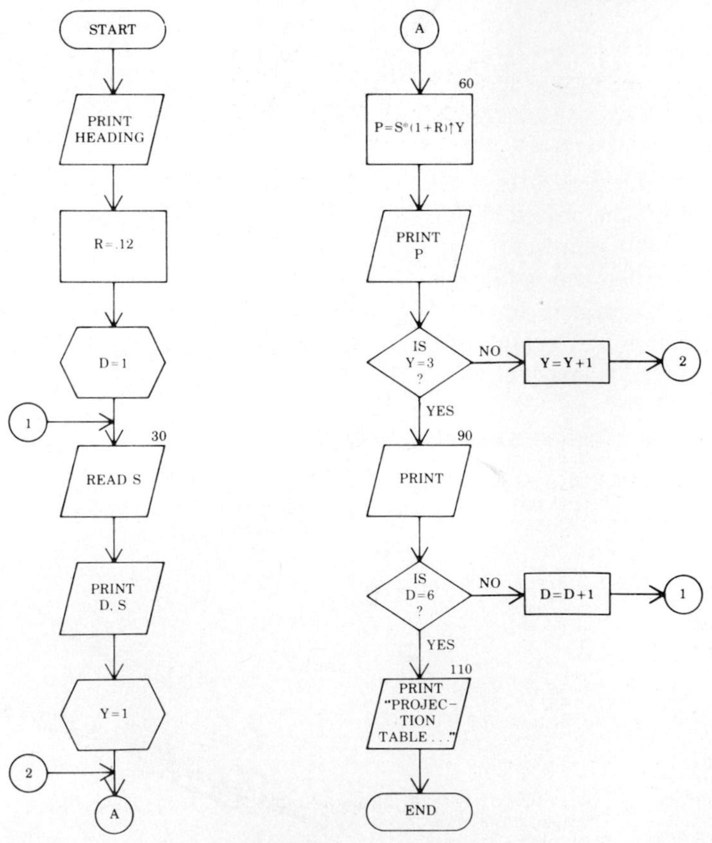

FIGURE 7.10 Flowchart for Program 7.9, Case 7.3, Sales Projections

Before we look at the next case, consider the following BASIC statements:

```
10 FOR A = 1 TO 60
20 PRINT "–";
30 NEXT A
```

These statements will result in a line of 60 dashes being outputted. Such a FOR/NEXT loop is useful for underlining and producing graphic output. Case 7.4 illustrates these points.

CASE 7.4 It is desired to develop a bar chart for the sales data shown below. Such charts provide a graphic display that is useful when comparing different groups, items, or activities.

Division	Sales (million $)
1	15
2	22
3	18
4	30

Program 7.10 produces a bar chart for the data supplied. The underlined heading is a result of the FOR/NEXT loop in lines 20 to 30. The bars are produced by the FOR/NEXT statements in lines 55 to 65. The lengths of the bars are determined by a variable, *D*, read by the statement 45 READ D. The outer loop (lines 40, 80) controls how many data values will be read and graphed.

PROGRAM 7.10 Case 7.4 Sales Data Bar Chart

```
10 REM PROGRAM TO DEVELOP A BAR CHART
15 PRINT " ","SALES DATA - BAR CHART"
20 FOR A = 1 TO 50
25 PRINT "-";
30 NEXT A
35 PRINT
40 FOR I= 1 TO 4
45 READ D
50 PRINT "DIVISION";I;":";
55    FOR P = 1 TO D
60    PRINT"=";
65    NEXT P
70 PRINT ":   ";D
75 PRINT
80 NEXT I
85 DATA 15,22,13,30
90 END
```

```
RUN
                  SALES DATA - BAR CHART
--------------------------------------------------
DIVISION 1 :===============:   15

DIVISION 2 :======================:   22

DIVISION 3 :=============:   13

DIVISION 4 :==============================:   30
```

There is no limit to the number of levels of nesting, as long as no inner loop overlaps any outer loop. Some examples follow.

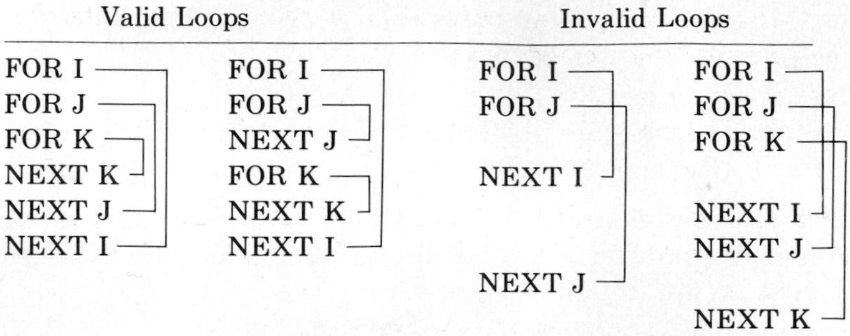

Valid Loops		Invalid Loops	
FOR I FOR J FOR K NEXT K NEXT J NEXT I	FOR I FOR J NEXT J FOR K NEXT K NEXT I	FOR I FOR J NEXT I NEXT J	FOR I FOR J FOR K NEXT I NEXT J NEXT K

Programs 7.11a and 7.11b illustrate the two valid loops.

PROGRAM 7.11a Three Nested Loops

```
10 FOR I= 1 TO 2
15     FOR J=12 TO 14
20       FOR K=26 TO 29
25       PRINT  I;J;K,
30       NEXT K
32       PRINT
35     NEXT J
37     PRINT
40 NEXT I
45 END

RUN
 1  12  26       1  12  27       1  12  28       1  12  29
 1  13  26       1  13  27       1  13  28       1  13  29
 1  14  26       1  14  27       1  14  28       1  14  29

 2  12  26       2  12  27       2  12  28       2  12  29
 2  13  26       2  13  27       2  13  28       2  13  29
 2  14  26       2  14  27       2  14  28       2  14  29
```

PROGRAM 7.11b Three Nested Loops

```
10 FOR I=1 TO 2
15     FOR J=12 TO 16
20     PRINT I;J,
25     NEXT   J
30     FOR   K=26 TO 30
35     PRINT    I;K,
40     NEXT    K
45 NEXT    I
50 END

RUN
 1  12        1  13        1  14        1  15        1  16
 1  26        1  27        1  28        1  29        1  30
 2  12        2  13        2  14        2  15        2  16
 2  26        2  27        2  28        2  29        2  30
```

Case 7.5 illustrates three levels of nesting.

CASE 7.5 A bank wishes to print a table of the amounts of money available when various principals are invested at varying interest rates for several time periods, as indicated below.

Principal	Rate (%)	Time (years)
1000, 2000	7, 7½, 8	5, 10, 15, 20

Program 7.12 prints such a table using three levels of nesting.

PROGRAM 7.12 Table Using Three Levels of Nesting

```
5  PRINT "PRINCIPAL","RATE","TIME","AMOUNT"
10 FOR P=1000 TO 2000 STEP 1000
15    FOR R=.07 TO .08 STEP .005
20       FOR T=5 TO 20 STEP 5
25       PRINT P,R,T,P*(1+R)↑(T-1)
30       NEXT T
31       PRINT
35    NEXT R
36    PRINT
40 NEXT P
45 END

RUN
PRINCIPAL       RATE            TIME            AMOUNT
 1000           .07             5               1310.8
 1000           .07             10              1838.46
 1000           .07             15              2578.53
 1000           .07             20              3616.53

 1000           .075            5               1335.47
 1000           .075            10              1917.24
 1000           .075            15              2752.44
 1000           .075            20              3951.49

 1000           .08             5               1360.49
 1000           .08             10              1999.
 1000           .08             15              2937.19
 1000           .08             20              4315.7


 2000           .07             5               2621.59
 2000           .07             10              3676.92
 2000           .07             15              5157.07
 2000           .07             20              7233.06

 2000           .075            5               2670.94
 2000           .075            10              3834.48
 2000           .075            15              5504.89
 2000           .075            20              7902.98

 2000           .08             5               2720.98
 2000           .08             10              3998.01
 2000           .08             15              5874.39
 2000           .08             20              8631.4
```

The PRINT statements on lines 31 and 36 improve the readability of the output by skipping lines whenever the interest rate and principal change.

SUMMARY

Whenever one wants to perform an operation a fixed number of times, the FOR/NEXT statements should be used. The FOR/NEXT statements are equivalent to a LET, an IF THEN, and a GO TO. The STEP option allows the programmer to increment the index variable by numbers other than one.

When developing a program, certain logical structures should be considered to simplify the coding and to improve the clarity of the program.

They are: a simple sequence, a selection sequence (IFTHENELSE), a repetition sequence (DOWHILE and DOUNTIL), and the CASE structure.

FOR/NEXT Loops may be nested. Such loops are permissible as long as they don't overlap.

EXERCISES

* 7.1 What will the following program do?

```
10 READ A,B,C
15 FOR I = A TO B/C STEP C*A
20 PRINT I;
25 NEXT I
30 DATA 1, 10, 1
35 END
```

7.2 What will the program in *exercise 7.1* do if line 30 is changed to:
a. 30 DATA 2, 12, 1?
b. 30 DATA .5, 5, 1?
c. 30 DATA 10, 1, −.5?
d. 30 DATA 1, 2, 3?

7.3 Write a program that will print all of the even numbers between 1 and 20. Use FOR/NEXT statements.

7.4 Rewrite **Program 6.6** so that data for exactly 10 employees are processed without having the program test if $N = 0$ to signal the end. Use FOR/NEXT statements.

7.5 Rewrite the programs in the following exercises using the FOR/NEXT statements:
   a. *exercise 6.12*
 * b. *exercise 6.14*
   c. *exercise 6.15*
   d. *exercise 6.17*
   e. *exercise 6.18*

7.6 What will **Program 7.3** do if
   a. line 20 is changed to 20 FOR N=1 TO 5 STEP 2?
   b. line 20 is changed to 20 FOR N=1 TO 5 STEP 3?
   c. lines 20 and 45 are changed as follows:

```
20 FOR X = 1 TO 5
45 NEXT X
```

   d. line 30 is changed to 30 LET N=N+X?

7.7 What will **Program 7.5** do if
   a. line 30 is changed to

```
30 FOR I = 11 TO 20?
```

   b. line 30 is changed to

```
30 FOR I = 1 TO 20?
```

   c. the RESTORE statement on line 65 is omitted?

   For each of the above parts, assume that the same numbers are input, as in the illustration.

7.8 What will **Program 7.5** do if line 55 is changed to 55 GO TO 15?

7.9 Rewrite **Program 7.6** without using any FOR/NEXT statements.

7.10 Compare and contrast the DOWHILE and DOUNTIL control structures.

7.11 Identify the control structures shown in
   a. Figure 6.2
   b. Figure 6.3
   c. Figure 6.4

7.12 What control structures can be found in Figure 7.2?

7.13 The United Store Chain, operators of six retail stores, reported the following sales for last week:

Store 1	$1200	Store 4	$1600
Store 2	1900	Store 5	1900
Store 3	2100	Store 6	2200

Develop a program similar to **Case 7.4** to produce a bar chart for this data. (Hint: scale down the data by dividing by a constant large enough so that the bars can fit on the output page.)

7.14 Write and run a program that will develop a compound interest table using the formula

$$I = (1 + r)^n$$

The interest rate r will vary from 8–9 percent by ¼ percent going across the table. The number of years ^{n} will go from 1 to 10 down the left margin. Use nested FOR/NEXT loops.

7.15 For the compound interest *exercise 7.14*, write and run a program that will output three tables, each one for a 10-year period; the first with r going from 10 to 11 percent; the second with r going from 11 to 12 percent; and the third with r going from 12 to 13 percent. In each case the increment is by ¼ percent.

7.16 What will the following program print when it is run?

```
10 FOR I = 1 TO 20 STEP 6
15       FOR J = 3 TO 10 STEP 2
20       PRINT I; J,
25       NEXT J
30 PRINT
35 NEXT I
40 END
```

7.17 What will the following program print when it is run?

```
10 FOR I = 1 TO 11 STEP 3
15       FOR J = 5 TO -1 STEP -2
20             FOR K = 2 TO 3 STEP .25
25             PRINT I; J; K,
30             NEXT K
35       PRINT
40       NEXT J
45 PRINT
50 NEXT I
55 END
```

* 7.18 Write a program that will print a 10 × 10 table with zeros everywhere except along the major and minor diagonals. Those positions should contain ones. That is, have the computer print an "X" of ones in a field of zeros.

7.19 Rewrite **Program 7.12** for a principal that goes from \$5000 to \$20,000 in increments of \$5000, the interest rate varies from 8 to 10 percent in increments of ½ percent, and the time goes from 10 to 20 years in increments of two years.

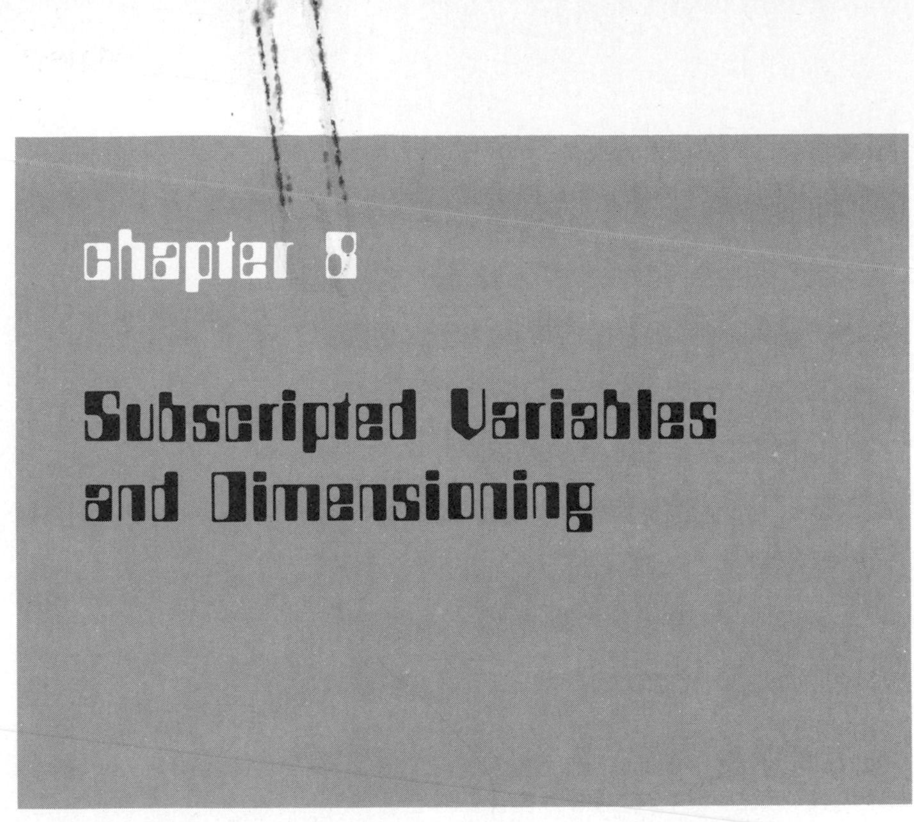

SUBSCRIPTED VARIABLES

In Chapter 3 it was pointed out that in BASIC the set of variable names consists of the alphabetic letters *A* to *Z* (26 names) plus each of these letters combined with a single number *A*0,. . . , *A*9, *B*0,. . . , *B*9,. . . , *Z*0,. . . , *Z*9 (260 names), which gives a total of 286 possible variable names. For simple programs this may be a sufficient number of names. For more complex programs, a much larger list of names may be necessary.

For example, it is not unusual for a company, a bank, or any large organization to have hundreds of employees, thousands of accounts, or thousands of customers. Each account, customer, and employee could require its own variable name. With only 286 variable names presently available, it would be very difficult to handle any problem dealing with hundreds or thousands of items.

The way out of this predicament is by using subscripted variables. A subscripted variable could be B_1 (*B* sub 1) or M_{25} (*M* sub 25). The letters *B* and *M* are the names of groups of similar items. Such a group of similar items having a single name is referred to as an *array*.

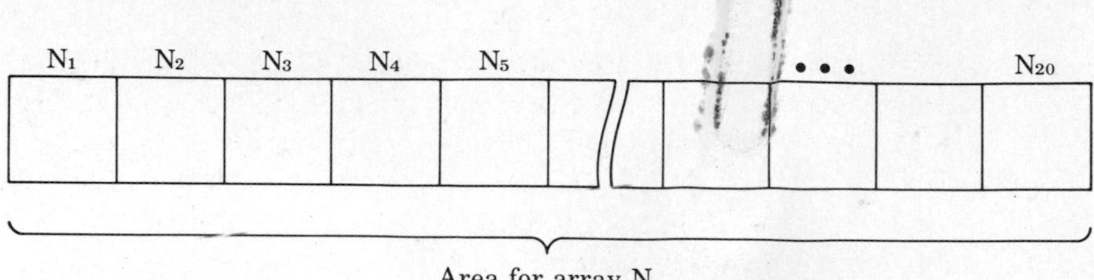

FIGURE 8.1 Storage Area for an Array with Subscripts

With subscripted variables a complete storage area is set aside for the values read in. This storage area has a single name and each value in the array has a subscript giving it a position in the storage area. If 20 values were to be treated as an array having a common name, *N*, read in and assigned by subscripting, Figure 8.1 would represent the storage area being discussed.

In Figure 8.1 the subscripts show that position in the array follows from left to right (low to high). The subscripts are always whole numbers, never fractional or decimal.

Each of the 286 "regular" variable names can be treated as an array having individual values identified with a subscript. For example, if each of 286 arrays had 100 items, the result would be 28,600 subscripted variables. With this many possible variables it becomes less difficult to "handle any problem dealing with hundreds or thousands of items." The way that subscripted variables are programmed in BASIC follows.

Suppose a company has insurance policies in various amounts for its 20 senior executives. We can assign a single variable name to these policies, say *P*. The mathematical notation and the BASIC notation for these 20 policies are as follows:

Mathematical	BASIC	Policy Face Value
P_1	P(1)	$20,000
P_2	P(2)	25,000
P_3	P(3)	15,000
.	.	.
.	.	.
.	.	.
P_{20}	P(20)	28,000

The subscript in the mathematical notation is slightly below the variable name. Since the terminal keyboard does not permit such notation, the subscript identification number is placed in parentheses next to the variable name. When these policy amounts are read into the computer, each is assigned to a location referred to by the *P*, and given a position with a specific (unique) identification number. In this way P(1) will be set equal to $20,000, P(2) will be set equal to $25,000, and so on, through P(20).

For only 10 policies a simple program illustrating how values are read, printed, and stored as subscripted variables is shown in Program 8.1. The FOR/NEXT loop provides the identification numbers for each of the *P* variables. When line 15, READ P(I), is executed, each data value gets the same variable name, *P*, but a different identification number. To print out the values of these variables we need a PRINT statement, as shown in line 20.

PROGRAM 8.1 Reading, Printing, and Storing Subscripted Variables

```
10 FOR I=1 TO 10
15 READ P(I)
20 PRINT P(I);
25 NEXT I
30 DATA 20000,25000,15000,16500,18500,32000,19500,17500,22000,26000
99 END


RUN
 20000  25000  15000  16500  18500  32000  19500  17500  22000  26000
```

The 10 values in Program 8.1 formed an array named *P*. Each value is now stored in a specific location, P(1), . . . , P(10). If lines 15 and 20 in Program 8.1 had been

15 READ P
20 PRINT P;

the output obtained would have been the same. The difference in programs is reflected in the variables used. An "ordinary" variable such as *P* provides only a single storage location for a single value at any one time. The subscripted variable P(I) provides a storage area that can contain more than a single value at any one time. In addition specific values of a subscripted array can be printed and used in subsequent processing if need be. With the ordinary variable approach mentioned above, it would not be possible to print out a specific *P* value, say the fourth or sixth value.

Program 8.2 shows in line 27 how the fourth, sixth, second, and seventh policy values are printed out because each has been assigned to a subscripted variable.

PROGRAM 8.2 Printing Specific Array Values

```
10 FOR I=1 TO 10
15 READ P(I)
20 PRINT P(I);
25 NEXT I
27 PRINT P(4),P(6),P(2),P(7)
30 DATA 20000,25000,15000,16500,18500,32000,19500,17500,22000,26000
99 END

RUN
 20000  25000  15000  16500  18500  32000  19500  17500  22000  26000
 16500            32000            25000            19500
```

At times subscripted variables may be stated directly rather than using FOR/NEXT loops to give identification numbers. Values may be assigned to subscripted variables by using one of the following:

READ/DATA statements,

```
10 READ M(1), M(2), M(3)
20 DATA 2, 3, 70
```

INPUT statement,

```
10 INPUT M(1), M(2), M(3)
```

or LET statements,

```
10 LET M(1) = 2
20 LET M(2) = 3
30 LET M(3) = 70
```

From this discussion it can be seen that other subscripts are possible besides P(I). In BASIC, examples of acceptable subscripts are S(4), X2(37), M(I+6), L(2*J), and E(B−1). Thus a subscript can be any expression that uses the operators ↑,*,/,+, and −. In addition, it is possible to subscript a subscripted variable so that if B(I) is a value, we can have the variable N(B(I)).

Subscript values should be positive integers. If not, some systems will truncate the subscript; other systems will round to the nearest integer.

DIMENSIONING

When subscripted variables are read into the computer they are placed in storage with a specific memory location. You are permitted up to 10 "free" subscripted variables for each of the variable names in your program. But since total storage available is limited, if you have more than 10 subscripted variables you must reserve storage space for them in the computer. Such reservations are made by using a DIM (dimension) statement at the start of your program. This statement will be illustrated within the discussion of lists and tables that follows.

Lists

A single column or row of values comprises a list or array. Such a list was formed by the 10 policies in Program 8.2. Since the list did not have more than 10 values, no dimension statement was required. If the list were larger, a DIM statement in the following form would be needed:

line # DIM variable name (# of storage spaces desired)

Example of such statements are:

20 DIM B(35)

suitable for a single list; or

20 DIM B(35), K(20), M(42)

dimensioning for more than one list. Program 8.3 illustrates, for the amounts of the 20 insurance policies shown earlier, how these values can be stored and might be printed out.

PROGRAM 8.3 Dimensioning for a List of 20 Insurance Policies

```
5 DIM P(20)
11 FOR I= 1 TO 20
15 READ P(I)
30 NEXT I
32 PRINT "POLICY","AMOUNT","POLICY","AMOUNT"
33 PRINT
34 FOR I= 20 TO 1 STEP -2
35 PRINT I,"$";P(I),I-1,"$";P(I-1)
38 NEXT I
40 DATA 20000,25000,15000,16500,18500,32000,19500,17500,22000,26000
45 DATA 18000,22000,16500,21500,22500,20000,18000,17000,19000,28000
99 END

RUN
POLICY        AMOUNT        POLICY        AMOUNT

 20           $ 28000        19           $ 19000
 18           $ 17000        17           $ 18000
 16           $ 20000        15           $ 22500
 14           $ 21500        13           $ 16500
 12           $ 22000        11           $ 18000
 10           $ 26000        9            $ 22000
 8            $ 17500        7            $ 19500
 6            $ 32000        5            $ 18500
 4            $ 16500        3            $ 15000
 2            $ 25000        1            $ 20000
```

Line 5 indicates that 20 storage areas are to be reserved for variable *P*. If the DIM statement was left out of the program, an error message would occur upon running the program. The DIM specification should always be equal to or greater than the size of the data list. Overdimensioning is permissible; underdimensioning is an error. Note the use of the variable designation P(I−1) in line 35. With this designation the program prints out the amount of each odd-numbered policy starting with the 19th and continuing down until the first policy.

Program 8.4, using the information of Case 8.1, incorporates dimensioning and subscripted variables.

CASE 8.1 The B and N Department Store Company wants to estimate the average amount of a charge sale as well as the percent of charges that are above the average. A random sample of 15 charges was recorded one day last week as follows:

Charge	Amount	Charge	Amount
1	\$ 3.47	9	\$33.21
2	97.74	10	57.60
3	16.76	11	18.18
4	12.56	12	25.62
5	55.59	13	23.42
6	16.22	14	52.36
7	84.42	15	37.85
8	63.01		

Program 8.4 shows how the desired results for Case 8.1 can be obtained. With subscripting, all that is needed is a loop like lines 30–50, and a comparison test as in line 35. Remarks within the program explain what each of the statements following them (REM) does. A flowchart for the program is shown in Figure 8.2.

PROGRAM 8.4 Case 8.1, B and N Department Store Company, Percent of Charges above the Average

```
1 DIM C(15)
2 PRINT "CHARGE","AMOUNT"
5 LET T1 = 0
6 LET T2 = 0
8 FOR I = 1 TO 15
10 READ C(I)
12 PRINT I,"$";C(I)
13 REM FIND THE TOTAL OF ALL CHARGES
15 LET T1=T1+C(I)
20 NEXT I
22 REM GET THE AVERAGE:DIVIDE TOTAL BY NUMBER OF CHARGES
25 LET A1=T1/15
30 FOR I=1 TO 15
32 REM TEST TO COMPARE WHICH CHARGES ARE GREATER THAN AVERAGE
35 IF C(I)>A1 THEN 45
40 GO TO 50
42 REM COUNT NUMBER OF CHARGES ABOVE AVERAGE
45 LET T2=T2+1
50 NEXT I
55 PRINT " ","--------"
60 PRINT "SAMPLE TOTAL $";T1
65 PRINT "EST.AVE.CHARGE $"A1
70 PRINT "% OF CHARGES ABOVE THE AVERAGE";(T2/15)*100
80 DATA 3.47,97.74,16.76,12.56,55.59,16.22,84.42,63.01,33.21,57.60
82 DATA 18.18,25.62,23.42,52.36,37.85
99 END
```

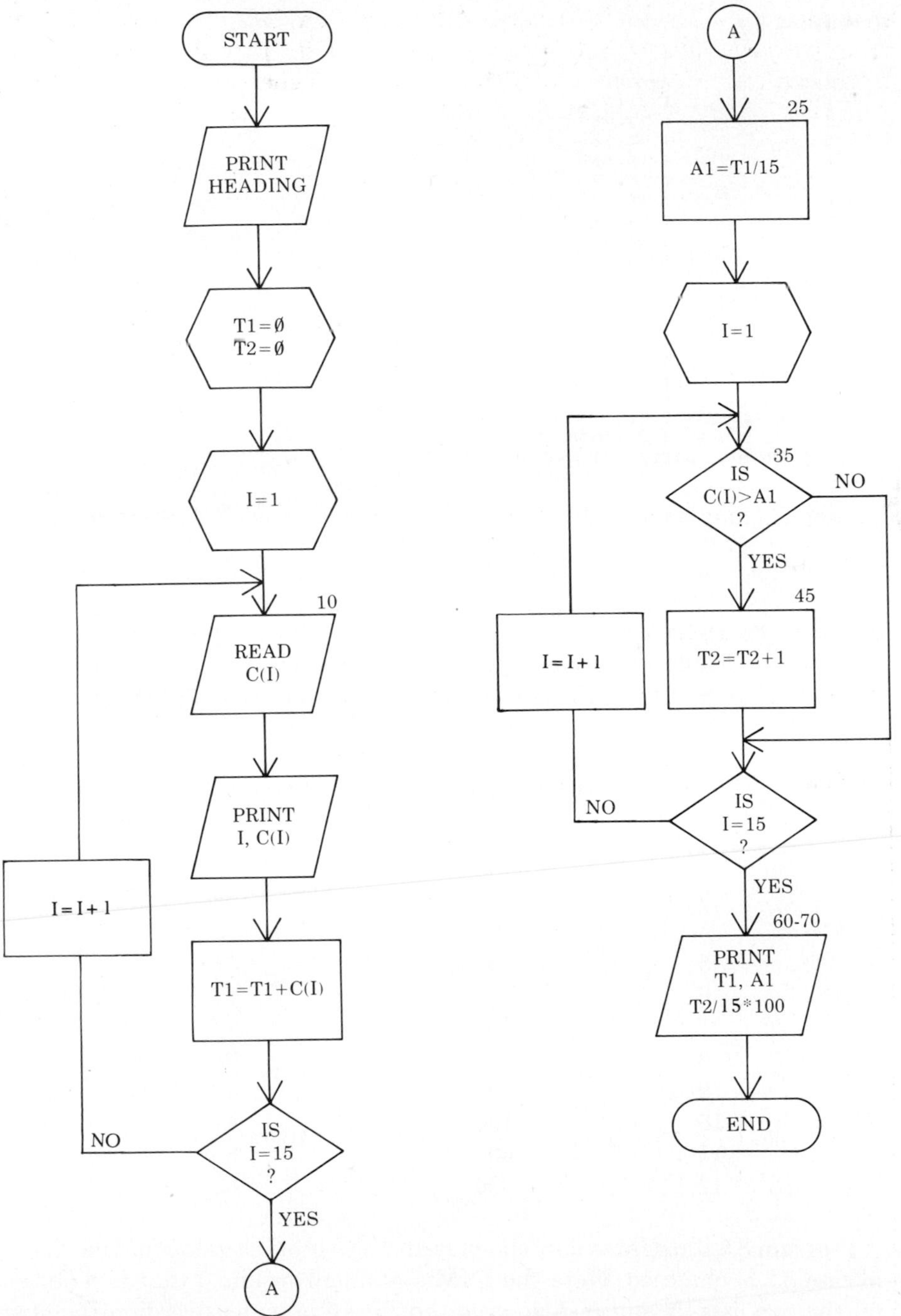

FIGURE 8.2 Flowchart for Program 8.4, Case 8.1, B and N Department Store Company

PROGRAM 8.4 continued

```
RUN
CHARGE          AMOUNT
 1              $ 3.47
 2              $ 97.74
 3              $ 16.76
 4              $ 12.56
 5              $ 55.59
 6              $ 16.22
 7              $ 84.42
 8              $ 63.01
 9              $ 33.21
 10             $ 57.6
 11             $ 18.18
 12             $ 25.62
 13             $ 23.42
 14             $ 52.36
 15             $ 37.85
                --------
SAMPLE TOTAL $ 598.01
EST.AVE.CHARGE $ 39.8673
% OF CHARGES ABOVE THE AVERAGE 40
```

A problem may have multiple data lists. Case 8.2 is such a situation.

CASE 8.2 An investment advisor wants to computer the present total market value of one investment portfolio. The advisor has the number of shares of each of 12 stocks and its current market price. These figures are as follows:

Stock	Number of Shares	Market Price
1	300	$50
2	400	42
3	500	32
4	900	5
5	300	31
6	500	17
7	500	77
8	100	98
9	800	52
10	100	49
11	400	80
12	800	83

Program 8.5 illustrates how the present total market value for the stocks in case 8.2 is obtained. Note the DIM statement in line 5 that is required for the two lists, *N* and *P*. Also note that line 5 provides overdimensioning

for variables *N* and *P*. The program contains four FOR/NEXT loops in a series. The first loop (lines 12–14) reads in the number of shares; the second loop (lines 18–22) reads in the market price; the third loop (lines 24–32) causes the printing of stock numbers, number of shares, and market price and then accumulates the market price. The last loop results in underlining by dashes across the page.

PROGRAM 8.5 Case 8.2, Stock Portfolio Present Market Value

```
5 DIM N(15),P(15)
10 PRINT "STOCK","# SHARES","MARKET PRICE"
11 LET T=0
12 FOR I=1 TO 12
13 READ N(I)
14 NEXT I
18 FOR I= 1 TO 12
20 READ P(I)
22 NEXT I
24 FOR I=1 TO 12
25 PRINT I,N(I),"$";P(I)
30 LET T=T+N(I)*P(I)
32 NEXT I
40 FOR A=1 TO 45
45 PRINT "-";
50 NEXT A
55 PRINT
60 PRINT "THE PRESENT VALUE OF PORTFOLIO IS $";T
70 DATA 300,400,500,900,300,500,500,100,800,100,400,800
75 DATA 50,42,32,5,31,17,77,98,52,49,80,83
99 END
```

```
RUN
STOCK          # SHARES          MARKET PRICE
 1             300               $ 50
 2             400               $ 42
 3             500               $ 32
 4             900               $ 5
 5             300               $ 31
 6             500               $ 17
 7             500               $ 77
 8             100               $ 98
 9             800               $ 52
 10            100               $ 49
 11            400               $ 80
 12            800               $ 83
---------------------------------------------
THE PRESENT VALUE OF PORTFOLIO IS $ 263300
```

Program 8.6 in a simple illustration of how it is possible to have values assigned to subscript variables using the INPUT statement (line 20). Note how line 35 causes the inputted values to be printed out in reverse sequence.

PROGRAM 8.6 Subscripting Variables Using the INPUT Statement

```
10 FOR I= 1 TO 5
20 INPUT A(I)
25 NEXT I
30 PRINT
35 FOR I= 5 TO 1 STEP -1
40 PRINT A(I);
50 NEXT I
99 END

RUN
 ?22
 ?25
 ?38
 ?46
 ?59

 59  46  38  25  22
```

Case 8.3 is based on the idea of using INPUT to assign values to subscripted variables.

CASE 8.3 Town Food Stores, Inc., has a sophisticated management information system (MIS) that keeps track of daily operations for its 13 stores. At the end of each day, each store telephones in the total daily receipts to the main computer room clerk. The clerk then responds to a conversational program that requests the sales figures for each store. This information is stored and a daily summary giving a total for the day for all the stores is printed out. Today's sales figures are:

Store	Sales	Store	Sales
1	$3,696	2	$4,281
3	5,650	4	6,969
5	3,854	6	4,955
7	5,724	8	1,695
9	7,864	10	1,947
11	4,417	12	5,092
13	2,611		

Program 8.7 shows a conversational program that carries out the objectives of Case 8.3. Line 30, INPUT D(I), is within a FOR/NEXT loop that causes values to be assigned to variables D(1) through D(13).

PROGRAM 8.7 Case 8.3, Town Food Stores, Inc., Conversational Program

```
5 DIM D(15)
10 PRINT "PLEASE TYPE IN THE DAILY SALES FOR EACH STORE AFTER"
12 PRINT "THE ? MARK."
15 LET S1 =0
20 FOR I= 1 TO 13
25 PRINT "STORE";I;
30 INPUT D(I)
40 LET S1 = S1 + D(I)
45 NEXT I
50 PRINT "     TODAY'S SALES REPORT"
55 PRINT "     --------------------"
60 PRINT "STORE","SALES"
65 FOR I = 1 TO 13
70 PRINT I,"$";D(I)
75 NEXT I
80 PRINT
85 PRINT "TOTAL","$";S1
99 END


RUN
PLEASE TYPE IN THE DAILY SALES FOR EACH STORE AFTER
THE ? MARK.
STORE 1   ?3696
STORE 2   ?4281
STORE 3   ?5650
STORE 4   ?6969
STORE 5   ?3854
STORE 6   ?4955
STORE 7   ?5724
STORE 8   ?1695
STORE 9   ?7864
STORE 10   ?1947
STORE 11   ?4417
STORE 12   ?5092
STORE 13   ?2611
     TODAY'S SALES REPORT
     --------------------
STORE          SALES
 1             $ 3696
 2             $ 4281
 3             $ 5650
 4             $ 6969
 5             $ 3854
 6             $ 4955
 7             $ 5724
 8             $ 1695
 9             $ 7864
 10            $ 1947
 11            $ 4417
 12            $ 5092
 13            $ 2611

TOTAL          $ 58755
```

Tables

Many times, data takes the form of a table that is simply several lists grouped together. Rather than reading each list as a separate variable, it is easier to treat them all as a single variable with two subscripts instead of one. In this manner we have a table with one subscript representing the row locations and the other representing the column locations.

As was the case with lists, tables containing data must be appropriately dimensioned to reserve storage space. The general form of the statement to be used is:

line # DIM variable name (table size: # rows, # columns)

An example for a single table five rows by eight columns could be:

```
10 DIM C(5,8)
```

If there are several tables in a program, the following statement could apply:

```
10 DIM C(5,8), A(12,8), R(10,20)
```

With tables and lists in a program, this statement may be used:

```
10 DIM C(5,8), S(15), R(10,20), B(50), X(35)
```

Suppose the Better Gum Company has test-marketed a new chewing gum in five types of outlets (candy store, gum machine, supermarket, etc.) in three regions for one month and has obtained the following sales figures in dozens of units sold:

Type of Outlet	Region		
	1	2	3
1	15	17	13
2	18	15	16
3	12	18	15
4	14	15	14
5	17	12	13

This table data has five rows with three columns. If the table is given the name "G," a program can then be written to read in and store the table. The "reading" of all the table will follow a row-by-row sequence, going from left to right across each column. The operation of nested loops does this reading process for us.* In Program 8.8 the outer loop bounded by lines 20 and 60, provides the row designation, and the inner loop (lines 30 through 50) provides the column designation.

*It may be useful for you at this point to review the material in Chapter 7 covering the operation of nested FOR/NEXT loops.

Line 10 in Program 8.8 shows the appropriate dimension, G(5,3), for a 5 × 3 table. The data in line 70 shows each row in sequence.

PROGRAM 8.8 Reading and Storing a 5 × 3 Table

```
10 DIM G(5,3)
20 FOR I= 1 TO 5
30    FOR J= 1 TO 3
40    READ G(I,J)
50    NEXT J
60 NEXT I
65 PRINT G(3,2), G(5,1)
70 DATA 15,17,13,18,15,16,12,18,15,14,15,14,17,12,13
99 END


RUN
 18            17
```

When the program is executed, each data value is represented by the variable name followed by a unique identification number corresponding to its row, *I*, and column, *J*, location. Variable G(3,2) is assigned the value 18, variable G(5,1) is assigned the value 17, and similarly for the rest of the data. The PRINT statement in line 65 shows how the values of individual subscripted variables like G(3,2) and G(5,1) can be printed out. To print all of Table G a PRINT statement such as line 45, PRINT G(I,J), in Program 8.9 is required.

Figure 8.3 shows Table G subscripted variables and their values.

To obtain a total for all of the data in Table G, an accumulator needs to be added to Program 8.8. To accomplish the task, lines 12 and 42 are added to the program. The revised program and resulting output are shown as Program 8.9.

		J: Columns		
		1	2	3
I: Rows	1	G(1,1) = 15	G(1,2) = 17	G(1,3) = 13
	2	G(2,1) = 18	G(2,2) = 15	G(2,3) = 16
G(I,J)	3	G(3,1) = 12	G(3,2) = 18	G(3,3) = 15
	4	G(4,1) = 14	G(4,2) = 15	G(4,3) = 14
	5	G(5,1) = 17	G(5,2) = 12	G(5,3) = 13

FIGURE 8.3 Table G Variables and Values

PROGRAM 8.9 Finding the Total Value of Table G

```
10 DIM G(5,3)
12 LET T1=0
15 PRINT " ","                    REGION"
16 PRINT "OUTLET", 1,2,3
17 PRINT
20 FOR I= 1 TO 5
25 PRINT I,
30    FOR J= 1 TO 3
40    READ G(I,J)
42    LET T1= T1 + G(I,J)
45    PRINT G(I,J),
50    NEXT J
55 PRINT
60 NEXT I
65 PRINT "TOTAL SALES";T1;"GROSS"
69 DATA 15,17,13,18,15,16,12,18,15,14,15,14,17,12,13
99 END

RUN
                                      REGION
OUTLET            1                    2                    3

 1                15                   17                   13
 2                18                   15                   16
 3                12                   18                   15
 4                14                   15                   14
 5                17                   12                   13
TOTAL SALES 224 GROSS
```

A flowchart of Program 8.9 is shown in Figure 8.4.

After values have been read in and stored as a table, it is possible to manipulate them. For instance, it may be desired to retrieve a part of a table. This can be accomplished by changing the starting point of the nested loops. Program 8.10 shows how the sales data for outlets 3 to 5 in regions 2 and 3 of the Better Gum Company test marketing could be printed out. Lines 70 and 80 are responsible for the partial output of Table G. The outer loop restricts printing to rows 3 through 5, while the inner loop restricts printing to columns 2 through 3.

PROGRAM 8.10 Printing Out Part of Table G

```
10 DIM G(5,3)
20 FOR I= 1 TO 5
    30 FOR J= 1 TO 3
    40 READ G(I,J)
    50 NEXT J
60 NEXT I
69 DATA 15,17,13,18,15,16,12,18,15,14,15,14,17,12,13
70 FOR I= 3 TO 5
80 FOR J= 2 TO 3
90 PRINT G(I,J),
100 NEXT J
110 PRINT
115 NEXT I
199 END

RUN
 18               15
 15               14
 12               13
```

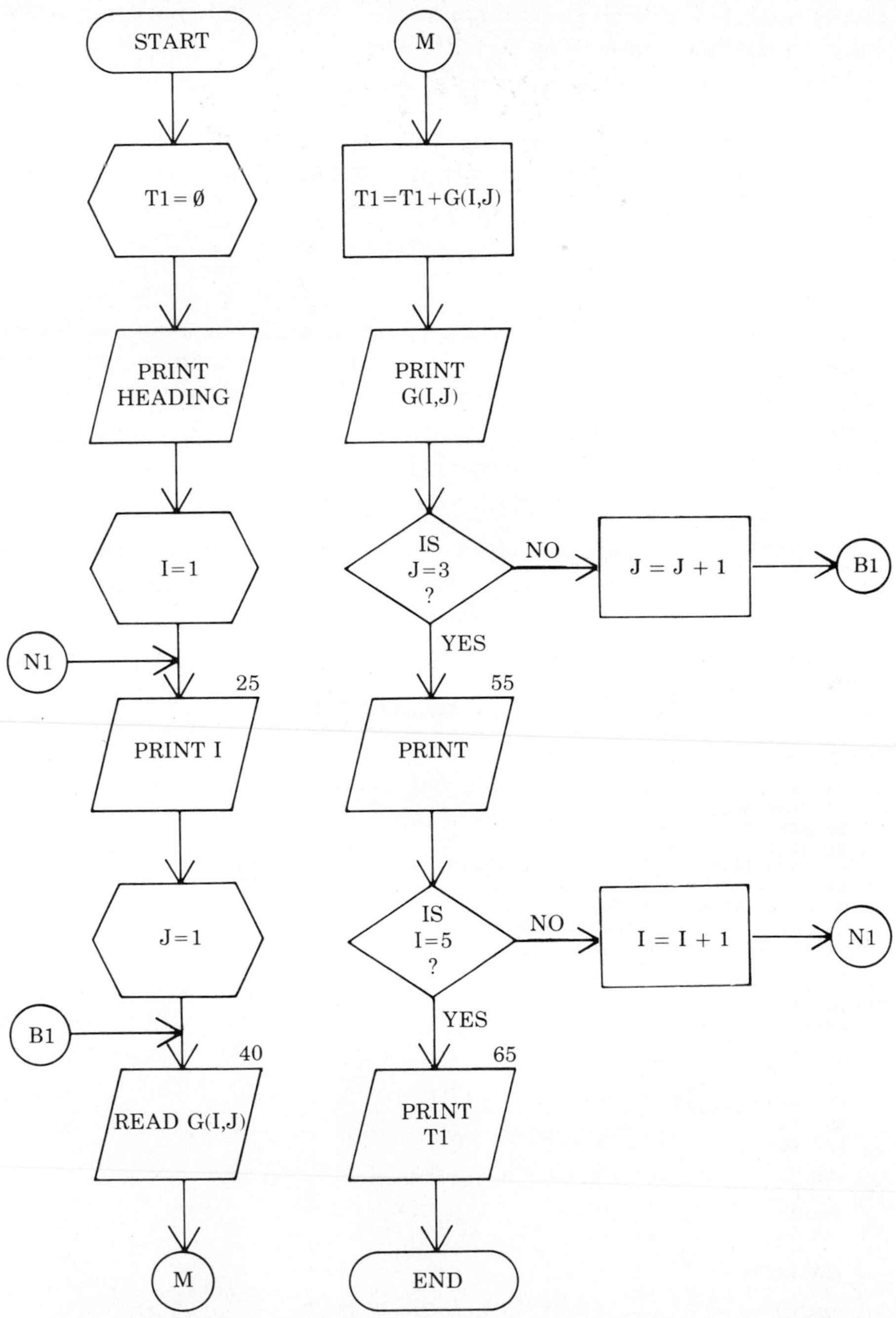

FIGURE 8.4 Flowchart for Program 8.9, Finding the Total Value of Table G

To obtain a specific row or column of a table that has been read in and stored (such as Table G), several approaches can be used. With only a few columns a statement such as

73 PRINT G(2,1), G(2,2), G(2,3)

would output the values of row 2 of Table G (18, 15, and 16, respectively). This could have also been done with the following statements:

```
77 FOR J = 1 TO 3
78 PRINT G(2,J),
80 NEXT J
```

Notice that G(2,J) holds the printing to row 2, while the columns, J, vary from 1 to 3. The same approach could be used to obtain a single column of a table. To print out the third column of Table G would require the following statements:

```
84 FOR I = 1 TO 5
85 PRINT G(I,3)
86 NEXT I
```

In the PRINT statement with G(I,3), the rows will vary from 1 to 5, while the printing is fixed on the third column. Program 8.11 summarizes these ideas based on the program (8.8) shown earlier.

PROGRAM 8.11 Printing Out a Row and Column of Table G

```
10 DIM G(5,3)
20 FOR I= 1 TO 5
30 FOR J= 1 TO 3
40 READ G(I,J)
50 NEXT J
60 NEXT I
69 DATA 15,17,13,18,15,16,12,18,15,14,15,14,17,12,13
70 PRINT
71 PRINT "OUTLET 2:"
73 PRINT G(2,1),G(2,2),G(2,3)
75 PRINT
76 PRINT "OUTLET 2:"
77 FOR J= 1 TO 3
78 PRINT G(2,J),
80 NEXT J
81 PRINT
82 PRINT "REGION 3:"
84 FOR I= 1 TO 5
85 PRINT G(I,3)
86 NEXT I
199 END

RUN

OUTLET 2:
 18             15             16

OUTLET 2:
 18             15             16
REGION 3:
 13
 16
 15
 14
 13
```

The following case (8.4) requires a single program that uses data in the form of two tables and one list.

CASE 8.4 The Computer Components Company pays its workers according to the number of units of each type of component (*A*, *B*, or *C*) they have assembled. The piecework rate is as follows:

Component	*A*	*B*	*C*
Rate per unit	$.25	$.35	$.50

Each worker's gross wages are based on a two-week period. Output for the last two weeks is as follows:

	Week 1			Week 2		
	Components			Components		
Worker	*A*	*B*	*C*	*A*	*B*	*C*
1	200	100	20	185	110	22
2	150	125	30	160	115	25
3	320	75	15	275	100	30
4	275	100	15	275	90	20
5	100	200	10	150	150	10

Program 8.12 shows how two tables (one for each week) and one list (the rates) are treated so as to obtain the gross wage per worker.

PROGRAM 8.12 Case 8.4, Computer Components Company, Gross Wage Calculations

```
5 DIM W1(5,3), W2(5,3), A(5,3)
10 FOR I= 1 TO 5
15 FOR J= 1TO 3
20 READ W1(I,J)
30 NEXT J
32 NEXT I
33 FOR I = 1 TO 5
34 FOR J = 1 TO 3
35 READ W2(I,J)
36 NEXT J
37 NEXT I
40 FOR J= 1 TO 3
45 READ R(J)
50 NEXT J
55 FOR I= 1 TO 5
60 LET G=0
65 FOR J= 1 TO 3
69 LET A(I,J)=W1(I,J)+W2(I,J)
70 LET G= G + A(I,J)*R(J)
75 NEXT J
80 PRINT "WORKER";I, "GROSS WAGE $";G
85 NEXT I
90 DATA 200,100,20,150,125,30,320,75,15,275,100,15
95 DATA 100,200,10,185,110,22,160,115,25,275,100,30
100 DATA 275,90,20,150,150,10,.25,.35,.50
199 END
```

PROGRAM 8.12 continued

```
RUN
WORKER 1        GROSS WAGE $ 190.75
WORKER 2        GROSS WAGE $ 189
WORKER 3        GROSS WAGE $ 232.5
WORKER 4        GROSS WAGE $ 221.5
WORKER 5        GROSS WAGE $ 195
```

In the program, line 5 provides the necessary dimensioning for each of the two tables. The "output" for week 1 is designated Table W1, and the "output" for week 2 is Table W2. Note the dimensioning for a Table A. The values in this table are developed further on in the program, and since they are to be stored, dimensioning prior to their creation is necessary. Table W1 is read in with a nested FOR/NEXT loop (lines 10–32). Table W2 is read in with a nested FOR/NEXT loop (lines 33–37). The piecework rates are list designated R, and are read in with a single FOR/NEXT loop (lines 40–50).

Within the nested FOR/NEXT loops (lines 55–85), the following calculations occur: In the inner loop (lines 65–75), line 69 accumulates the number of units each worker produced, by component for 2 weeks; in line 70 the "gross wage" for each worker is calculated by multiplying the total number of units of each component produced by the piecework rate for each component.

Below are the step-by-step calculations carried out for "Worker 1." Assume that line 65 has been executed, then $I = 1, J = 1$.

line 69: A(1,1) = W1(1,1) + W2(1,1) = 200 + 185 = 385
line 70: G = G + A(I,J)*R(J) = 0 + A(1,1)*R(1)
G = 0 + 385*.25 = 96.25

The NEXT J brings us to $I = 1, J = 2$,

line 69: A(1,2) = W1(1,2) + W2(1,2) = 100 + 110 = 210
line 70: G = 96.25 + A(1,2)*R(2) = 96.25 + 210*.35
G = 96.25 + 73.5 = 169.75

The NEXT J brings us to $I = 1, J = 3$,

line 69: A(1,3) = W1(1,3) + W2(1,3) = 20 + 22 = 42
line 70: G = 169.75 + A(1,3)*R(3) = 169.75 + 42*.50
G = 169.75 + 21 = 190.75

After $J = 3$, line 80 is executed, causing the results for Worker 1 to be printed out. The execution of line 85, the NEXT I, starts the process over again, but this time for $I = 2$, the second worker. Note how line 60 reinitializes G at zero before starting the next worker. This process ensures that the accumulation for G starts at zero for each worker.

Array Subscripts

As described above the dimension statement is used to specify how much space should be reserved for an array. Without a dimension statement, the array subscripts go from a lower bound of zero to an upper bound of 10. Using the dimension statement enables us to increase the upper bound of an array beyond 10.

ANSI minimal BASIC provides a means of specifying what the lower bounds of the subscripts for all the arrays in a program should be.* To declare that the arrays start at either zero or one requires the use of the OPTION BASE keywords. The general form of the declaration statement is:

line # OPTION BASE *n*

where *n* is either a 0 or 1. For example, the statement

5 OPTION BASE 1

will cause *all* arrays in a program to begin with subscripts one. This applies to both lists and tables. When used in a program, the OPTION BASE statement must have a lower line number than any dimension statement.

SUMMARY

This chapter introduced the concept of subscripted variables. Such variables identify individual storage locations. The subscripting process can be accomplished within a single FOR/NEXT loop if the data consists of a list; or within nested FOR/NEXT loops if the data forms a table.

Subscripted variables may be stated directly with READ/DATA, INPUT, or LET statements. To reserve storage space for subscripted variables, dimensioning is necessary. The DIM statement is used to dimension both lists and tables of data. The OPTION BASE statement provides a means to specify a lower bounds for all array subscripts.

EXERCISES

8.1 Revise **Program 8.5** for **Case 8.2** to add a column showing the present market value for each stock along with a total for this column.

8.2 Suppose that for the 12 stocks listed in **Case 8.2,** there are also available the following purchase prices: $46, $42, $32, $5, $31, $17, $77, $98,

*This capability may not be available on all systems. Check your system's BASIC manual for this procedure.

$52, $49, $79, and $83. Revise **Program 8.5** so that two additional columns will be produced, one showing the cost of purchase of each stock, and the other showing the gain or loss for each stock. The output should end with the total gain or loss for the entire portfolio.

8.3 Revise **Program 8.5 (Case 8.2)** such that the data lines are in this form:

```
70 DATA 300, 50, 400, 42, 500, 32, 900, 5, 300, 31, 500, 17
75 DATA 500, 77, 100, 98, 800, 52, 100, 49, 400, 80, 800, 83
```

Use READ N(I), P(I).

8.4 Revise **Program 8.7** (**Case 8.3**) to add an additional column that shows for each store the "% of total sales."

8.5 Using the weekly data shown in **Case 8.4,** write a program that reads in both tables, stores them, prints out each one, and shows for each week how many units each worker has produced (row totals).

	Week 1			Week 2		
	Components			Components		
Worker	*A*	*B*	*C*	*A*	*B*	*C*
1	200	100	20	185	110	22
2	150	125	30	160	115	25
3	320	75	15	275	100	30
4	275	100	15	275	90	20
5	100	200	10	150	150	10

8.6 Using the weekly data shown in **Case 8.4,** (see *exercise 8.5*), write a program that reads in and stores this data, prints out each table, and generates how many units of each type were produced (column totals).

8.7 Write a single program that carries out the requirements of *exercises 8.5* and *8.6,* and in addition, gets a grand total for each weekly table.

* 8.8 Using the weekly data shown in **Case 8.4** (see *exercise 8.5*), write a program that reads in and stores both tables, and then generates a new table that gives the combined week 1 and week 2 output by worker and component. This new table should also have column and row totals as well as a grand total.

* 8.9 Below are the prices at which four models of minicomputers are sold. Also shown are the numbers of units sold by the five salespersons selling these products. Prepare a program that will store this information and generate the total dollar volume for each salesperson. This total is equal to price per unit times number of units sold.

Model	1	2	3	4
Price	$10,000	$12,500	$17,200	$20,000

Salesperson	No. of Units Sold This Month, by Model			
	1	2	3	4
1	6	8	2	1
2	5	4	3	1
3	7	6	1	2
4	3	9	5	0
5	4	2	4	3

8.10 Write a program for *exercise 8.9* and in addition have it obtain the total dollar sales volume for all the salespersons.

8.11 For the information given in *exercise 8.9* prepare a program that will generate the following:

a. the total number of units of each model sold
b. the total dollar value of each model sold
c. the total dollar value of all the units sold
d. the percent of the total number of units sold, by model
e. the percent distribution of the total dollar value for each model sold

8.12 Assume in *exercise 8.9* that each salesperson telephones in monthly sales figures to company headquarters. Write a conversational program that a clerk could run so as to generate a monthly sales report for the items requested in *exercises 8.10* and *8.11*.

8.13 The following table shows the sales (millions of dollars) for the first 6 months of the XYZ Company, by division.

Month	Division			
	1	2	3	4
1	2.1	3.2	1.8	.9
2	2.0	2.7	1.4	.8
3	1.7	3.1	1.5	.6
4	2.3	3.3	1.7	.7
5	1.8	3.0	1.9	.9
6	1.4	3.1	2.0	.9

Write a program that will do the following:

a. Read in and store this information.
b. Output the data for the 1st quarter (months 1–3).
c. Output the data for the 2nd quarter (months 4–6).
d. Output the data for divisions 2, 3, and 4.
e. Output the data for divisions 1 and 3.
f. Output the data for months 1 and 6.
g. Provide total sales by each quarter for all divisions.

8.14 What would **Program 8.5** do if

a. lines 22 and 24 were omitted?

b. lines 14 and 18 were omitted?

c. How can we get the program to work with leaving out lines 14, 18, 22 and 24 by changing the DATA statements in lines 70 and 75?

8.15 Redo *exercise 8.2* but instead of reading in three lists, read in a 3 × 12 table where the first row contains the numbers of shares, the second row contains the market price, and the third row contains the purchase prices. The output should be the same as in *exercise 8.2*. Use nested FOR/NEXT loops.

8.16 What will the following program print?

```
10 DIM X(10)
15 FOR I=1 TO 10 STEP 2
20 READ X(I)
25 LET X(I+1)=10-I
30 NEXT I
35 FOR N=1 TO 10
40 PRINT X(N); X(X(N))
45 NEXT N
50 DATA 4,7,2,6,3
55 END
```

8.17 What will the following program print?

```
10 DIM B(2,4)
20 FOR I=1 TO 2
30 FOR J=1 TO 4
40 READ B(I,J)
50 NEXT J
55 RESTORE
60 NEXT I
70 DATA 1,3,5,7,9,11,13,15,17,19,21,23
80 PRINT B(1,3), B(2,1), B(1,4), B(B(1,1),B(1,2))
90 END
```

8.18 Contrast the dimension statement with the OPTION BASE statement.

8.19 Revise **Program 8.12** so that all arrays in the program will start with a subscript of zero.

chapter 9

Functions and Subroutines

STORED FUNCTIONS

There are a number of mathematical operations that the computer can be directed to perform without the individual user-programmer having to write detailed instructions for those operations. For example, we can get the square root of a number directly without giving the computer detailed instructions. Such operations are possible because of stored (library) functions included in the BASIC language. They are summarized below:

Function	Description
SIN (X)	The trigonometric sine function
COS (X)	The trigonometric cosine function
TAN (X)	The trigonometric tangent function
ATN (X)	The trigonometric arctangent function
LOG (X)	The natural logarithm function
EXP (X)	e raised to the X power
INT (X)	The greatest integer less than or equal to X
SGN (X)	The sign of X
ABS (X)	Absolute value of X
SQR (X)	The square root of X
RND	Random number between 0 and 1.

We shall confine our attention here to the last five functions. The (X) in the function references a value, or *argument* passed to the function.

The INT function (integer function) will assign the greatest integer that is less than or equal to its argument. For example,

X	INT (X)
5	5
7.2	7
6.9	6
0.5	0
−2.3	−3
−1.7	−2
−.4	−1
10 E−3	0

Note that INT (6.9) = 6. The number is not rounded. It is truncated. Note also the INT (−2.3) = −3, since −3 is the greatest integer less than −2.3.

The SGN function (sign function) gives three possible values: −1, 0, and +1. If $X > 0$, SGN (X) = 1; if $X = 0$, SGN (X) = 0; and if $X < 0$, SGN (X) = −1.

X	SGN (X)
5	+1
−5.7	−1
1.0	+1
0.5	+1
0	0
−4	−1
−1	−1
10 E−3	+1

The ABS function (absolute value function) returns the number in the parentheses without any sign. If $X >= 0$, ABS (X) = X; if $X < 0$, ABS (X) = −1*X.

X	ABS (X)
−4.8	4.8
0	0
5.1	5.1
− .5	.5
1.1	1.1
10 E−3	10 E−3

Note that SGN (X) * ABS (X) = X for any X.

The SQR function gives the positive square root of the number or variable in the parentheses. The value in the parentheses should be positive, although some systems will allow negative numbers but ignore their sign. Programs 9.1 and 9.2 summarize the INT, ABS, SGN, and SQR functions. In Program 9.1 the square roots of negative numbers were not printed.

PROGRAM 9.1 Library Functions

```
10 PRINT "NUMBER","INTEGER","SIGN","ABS. VALUE","SQ. ROOT"
20 READ A,B,C,D,E,F
30 PRINT A,INT(A),SGN(A),ABS(A),SQR(A)
40 PRINT B,INT(B),SGN(B),ABS(B),SQR(B)
50 PRINT C,INT(C),SGN(C),ABS(C),SQR(C)
60 PRINT D,INT(D),SGN(D),ABS(D),SQR(D)
70 PRINT E,INT(E),SGN(E),ABS(E)," -"
80 PRINT F,INT(F),SGN(F),ABS(F)," -"
100 DATA 2,1.44,.09,0,-10.6,-5.1
110 STOP
199 END
```

```
RUN
NUMBER          INTEGER         SIGN            ABS. VALUE      SQ. ROOT
 2               2               1               2               1.41421
 1.44            1               1               1.44            1.2
 .09             0               1               .09             .3
 0               0               0               0               0
-10.6           -11             -1               10.6            -
-5.1            -6              -1               5.1             -
```

The parentheses may enclose a single variable, a constant, or an expression. The variable must have been given a value previously, as in the LET statement. The parentheses may also enclose another function, as illustrated in Program 9.2.

PROGRAM 9.2 Function of Functions

```
10 READ X,Y,Z
15 DATA 5,-1.7,3.8
20 PRINT ABS(Y),SGN(Z),INT(Y)
25 LET W=SGN(X)+ABS(X)
30 PRINT INT(W*2),SGN(INT(ABS(Y)))
35 END
```

```
RUN
 1.7             1              -2
 12              1
```

Note that in line 30 of Program 9.2 we wish to print the sign of the greatest integer less than or equal to the absolute value of variable *Y*.

A practical application of the INT function is when we want to *round* a number *to the nearest* integer or tenth. We can use the INT function to accomplish this, as shown in Program 9.3.

PROGRAM 9.3 Rounding Numbers

```
10 READ A,B,C,D,E
15 DATA 5.11,3.63,9.37,4.46,2.58
20 PRINT "ROUNDING TO THE NEAREST WHOLE NUMBER"
25 LET A0 = INT(A+.5)
30 LET B0 = INT(B+.5)
35 LET C0 = INT(C+.5)
40 LET D0 = INT(D+.5)
45 LET E0 = INT(E+.5)
50 PRINT A,B,C,D,E
51 PRINT A0,B0,C0,D0,E0
55 PRINT
60 PRINT "ROUNDING TO THE NEAREST DECIMAL"
65 LET A1 = INT((A+.05)*10)/10
70 LET B1 = INT((B+.05)*10)/10
75 LET C1 = INT((C+.05)*10)/10
80 LET D1 = INT((D+.05)*10)/10
85 LET E1 = INT((E+.05)*10)/10
95 PRINT A,B,C,D,E
96 PRINT A1,B1,C1,D1,E1
100 END
```

```
RUN
ROUNDING TO THE NEAREST WHOLE NUMBER
 5.11           3.63           9.37           4.46           2.58
 5              4              9              4              3

ROUNDING TO THE NEAREST DECIMAL
 5.11           3.63           9.37           4.46           2.53
 5.1            3.6            9.4            4.5            2.6
```

Note that when we round a number to the nearest whole number, we add ½ or .5 to it and take the INT function of the sum. For example, to round off 4.7 to the nearest whole number, we add .5 to 4.7 giving 5.2, and when we take INT of 5.2 we get 5. To round off 6.3 to the nearest whole number, we add .5 to 6.3 getting 6.8, and when we take INT of 6.8 we get 6. To round a number to the nearest tenth, we just add .05 to the number, multiply the sum by 10, take the INT function of that product, and then divide by 10. For example, to round 3.46 to the nearest tenth, we get $3.46 + .05 = 3.51$, $3.51 * 10 = 35.1$, $\text{INT}(35.1) = 35$, and $^{35}/_{10} = 3.5$.

Another program that rounds numbers to the nearest whole number and uses the SGN, ABS, and INT functions is given in Program 9.4. Note that the intermediate values are given as well. Programs 9.3 and 9.4 work for both positive and negative numbers.

PROGRAM 9.4 Rounding Numbers Using SGN, INT, and ABS

```
5 PRINT "X","SGN(X)","INT(ABS(X)+.5)","NEAREST WHOLE NUMBER"
10 READ X
15 LET S=SGN(X)
20 LET R=INT(ABS(X)+.5)
25 LET N=S*R
30 PRINT X,S,R,N
35 DATA -1.6,-5.4,7.5
36 GO TO 10
40 END

X              SGN(X)         INT(ABS(X)+.5) NEAREST WHOLE NUMBER
-1.6           -1              2             -2
-5.4           -1              5             -5
 7.5            1              8              8

OUT OF DATA- LN #  10
```

Program 9.5, based on Case 9.1, makes use of the SQR function.

CASE 9.1 The management of many firms involves the development of inventory policies that keep the total costs of ordering and carrying inventory at a minimum. Two useful formulas for inventory analysis and control are:

$$(1)\ Q_o = \sqrt{\frac{2\,R\,S}{I\,C}} \qquad \text{and} \qquad (2)\ T_{\min} = \sqrt{2\,R\,I\,S\,C}$$

where

Q_o = the optimum order quantity or the number of units to order that will minimize the firm's total inventory costs; also referred to as the *economic order quantity* (EOQ)

C = the total cost of a single unit

R = the number of units required per year

S = the cost of placing a single order

I = the inventory carrying costs which are a percentage figure based on the value of the average inventory

$T_{\min}$ = the minimum total cost for carrying and ordering Q_o

A conversational program is needed to compute Q_o and $T_{\min}$ whenever such information is required.

Program 9.5 carries out the computation of Q_o and $T_{\min}$. The values entered for C, R, S, and I were \$2.00, 4000 units, \$15.00, and 10%, respectively.

Note lines 80 and 85 in the program. Formulas (1) and (2) require a square root operation; these two lines and the LET statements in them carry out the evaluation required by using the SQR function.

PROGRAM 9.5 Case 9.1, Economic Order Quantity

```
10 PRINT "*****INVENTORY ANALYSIS PROGRAM*****"
25 PRINT "INSTRUCTIONS:  AFTER EACH ? MARK TYPE THE INFORMATION"
26 PRINT "REQUESTED FOLLOWED BY A RETURN."
35 PRINT "WHAT IS THE COST OF A SINGLE UNIT";
40 INPUT C
45 PRINT "HOW MANY UNITS ARE REQUIRED FOR THE YEAR";
50 INPUT R
55 PRINT "WHAT IS THE COST OF PLACING AN ORDER";
60 INPUT S
65 PRINT "WHAT IS THE PERCENTAGE OF THE AVERAGE INVENTORY VALUE"
66 PRINT "THAT IS FOR CARRYING COSTS";
70 INPUT I
75 REM COMPUTE EOQ AND T-MIN
80 LET Q=SQR(2*R*S/(I*C))
85 LET T=SQR(2*R*I*S*C)
90 PRINT
95 PRINT "*****INVENTORY ANALYSIS REPORT*****"
105 PRINT "THE OPTIMUM ORDER QUANTITY,EOQ IS";Q;"UNITS PER ORDER"
115 PRINT "THE MINIMUM TOTAL COST FOR ORDERING AND CARRYING THE"
116 PRINT "EOQ IS $";T
120 PRINT
125 PRINT "THE ABOVE RESULTS ARE BASED ON THE FOLLOWING:"
130 PRINT "A COST PER UNIT OF $";C;
135 PRINT " NUMBER OF UNITS REQUIRED";R;" UNITS"
140 PRINT "A COST OF PLACING AN ORDER OF $";S
150 PRINT "A CARRYING COST PERCENT OF AVG. INVENTORY VALUE";
151 PRINT "OF";I*100;"%"
190 END
```

```
RUN
*****INVENTORY ANALYSIS PROGRAM*****
INSTRUCTIONS:  AFTER EACH ? MARK TYPE THE INFORMATION
REQUESTED FOLLOWED BY A RETURN.
WHAT IS THE COST OF A SINGLE UNIT ?2
HOW MANY UNITS ARE REQUIRED FOR THE YEAR ?4000
WHAT IS THE COST OF PLACING AN ORDER ?15
WHAT IS THE PERCENTAGE OF THE AVERAGE INVENTORY VALUE
THAT IS FOR CARRYING COSTS ?.10

*****INVENTORY ANALYSIS REPORT*****
THE OPTIMUM ORDER QUANTITY,EOQ IS 774.597 UNITS PER ORDER
THE MINIMUM TOTAL COST FOR ORDERING AND CARRYING THE
EOQ IS $ 154.919

THE ABOVE RESULTS ARE BASED ON THE FOLLOWING:
A COST PER UNIT OF $ 2  NUMBER OF UNITS REQUIRED 4000  UNITS
A COST OF PLACING AN ORDER OF $ 15
A CARRYING COST PERCENT OF AVG. INVENTORY VALUEOF 10 %
```

The RND function generates a random number between 0 and 1. A random number is a number selected "at random." Imagine the computer having a round card with a spinner at the center and a scale going from 0 to 1 around the edge of the card. When the RND function is used, the spinner spins and the number to which the spinner points is recorded, and RND takes that value. Thus every number between 0 and 1 has an equal chance of being selected each time the RND function is used. (In point of fact, there is no spinner inside the computer. The actual method used to generate random numbers is beyond the scope of this book.) This function is useful when it is necessary to create artificial data.

Random numbers will be generated from the same starting point each time this function is used. If different sets of random numbers are desired, the following statement must precede the RND function

line # RANDOMIZE

Programs 9.6 and 9.7 show the use of the RND function. Program 9.6 is without the RANDOMIZE statement, and Program 9.7 is with it.

PROGRAM 9.6 RND without RANDOMIZE

```
10 PRINT RND,RND,RND
15 END
RUN
 .499592          .527304          .670495
RUN
 .499592          .527304          .670495
```

PROGRAM 9.7 RND with RANDOMIZE

```
5 RANDOMIZE
10 PRINT RND,RND,RND
15 END
RUN
 .15936           .956071          .302136
RUN
 .495311          .971736          .372618
```

Program 9.6 will print the same sequence of numbers each time the program is run, whereas Program 9.7 will print a different set of numbers each time.

Because the RND function gives numbers *between* 0 and 1, it is necessary to use the following procedure if *exact* limits are required.

If the range of values desired is from low (L) to high (H), inclusive, then the RND function should look like this:

INT((D+1)*RND + L)

where D is equal to the difference or range between H and L. For example, if random numbers from 10 to 20, inclusive, had to be generated, an appropriate statement would be:

40 LET R = INT(11*RND + 10)

Since RND gives numbers between 0 and 1, or from .000001 to .999999, then 11*RND will produce values from .000011 to 10.999989. By adding 10 to this range, we have values from 10.000011 to 20.999989. The integer part of this range is from 10 to 20, which is the desired range of values.

Case 9.2 requires a program using numbers that are generated by the RND function.

CASE 9.2 In order to check the quality of the product coming off its assembly line, the National Electronics Company quality control department examines samples of output twice a day. One inspection is in the morning between 9 a.m. and 12:59 p.m. The other is in the afternoon between 1 p.m. and 5:59 p.m. The times that the samples are taken each day are selected at random.

Program 9.8 shows how times can be randomly obtained for the quality control department. The program will generate the hours and minutes for each time interval by using the RND functions in lines 15, 25, 30, and 45.

PROGRAM 9.8 Case 9.2, Random Inspection Times

```
10 RANDOMIZE
15 LET H1=INT(4*RND +9)
25 LET M1=INT(60*RND)
30 LET H2=INT(5*RND +1)
45 LET M2=INT(60*RND)
60 PRINT "  **********INSPECTION TIMES*************"
70 PRINT "MORNING TIME";H1; ":" ;M1
75 PRINT
80 PRINT "AFTERNOON TIME";H2; ":" ;M2
99 END


RUN

  **********INSPECTION TIMES*************
MORNING TIME 10 : 31

AFTERNOON TIME 4 : 16
```

The next case, 9.3, requires the generation of random numbers.

CASE 9.3 A manager must plan the vacation schedules for six employees. Each employee is entitled to one week out of the six weeks available for vacations. There are six employees, and the manager does not want to give anyone preferential treatment in the assignment of vacation weeks. The manager wants a computer program that will randomly schedule each of the six employees to one of the six available weeks.

Program 9.9 shows how a list of six numbers, 1 to 6, representing the six employees can be scrambled. The employee numbers are read into the array R(I) by lines 15–25. A random number X from one to six is picked by line 40. Once a number, X, is picked it is processed through the FOR/NEXT loop, lines 45–80. The following tasks are performed within this loop.

Line 50 tests to see if a particular employee number has been picked before by checking for a -9 in the array location R(I). If a -9 is found, the program will go on to the NEXT I, or R(2). If the number in the array has not already been picked, is it equal to the random number X? If it is not equal to X, the program keeps searching for the value of R(I) equal to X. Once found, the value of X is assigned by line 60 to the array V(C). A -9 is placed into the location R(I) so that duplicates in the vacation schedule do not occur. Once all six employee numbers have been randomly picked, from the array R(I), transferred to the array V(C), and replaced in R(I) by -9's, the program continues to the FOR/NEXT loop in lines 95–105, where the vacation schedule is printed out.

PROGRAM 9.9 Case 9.3, A Randomly Assigned Vacation Schedule

```
10 RANDOMIZE
15 FOR I= 1 TO 6
20    READ R(I)
25 NEXT I
30 DATA 1,2,3,4,5,6
35 LET C=0
40 LET X=INT(6*RND+1)
45 FOR I= 1 TO 6
50    IF R(I)= -9 THEN 80
55       IF R(I)<>X THEN 80
60          LET C=C+1
65          LET V(C)=X
70          LET R(I)= -9
75    IF C=6 THEN 90
80 NEXT I
85 GO TO 40
90 PRINT "EMPLOYEE","VACATION WEEK"
95 FOR C= 1 TO 6
100      PRINT C,V(C)
105 NEXT C
110 END

RUN
EMPLOYEE          VACATION WEEK
 1                 5
 2                 6
 3                 1
 4                 2
 5                 3
 6                 4
```

Figure 9.1 shows how the array R(I) and V(C) might appear after one cycle of the program loop and ultimately after all six numbers have been randomly scrambled. Figure 9.2 is a flowchart for Program 9.9.

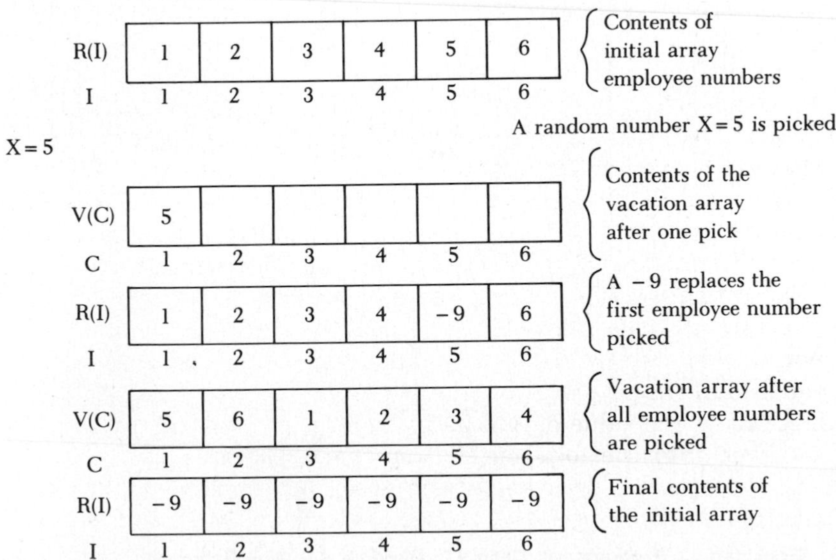

FIGURE 9.1 Storage Arrays, Program 9.9 Vaction Scheduling, Case 9.3

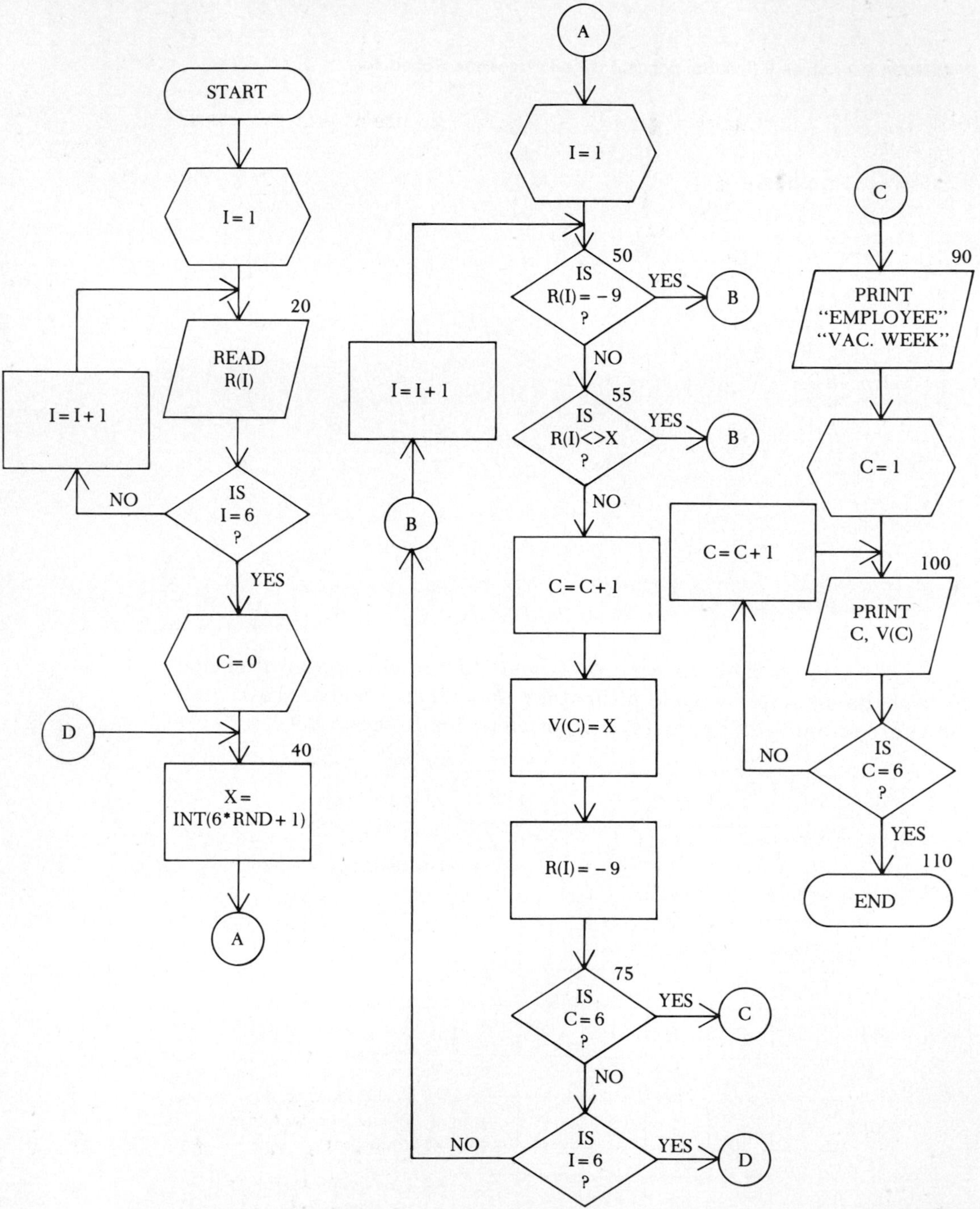

FIGURE 9.2 Flowchart for Program 9.9, Case 9.3, Random Vacation Schedule

A simulation application of the RND function is given in Case 9.4.

CASE 9.4 A Microcomputer Company would like to use as part of a game package that it offers—the tossing of a pair of dice. Program 9.10 simulates the tossing of a pair of dice using the RND function. It prints the outcomes of 10 tosses of a red and blue die and the sum of both dice.

PROGRAM 9.10 Case 9.4, Simulating a Pair of Dice

```
5 RANDOMIZE
10 PRINT "RED","BLUE","TOTAL"
15 FOR I=1TO10
20 LET R=INT(6*RND+1)
25 LET B=INT(6*RND+1)
30 PRINT R,B,R+B
35 NEXT I
40 END
RUN
RED           BLUE          TOTAL
 4             1             5
 4             2             6
 4             6             10
 6             2             3
 2             6             3
 2             6             3
 6             3             9
 4             6             10
 5             1             6
 4             1             5
```

THE DEF STATEMENT

The DEF statement allows the programmer to define functions. For example, suppose you are interested in the amount of money that would be on deposit if $100 were invested at 6 percent compounded annually after n years for $n = 1, 5, 10$, and 20. We would use the compound interest formula described in Chapter 3, under *Variables*.

$$A = P(1 + r)^n$$

Without the DEF statement we could write Program 9.11.

PROGRAM 9.11 Compound Interest without DEF

```
10 READ P,R
15 PRINT P*(1+R)↑1,P*(1+R)↑5,P*(1+R)↑10,P*(1+R)↑20
20 DATA 100,.06
25 END

RUN
 106           133.823         179.085         320.714
```

With the DEF statement, we have Program 9.12.

PROGRAM 9.12 Compound Interest with DEF

```
10 READ P,R,N
15 DEF FNA(N)=P*(1+R)↑N
20 PRINT FNA(1),FNA(5),FNA(10),FNA(20)
25 DATA 100,.06,5
30 END

RUN
 106            133.823          179.085          320.714
```

The statement on line 15 defines the function of the dummy variable *N*. The variable *N* need not have been given a value previously. Line 20 then prints the values of the function for the values of the numbers in parentheses. That is, FNA(1) assigns the value of 1 to *N* and evaluates the function on line 15.

The form of the DEF statement is

line # DEF FN – (V) = expression

The dash can be any letter. Thus at most we can have 26 different functions in any one program—one designated by each letter of the alphabet. *V* can be any variable. Normally the variable would appear in the expression to the right of the equal sign.

If we would replace line 15 in Program 9.12 with

15 DEF FNA(P) = P * (1+R) ↑ N

line 20 would print the amount on deposit after 5 years if $1, $5, $10, and $20 were deposited at 6 percent interest compounded annually. Note that all we changed was the variable in parentheses, and now we are defining a function of *P*, the principal, rather than a function of *N*, the number of years.

THE GO SUB AND RETURN STATEMENTS

Suppose you wanted to find the largest of three numbers for two different sets of three numbers. You could write the program as Program 9.13. Note that lines 20–60 are almost identical to lines 70–110. It is wasteful to have those lines appear twice in the same program. To avoid this redundancy, we can use the GO SUB and RETURN statements, as in Program 9.14.

PROGRAM 9.13 The Largest of Three Numbers without GO SUB

```
10 READ A,B,C
15 DATA 1,2,3,4,1,2
20 LET D=A
25 IF D<B THEN 45
30 IF D<C THEN 55
35 PRINT A,B,C,D
40 GO TO 65
45 LET D=B
50 GO TO 30
55 LET D=C
60 GO TO 35
65 READ A,B,C
70 LET D=A
75 IF D<B THEN 95
80 IF D<C THEN 105
85 PRINT A,B,C,D
90 GO TO 999
95 LET D=B
100 GO TO 80
105 LET D=C
110 GO TO 85
999 END

RUN
 1              2              3              3
 4              1              2              4
```

PROGRAM 9.14 The Largest Three Numbers with GO SUB

```
10 READ A,B,C
15 DATA 1,2,3,4,1,2
20 GO SUB 500
25 PRINT A,B,C,D
30 READ A,B,C
35 GO SUB 500
40 PRINT A,B,C,D
45 STOP
500 LET D=A
510 IF D<B THEN 525
515 IF D<C THEN 535
520 RETURN
525 LET D=B
530 GO TO 515
535 LET D=C
540 RETURN
999 END

RUN
 1              2              3              3
 4              1              2              4
```

The GO SUB 500 in line 20 transfers control to line 500, just like a GO TO 500 would. However, the 20 GO SUB 500 stores the number of the line following line 20 (in this case line 25) in a special location internally. When the computer encounters the RETURN statement (in line 540), control is transferred to line 25.

Similarly, when 35 GO SUB 500 is executed, the number 40 is put in that special location. When the RETURN is encountered (now in line 520), control is transferred to line 40. The RETURN returns control to the line following the most recently executed GO SUB.

The statements 500 to 540 are a subroutine. This particular subroutine finds the largest of three numbers *A, B,* and *C*, and assigns the largest number to variable *D*, as was done in Program 9.13. Note that there are two RETURN statements in one subroutine. In general, the number of GO SUB statements can be more, the same as, or less than the number of RETURN statements. There need *not* be a one-to-one correspondence as there must be with the FOR and NEXT statements. The statements in Program 9.14 are executed in the following sequence:

10, 15, 20, 500, 510, 525, 530, 515, 535, 540, 25, 30
35, 500, 510, 515, 520, 40, 45

There are two essential applications of subroutines. One, as illustrated in Program 9.14, is to allow a series of statements to be executed several times during a program without having to actually rewrite those statements. Thus in Program 9.14, statements 500 through 540 are executed twice in the program although they appear only once.

The other application of subroutines is to aid in the writing of large computer programs. Thus if we are writing a payroll program, for example, we could write one subroutine to determine FICA taxes, others to determine federal, state, and city income taxes, another to determine insurance deductions, etc. Each of the subroutines can be written independently of the main program and checked individually. Then, the main program would consist primarily of a series of GO SUB statements. This type of programming is also part of structured programming.

Case 9.5 is an illustration of this application of subroutines.

CASE 9.5 The Luce Candy Company of New York City sells products at a discount, depending on the amount purchased, and collects sales tax based on the location of the purchaser, as given in Tables 9.1a and 9.1b.

Amount of Order	Discount
Less than $100	0
Between $100 and $500	5%
Over $500	10%

Table 9.1a Discount Percentages

Location of Purchaser	Sales Tax
New York City	8%
New York State	4%
Out of State	0%

Table 9.1b Sales Tax Percentages

Program 9.15 reads the customer's name, location code (1=city, 2=state, 3=out of state), and the amount of the order, and then prints a table showing the customer's name, amount of order, discount, sales tax, and net amount. It also prints the total amount ordered, total discount, total sales tax, and total net amount below. There are separate subroutines to calculate the discount, calculate the tax, and accumulate the totals.

Note that the use of subroutines improves program clarity and avoids unnecessary branching. These features are part of structured programming.

PROGRAM 9.15 Case 9.5, Structured Program Using Subroutines

```
10 PRINT "I.D.","AMOUNT","DISCOUNT","SALES TAX","NET AMOUNT"
15 LET A1=0
20 LET D1=0
25 LET T1=0
30 LET N1=0
35 FOR I=1 TO 5
40 READ M,C,A
45 GO SUB 1000
50 GO SUB 2000
51 LET N=A-D+T
55 GO SUB 3000
60 PRINT M,A,D,T,N
65 NEXT I
66 PRINT
67 PRINT "TOTALS",A1,D1,T1,N1
70 DATA 632,3,512,314,2,480,711,1,400
75 DATA 342,2,65,759,1,550
80 STOP
1000    LET D=0
1005    IF A<100 THEN 1020
1007    IF A<500 THEN 1025
1010    LET D=.10*A
1020    RETURN
1025    LET D=.05*A
1030    RETURN
2000        LET T=0
2001        IF C=2 THEN 2015
2005        IF C=1 THEN 2025
2010        RETURN
2015        LET T=.04*(A-D)
2020        RETURN
2025        LET T=.08*(A-D)
2030        RETURN
3000            LET D1=D1+D
3002            LET A1=A1+A
3005            LET T1=T1+T
3010            LET N1=N1+N
3015            RETURN
9999 END
RUN
I.D.            AMOUNT          DISCOUNT          SALES TAX          NET AMOUNT
 632             512             51.2              0                  460.8
 314             480             24                18.24              474.24
 711             400             20                30.4               410.4
 342             65              0                 2.6                67.6
 759             550             55                39.6               534.6

TOTALS           2007            150.2             90.84              1947.64
```

NESTED SUBROUTINES

It is possible for one subroutine to cause the computer to branch to another subroutine. Observe Program 9.16.

PROGRAM 9.16 Nested Subroutines

```
10 READ A,B,D
15 DATA 3,4,0
20 GO SUB 100
25 PRINT A,B,C,D
30 GO SUB 200
35 PRINT A,B,C,D
40 STOP
100 LET C=A+B
105 GO SUB 200
110 RETURN
200 LET D=D+1
205 RETURN
300 END


RUN
 3              4              7              1
 3              4              7              2
```

The statements in Program 9.16 are executed in the following sequence:

10, 15, 20, 100, 105, 200, 205, 110, 25, 30, 200, 205, 35, 40

Note that the RETURN in 205 returns first to 110 and then to 25. As before, the RETURN always returns to the statement following the most recently executed GO SUB statement. That is, each GO SUB statement that is executed puts into that special location of memory (actually, an array) the line number of the following statement. If a second GO SUB is encountered before a RETURN statement, the line number of the statement following the second GO SUB statement is also put into that array. Then, when a RETURN is encountered, the last line number to be put into the array is the one to which control is transferred. In other words, last in, first out.

Note that the STOP statements in lines 45 and 40 in Programs 9.14 and 9.16, respectively, are necessary. For example, if line 45 were eliminated in Program 9.14, the computer would print:

```
1  2  3  3
4  1  2  4
RETURN ENCOUNTERED WITHOUT
PRIOR GO SUB IN LINE 520.
```

That is, after finishing the program as before, it would continue down to lines 500, 510, 515, 520. The RETURN in 520 does not know where to return to since the special location in memory mentioned above is empty.

SUMMARY

There are several stored functions in the BASIC language including SIN, COS, TAN, ATN, LOG, EXP, SQR, INT, SGN, ABS, and RND. In addition, you can define your own specialized functions using the DEF statement. The GO SUB and RETURN statements are used to write subroutines. A subroutine is useful when you have a series of statements that are to be executed more than once in a program (not in a loop) or when a very large program is being written and it is desired to test the different parts of the program independently.

EXERCISES

9.1 What value is assigned to the variables shown below?

- a. LET P = INT(−61.49)
- *b. LET C = INT(2*31.2 + .9)
- *c. LET W = SQR(.16)
- d. LET Y = INT(SQR(.25))
- e. LET X = SGN(−51.3)
- f. LET M = SQR(225) + INT(46/3)
- *g. LET R = ABS(−45.01)

*9.2 What value is assigned to *V*7 in line 80?

```
50 LET M = .6
60 LET B = 2
70 LET A = 7
80 LET V7 = 10 * INT(M + B + A*.30)
```

9.3 What will the following program cause to be printed?

```
10 READ X, Y, Z
15 PRINT ABS(X), SGN(Y+Z), INT(Y)
20 PRINT ABS(SGN(INT(X)))
25 PRINT INT(ABS(SGN(X)))
30 DATA −4.1, 7.8, −7.8
35 END
```

9.4 Write a program to read one number and print it rounded off to the nearest thousandth.

9.5 Revise **Program 9.5** to produce:

- a. *Q* as an integer value, and
  T rounded to the nearest whole dollar.
- b. *Q* rounded to the nearest unit, and
  T rounded to the nearest penny.

9.6 What is the range of values in each case below:

a. LET R = 10*RND

*b. LET X = RND*2.5

c. LET L = −.5*RND

*d. LET T = INT(10*RND)

e. LET B9 = INT(RND*5*1)

*f. LET C2 = INT(50 + 101*RND)

g. LET K4 = INT(21*RND)+60

9.7 Suppose the National Electronics Company (**Case 9.2**) is operating on an overtime schedule; that is, from 8 a.m. to 12:59 p.m. and from 1 p.m. to 8:59 p.m. Revise **Program 9.8** to take these changes into account.

*9.8 Your club has sold 500 raffles, numbered from 001 to 500. Write a program to randomly select a winning number using the RND function.

9.9 Write a program to read one number and print whether that number is even or odd. Use the INT function.

9.10 What program modifications could you suggest be made if we wanted to check that the array R in **Program 9.9** contains all −9's?

9.11 Design a computer game in which the player must guess a random number from 1 to 100 picked by the computer. After each number guess, the player is informed to go "higher" or "lower." Upon guessing the random number, the player is given the number of guess attempts. If more than nine tries were needed, the player is given a "poor rating"; for four to nine tries, the player is given an "average rating"; and for three or fewer tries, an "excellent rating."

9.12 What will the following program print when it is run?

```
 5 DATA 1,2,3,4
10 READ A,B,C,X
15 DEF FNA(X)=A*X+B↑2+C
20 PRINT FNA(1),FNA(A),FNA(B),FNA(C),FNA(X)
25 END
```

9.13 What will the program in *exercise 9.12* do if line 15 is changed to

a. 15 DEF FNA(A)=A*X+B↑2+C?

b. 15 DEF FNA(B)=A*X+B↑2+C?

c. 15 DEF FNA(C)=A*X+B↑2+C?

d. 15 DEF FNA(D)=A*X+B↑2+C?

9.14 How would you change **Program 9.12** to print the amount on deposit after 5 years if $100 is deposited at 6%, 7%, 8%, and 8½%. Change only lines 15 and 20.

* 9.15 Write a program similar to **Program 9.14,** but with *D* set equal to the smallest of *A, B,* and *C* instead of the largest.

9.16 What will the following program print when it is run?

```
10 READ N
11 DATA 5,4,7
12 GO SUB 100
13 PRINT X,Y,Z
14 GO SUB 200
15 STOP
100 REM-SUBROUTINE A
101 LET X=N↑2
102 GO SUB 200
103 LET Y=X/Z
104 RESTORE
105 LET X=X+2
106 RETURN
200 REM-SUBROUTINE B
201 LET Z=X*N
203 PRINT Z+1,X
204 RETURN
205 END
```

9.17 Write any program with three levels of nested subroutines and state in what order the statements will be executed.

9.18 Write a program as in *exercise 9.4,* for three numbers. Use the DEF, GO SUB, and RETURN statements.

chapter 10

String Variables

Until now, the only data we can READ, PRINT, or compare is numeric data. Thus, for example, we could refer to an employee only via an employee number (in Program 6.6), not the employee's name, which might be more useful. Or (as in Program 7.5), we could refer to a product number, but not to a more meaningful product name. In this chapter we will correct this deficiency.

ORDINARY STRING VARIABLES

The first type of string variable that we will discuss is ordinary or nonsubscripted string variables. These are variables that can have assigned as their value any single string of characters–in the same way in which an ordinary or nonsubscripted numeric variable can be assigned one number.

Suppose we have five DATA statements. Each contains employee names, social security numbers, number of hours worked, and hourly rate. We wish to write a program (10.1) to PRINT employee names, social security numbers, and salaries (computed as numbers of hours worked multiplied by hourly rate). Let us assume that there is no overtime.

PROGRAM 10.1 String Variables

```
10 PRINT "NAME","S.S.NUMBER","HOURS","RATE","SALARY"
15 FOR I = 1 TO 5
20 READ N$,S$,H,R
25 LET S=H*R
30 PRINT N$,S$,H,R,S
35 NEXT I
40 DATA J.SUTTON,"123-45-6789",40,15.55
41 DATA E.KAPLAN,"352-31-7896",35,7.70
42 DATA R.NENNER,"098-76-5321",41,3.80
43 DATA B.SIROTA,"212-17-6034",50,10.50
44 DATA P.KAMBER,"696-40-3117",30,8.50
45 END

RUN
NAME          S.S.NUMBER     HOURS          RATE          SALARY
J.SUTTON      123-45-6789     40             15.55         622
E.KAPLAN      352-31-7896     35             7.7           269.5
R.NENNER      098-76-5321     41             3.8           155.8
B.SIROTA      212-17-6034     50             10.5          525
P.KAMBER      696-40-3117     30             8.5           255
```

Look at program 10.1. Note that the variable to which we assign the name of the employee is *N$*. Any variable to which we want to assign an alphabetic value (that is, a variable containing letters, as opposed to a numeric variable, which can contain only numbers) must consist of a single letter (or a single letter followed by a single digit) followed by a "$" sign. If in Program 10.1 on line 20 we had

20 READ N, S, H, R

we would have gotten an error message, since the variable *N* can contain only numeric data and the first item in the DATA statement is J. SUTTON, which is alphabetic data. *N$* and *S$* are called *string variables.* A string variable can contain alphabetic data exclusively, as *N$* does. It can contain digits, as *S$* does. A string variable can contain any string of characters, including the dashes in the social security number.

A string variable can appear in any statement in which a numeric variable can appear. Some examples follow:

Statement	Example
READ	READ N$, H, R
PRINT	PRINT N$, S
LET	LET G$="B+" or LET G$=Q$
IF	IF A$<B$ THEN 10 or IF R$ = "YES" THEN 10
INPUT	INPUT R$
DIM	DIM N$ (20)

Alphabetic data can also appear in DATA statements. Quotation marks around the alphabetic data are optional in most instances. They are only required when a comma is part of the data or if trailing blanks are part of the data. Thus, if the DATA statement in Program 10.1 contained the last names first, followed by a comma and the first initial, we would have written

40 DATA "SUTTON, J.","123–45–6789",40, 15.55

Similarly, if we want a string variable to contain the letters *ABC* followed by two blanks, we would write the DATA statement

60 DATA "ABC "

String variables find wide application in promotional letters generated by computer. The body of such a letter stays fixed within the program. Data for the the program consists of the names and addresses of the people who are to receive the letter. Case 10.1 illustrates how a program can be used to produce letters.

CASE 10.1 The World Airlines Company wants to promote its new Flyaway Credit Card. To carry out the promotion, a computer-generated letter is being used. The computer addresses each letter produced. It also inserts the person's name and the street name in appropriate places within the letter. The string variables used in the program are:

Variable	Item
L$	Tear line
N$	Title–Mr., Mrs., Ms., Dr.
N1$	First name
N2$	Last name
A$	Street number
A1$	Street name
C$	City and state

Program 10.2 produces the promotional letter. Only a few data lines have been included for illustration purposes. In actual practice there may be thousands of names and addresses processed for such a promotion.

PROGRAM 10.2 Case 10.1, Computer Letter Using Ordinary String Variables

```
10 REM COMPUTER LETTER PRORAM
15 LET L$ = "-------------------------------------------------------------"
20 READ N$,N1$,N2$,A$,A1$,C$
25 PRINT L$
30 IF N$ = "NO MORE DATA" THEN 160
35 PRINT
40 PRINT N$;" ";N1$;" ";N2$
45 PRINT A$;" ";A1$
50 PRINT C$
55 PRINT
60 PRINT "DEAR ";N$;" ";N2$;":"
65 PRINT
70 PRINT "     THIS IS A SPECIAL INVITATION FOR YOU TO RECEIVE"
75 PRINT "A WORLD AIRLINES FLYAWAY CREDIT CARD. A CARD HAS BEEN"
80 PRINT "RESERVED IN YOUR NAME, ";N$;" ";N2$;". JUST CALL OUR"
85 PRINT "TOLL FREE NUMBER (800-123-4567) FOR DETAILS. THIS "
90 PRINT "INVITATION HAS NOT BEEN SENT TO EVERYONE ON ";A1$;","
95 PRINT "ONLY SELECTED PEOPLE LIKE YOURSELF."
100 PRINT
105 PRINT "SINCERELY YOURS,"
110 PRINT
115 PRINT
120 PRINT "R. FRANCIS WALDMAN"
125 PRINT "PRESIDENT, WA "
130 PRINT
135 GO TO 20
140 DATA DR.,PATRICK,HILL,"1901","NORTH ROAD","CHICAGO IL 60620"
145 DATA MRS.,ALBERT,JONES,"17","UNION ST.","EDMOND OK 73034"
150 DATA MS.,MARILYN,BOLTON,"28-14","EDISON DRIVE","DENVER CO 80204"
155 DATA "NO MORE DATA",X,X,X,X,X
160 END

RUN
-------------------------------------------------------------

DR. PATRICK HILL
1901 NORTH ROAD
CHICAGO IL 60620

DEAR DR. HILL:

     THIS IS A SPECIAL INVITATION FOR YOU TO RECEIVE
A WORLD AIRLINES FLYAWAY CREDIT CARD. A CARD HAS BEEN
RESERVED IN YOUR NAME, DR. HILL. JUST CALL OUR
TOLL FREE NUMBER (800-123-4567) FOR DETAILS. THIS
INVITATION HAS NOT BEEN SENT TO EVERYONE ON NORTH ROAD,
ONLY SELECTED PEOPLE LIKE YOURSELF.

SINCERELY YOURS,


R. FRANCIS WALDMAN
PRESIDENT, WA

-------------------------------------------------------------
```

PROGRAM 10.2 continued

```
MRS. ALBERT JONES
17 UNION ST.
EDMOND OK 73034

DEAR MRS. JONES:

     THIS IS A SPECIAL INVITATION FOR YOU TO RECEIVE
A WORLD AIRLINES FLYAWAY CREDIT CARD. A CARD HAS BEEN
RESERVED IN YOUR NAME, MRS. JONES. JUST CALL OUR
TOLL FREE NUMBER (300-123-4567) FOR DETAILS. THIS
INVITATION HAS NOT BEEN SENT TO EVERYONE ON UNION ST.,
ONLY SELECTED PEOPLE LIKE YOURSELF.

SINCERELY YOURS,


R. FRANCIS WALDMAN
PRESIDENT, WA

-------------------------------------------------------

MS. MARILYN BOLTON
23-14 EDISON DRIVE
DENVER CO 30204

DEAR MS. BOLTON:

     THIS IS A SPECIAL INVITATION FOR YOU TO RECEIVE
A WORLD AIRLINES FLYAWAY CREDIT CARD. A CARD HAS BEEN
RESERVED IN YOUR NAME, MS. BOLTON. JUST CALL OUR
TOLL FREE NUMBER (300-123-4567) FOR DETAILS. THIS
INVITATION HAS NOT BEEN SENT TO EVERYONE ON EDISON DRIVE,
ONLY SELECTED PEOPLE LIKE YOURSELF.

SINCERELY YOURS,


R. FRANCIS WALDMAN
PRESIDENT, WA

-------------------------------------------------------
```

We can also compare the values of string variables. Suppose we want to print two names stored in *A*\$ and *B*\$ in alphabetical order, but we don't know which name will come first. This situation is illustrated in Program 10.3.

PROGRAM 10.3 Comparing String Variables

```
10 READ A$,B$
15 IF A$>B$ THEN 30
20 PRINT A$,B$
25 GO TO 40
30 PRINT B$,A$
35 DATA JACKY,JACKSON
40 END

RUN
JACKSON        JACKY
```

Note that JACKSON is lower alphabetically than JACKY, so it should appear first in order, just as these names would appear in a telephone book. It makes no difference that JACKSON has more letters than JACKY.

An example illustrating string variables in the INPUT statement appears in Program 10.4. In that program, the square root of any number will be printed.

PROGRAM 10.4 Inputting String Variables

```
10 PRINT "TYPE IN ANY POSITIVE NUMBER AND SQUARE ROOT WILL BE GIVEN"
15 PRINT "NUMBER =";
20 INPUT N
25 PRINT "THE SQUARE ROOT OF";N;"IS";SQR(N)
30 PRINT "ANY MORE NUMBERS (TYPE YES OR NO)"
35 INPUT A$
40 IF A$="YES" THEN 15
45 END


RUN
TYPE IN ANY POSITIVE NUMBER AND SQUARE ROOT WILL BE GIVEN
NUMBER = ?4
THE SQUARE ROOT OF 4 IS 2
ANY MORE NUMBERS (TYPE YES OR NO)
 ?YES
NUMBER = ?25
THE SQUARE ROOT OF 25 IS 5
ANY MORE NUMBERS (TYPE YES OR NO)
 ?YES
NUMBER = ?256
THE SQUARE ROOT OF 256 IS 16
ANY MORE NUMBERS (TYPE YES OR NO)
 ?YES
NUMBER = ?3
THE SQUARE ROOT OF 3 IS 1.73205
ANY MORE NUMBERS (TYPE YES OR NO)
 ?NO
```

Note how line 40 carries out an IF test on the word "YES." The only way this program will continue is if YES is typed after the INPUT query.

SUBSCRIPTED STRING VARIABLES

A subscripted string variable is similar to a subscripted numeric variable in that it can contain a list of items instead of only one item. For example, M$(3) refers to the third alphabetic string in the list of strings designated by M$.

Case 10.2, Program 10.5 illustrates how subscripted string variables are handled.

CASE 10.2 A company with monthly production data would like to print a report with the production figures grouped by quarters.

PROGRAM 10.5 Production Report Using Subscripted String Variables

```
10 DIM M$(12),P(12)
20 FOR I = 1 TO 12
30 READ M$(I),P(I)
40 NEXT I
50 DATA JANUARY,1500,FEBRUARY,1200,MARCH,1750,APRIL,1600,MAY,1550
51 DATA JUNE,1350,JULY,1400,AUGUST,1750,SEPTEMBER,1200,OCTOBER,1250
52 DATA NOVEMBER,1300,DECEMBER,1500
60 FOR I = 1 TO 4
61 PRINT "QUARTER NUMBER";I
62 PRINT "MONTH","PRODUCTION"
70      FOR J = 1 TO 3
100         PRINT M$(3*(I-1)+J),P(3*(I-1)+J)
110         NEXT J
115 PRINT
120 NEXT I
999 END
```

```
RUN
QUARTER NUMBER 1
MONTH               PRODUCTION
JANUARY              1500
FEBRUARY             1200
MARCH                1750

QUARTER NUMBER 2
MONTH               PRODUCTION
APRIL                1600
MAY                  1550
JUNE                 1350

QUARTER NUMBER 3
MONTH               PRODUCTION
JULY                 1400
AUGUST               1750
SEPTEMBER            1200

QUARTER NUMBER 4
MONTH               PRODUCTION
OCTOBER              1250
NOVEMBER             1300
DECEMBER             1500
```

Note that line 30 reads in data for the string variable array *M$* as well as for the numeric variable array *P*. By dimensioning *M$*, we can refer to the sixth month by *M$*(6), which will be printed out as JUNE. Note how the expressions in the parentheses in line 100 print the *J*th month in the *I*th quarter. Thus, for example, the second month in the third quarter corresponds to $J = 2$ and $I = 3$ and $3*(I - 1) + J = 8$, which is the eighth month of the year (August).

Another program that makes use of subscripted string variables is shown in Case 10.3.

CASE 10.3 A standard computer security procedure for users of computer terminals involves the use of passwords. If a user wishes to gain access to the computer, there is a sign-on procedure that requires the user to enter a password that is verified by the system. Passwords may be randomly generated and distributed to users. They are generally from four to six characters in length and are changed frequently in many organizations.

Program 10.6 can be used to generate random passwords, given the number of passwords needed and the number of alphabetic characters (4 to 6) desired. Passwords are picked randomly from a subscripted string array, P$(I), which contains the twenty-six letters of the alphabet. In the program, lines 130–150 set up the subscripted string array P$(I). The LET statement in line 250 causes one of the twenty-six characters stored in P$(I) to be randomly picked as part of the password having a length of C characters. This length is set by the INPUT C in line 210. Line 190 INPUT N provides the program user the ability to generate as many passwords as needed.

PROGRAM 10.6 Case 10.2, Password Generator Program

```
100 REM PROGRAM TO GENERATE SECURITY PASSWORDS
110 DIM P$(26)
120 RANDOMIZE
130 FOR I= 1 TO 26
140      READ P$(I)
150 NEXT I
160 DATA A,B,C,D,E,F,G,H,I,J,K,L,M
170 DATA N,O,P,Q,R,S,T,U,V,W,X,Y,Z
180 PRINT"HOW MANY PASSWORDS NEEDED";
190 INPUT N
200 PRINT "HOW MANY CHARACTERS IN EACH PASSWORD ";
210 INPUT C
220 FOR A= 1 TO N
230 PRINT "PASSWORD";A;
240     FOR B= 1 TO C
250       LET I = INT(26*RND + 1)
260       PRINT P$(I);
270     NEXT B
280 PRINT
290 NEXT A
300 END
RUN
HOW MANY PASSWORDS NEEDED ?5
HOW MANY CHARACTERS IN EACH PASSWORD  ?4
PASSWORD 1 RZZY
PASSWORD 2 VJUK
PASSWORD 3 FQCS
PASSWORD 4 NVFV
PASSWORD 5 CDZO
RUN
HOW MANY PASSWORDS NEEDED ?4
HOW MANY CHARACTERS IN EACH PASSWORD  ?6
PASSWORD 1 COPJWV
PASSWORD 2 LBKVHF
PASSWORD 3 PRUOHL
PASSWORD 4 HPBZHZ
RUN
HOW MANY PASSWORDS NEEDED ?6
HOW MANY CHARACTERS IN EACH PASSWORD  ?3
PASSWORD 1 VBV
PASSWORD 2 JPI
PASSWORD 3 RAB
PASSWORD 4 BXY
PASSWORD 5 OYO
PASSWORD 6 XEB
```

Case 10.4 also requires a program using subscripted string variables.

CASE 10.4 In a certain course, three class exams and a final exam are given. The final term average is based on the average of the three class exam grades averaged in with the final exam grade. A letter grade of *A, B+, B, C+,C,D+, D,* or *F* is also given. We wish to write a program to read the student's name, class, grades, and final grade, and print a table with the student's name, final term average, and letter grade. A letter grade of *A* is given to those whose term average is at least 90, a *B+* is given to those whose term average is at least 85 and less than 90, etc. There are 10 students in the class. We also wish to print the number of people receiving each of the grades.

PROGRAM 10.7 Case 10.4, Grading Program

```
5 DIM N(8),G$(8)
10 FOR I=1 TO 8
15 READ G$(I)
16 DATA A,B+,B,C+,C,D+,D,F
20 LET N(I)=0
25 NEXT I
30 PRINT "NAME","TERM AVERAGE","GRADE"
35 FOR I= 1 TO 10
40 READ N$,G1,G2,G3,F
45 LET A=((G1+G2+G3)/3+F)/2
50 IF A>=90 THEN 95
55 IF A>=85 THEN 105
60 IF A>=80 THEN 115
65 IF A>=75 THEN 125
70 IF A>=70 THEN 135
75 IF A>=65 THEN 145
80 IF A>=60 THEN 155
85 LET X=8
90 GO TO 160
95 LET X=1
100 GO TO 160
105 LET X=2
110 GO TO 160
115 LET X=3
120 GO TO 160
125 LET X=4
130 GO TO 160
135 LET X=5
140 GO TO 160
145 LET X=6
150 GO TO 160
155 LET X=7
160 LET N(X)=N(X)+1
165 PRINT N$,A,G$(X)
170 NEXT I
175 PRINT "GRADE","NUMBER"
180 FOR I=1 TO 8
185 PRINT G$(I),N(I)
190 NEXT I
200 DATA J.SAMBORN,65,76,80,90,P.FISHMAN,70,81,95,93,E.GOLD,76,84,68,78
210 DATA A.EINSTEIN,98,97,90,95,B.WEIN,86,88,89,89,S.LACHS,77,76,80,73
220 DATA M.FALIG,81,84,90,80,R.HERMAN,58,74,67,54,B.GILA,70,75,78,79
230 DATA J.LYNN,70,74,65,68
9999 END
```

PROGRAM 10.7 continued

```
RUN
NAME           TERM AVERAGE    GRADE
J.SAMBORN       81.8333        B
P.FISHMAN       87.5           B+
E.GOLD          77             C+
A.EINSTEIN      95             A
B.WEIN          88.3333        B+
S.DACHS         75.3333        C+
M.FALIG         82.5           B
R.HERMAN        60.1667        D
B.GILA          76.6667        C+
J.LYNN          68.8333        D+
GRADE          NUMBER
A               1
B+              2
B               2
C+              3
C               0
D+              1
D               1
F               0
```

In Program 10.7 an array *G$* contains each of the possible grades *A,B*+, *B, C*+, *C, D*+, *D,* and *F*. Similarly, the array *N* will contain the number of students receiving each grade. Thus, *G$*(3) = *B* and *N*(3) = the number of students receiving a *B,* and so on. Therefore, if the average is, say, at least 80 and under 85, the computer branches to line 115 where *X* is set to 3. Then, the computer branches to line 160 where *N*(*X*) or *N*(3) increases by 1, and then prints the name of the student, the term average, and *G$*(*X*) or *G$*(3), which is *B*. The values of the array *G$* were read in at the beginning of the program (lines 10–25), and the initial zero values of the array *N* were also set to zero within these lines.

Instead of reading the values of the array *G$*, we could have written

```
LET G$(1) = "A"
LET G$(2) = "B+"
LET G$(3) = "B"
```

and so on. See also exercise 10.4 that replaces all of the 22 statements between lines 50 and 155, inclusive, with only 7 statements.

SUMMARY

String variables are variables that can be assigned strings of characters, such as names of people or products. String variables can appear in any statement in which numeric variables can appear, including READ, PRINT, LET, IF/THEN, INPUT, and DIM. String variables can be ordinary or nonsubscripted, as well as subscripted.

EXERCISES

* 10.1 Write a program to read five product names, their prices, and quantity ordered, and print a table containing the column headings, "Product Name," "Price," "Quantity," and "Amount." The amount is the price times the quantity. The total of the amount column should also be printed. The data lines for the program are:

```
60 DATA HAND SOAP,24,.69.TOOTH PASTE,35,.76
62 DATA BROWN SUGAR,16,1.25
65 DATA COLA,24,.55,RYE BREAD,50,.20
```

* 10.2 Rewrite **Program 7.5** to use these data lines with product names instead of product numbers:

```
75 DATA SOAP,100,TISSUE,150,BREAD,50
77 DATA BRUSHES,25,ASPIRIN,12,SODA,250
80 DATA CHEESE,80,CEREAL,200,BEANS,500,SOUP,75
```

10.3 Write a program to read three names of people and print them out in alphabetical order.

10.4 Explain how the following 7 statements accomplish the same thing as the 22 statements between lines 50 and 155, inclusive, of **Program 10.7:**

```
50 IF A>94 THEN 70
55 IF A<60 THEN 80
60 LET X = INT((94.5 -A)/5)+1
65 GO TO 160
70 LET X = 1
75 GO TO 160
80 LET X = 8
```

10.5 What would **Program 10.4** do if, in response to the question "ANY MORE NUMBERS (TYPE YES OR NO)," you typed

a. DEFINITELY NOT
b. SURE
c. OF COURSE
d. YES!
e. NO!

*10.6 Write a program that will read a name from the terminal, one letter at a time, and print out the name backwards. End the name with a period. You must use a DIM statement to dimension the letters in the name.

10.7 The XYZ Company has five salespersons. They are listed on the following page, with the amount of goods each sold last month.

Salesperson	Amount Sold
Julie Shana	$12,000
Jay Joshua	$17,500
Shirley Efram	14,500
Al Bennet	18,250
Ari Lee	16,250

Using the concept of string variables for the above names, write a program that will output all the above information with a column showing commissions on sales. Commissions are 10 percent of sales.

10.8 Do *exercise 10.7*, treating first names and last names as separate string variables. Have the output show last names and then first names. Also have the totals of the amounts sold and commissions printed.

10.9 In order to prepare a budget for next year, the NARCO Company estimates that each of its sales regions will show a growth in sales above this year of 8½ percent. This year's sales by each region are as follows:

Region	Sales (million $)
Northern	4.65
Central	5.23
Western	2.81
Midwest	9.67
Eastern	3.56
Southern	8.89

Write a program which uses string variables for the regions and which outputs the expected sales for next year for each region.

10.10 Redo *exercise 6.33*, reading in the employee's name instead of number, using the idea of subscripting given in **Case 10.4** to determine the tax rate, and using different subroutines to determine the gross wages, tax rate, and insurance premium. Use as your DATA statements the following:

```
9 20 DATA K.GRIBETZ,Ø,37,3.5Ø,1,G.LANDA,2,42,3.75,2
9 3Ø DATA E.FROMEN,1,4Ø,4.1Ø,2,J.HILLER,Ø,47,4.5Ø,1
9 4Ø DATA Y.DAHAN,8,45,2.8Ø,2,G.MARK,4,5Ø,2.5Ø,1
9 5Ø DATA D.CHILL,2,4Ø,3.ØØ,1,J.TUCHMAN,5,42,2.6Ø,2
9 6Ø DATA N.MEISEL,7,38,4.25,2,S.KLEIN,Ø,41,2.8Ø,Ø
```

10.11 Redo **Program 9.15 Case 9.5** where the customer's name instead of his account number is used, and his city, state or out of state code is C, S, and O instead of 1, 2, and 3. Use the following DATA lines:

```
70 DATA R.NORTON,O,512,P.SCHWARTZ,S,480,M.LINK,C,400
75 DATA L.SHAPIRO,S,65,G.TAI,C,550
```

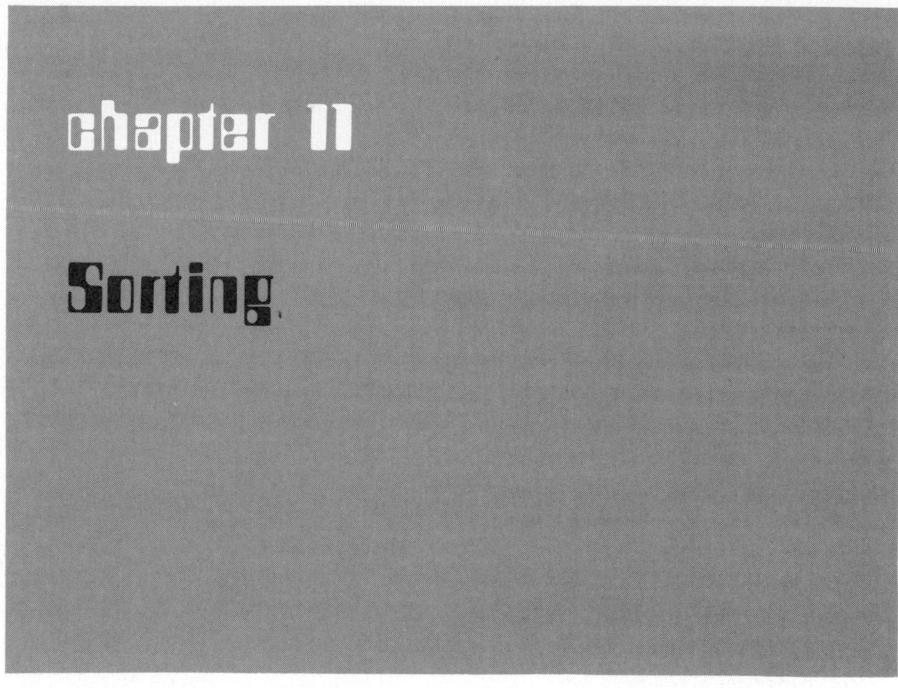

It is frequently desired to sort an array—that is, put the numbers in the array in ascending or descending order or to put alphabetic strings in alphabetical order. In this chapter, we will study several sorting programs for both numerical and alphabetical data. The concepts used in these programs are somewhat complicated. You are not expected to be able to write a sort program on your own but rather to understand how these programs were written and to use or modify them as needed.

NUMERICAL SORTING—THE SELECTION SORT

Suppose array A contains five numbers in a random order, and we would like to sort them in ascending order and put them into array B. Program 11.1 accomplishes this by repeated selection of the smallest element in array A. Once the smallest element of A is found, it is replaced with a very large number so that it will not be selected again. Figure 11.1 illustrates how this program works.

PROGRAM 11.1 The Selection Sort

```
10 FOR I=1 TO 5
15 READ A(I)
20 PRINT A(I),
22 NEXT I
27 FOR I=1 TO 5
30 LET X=1E10
35     FOR J=1 TO5
40     IF A(J)>=X THEN 65
45     REMEMBER THE SMALLEST
50     LET X=A(J)
55     REMEMBER ITS INDEX
60     LET S=J
65     NEXT J
70 LET B(I)=X
75 REM SET A(S)=A VERY BIG NUMBER
30 LET A(S)=1E10
35 NEXT I
90 FOR I=1 TO 5
95 PRINT B(I),
100 NEXTI
105 DATA 1,7,6,0,3
110 END

RUN
 1              7              6              0              3
 0              1              3              6              7
```

before first pass

A	X	B	S
1	1E10	*	*
7		*	
6		*	
0		*	
3		*	

after first pass

A	X	B	S
1	0	0	4
7		*	
6		*	
1E10		*	
3		*	

---

*means not yet defined

FIGURE 11.1 Illustration of Program 11.1

after second pass

A	*X*	*B*	*S*
1E10	1	0	1
7		1	
6		*	
1E10		*	
3		*	

after third pass

A	*X*	*B*	*S*
1E10	3	0	5
7		1	
6		3	
1E10		*	
1E10		*	

after fourth pass

A	*X*	*B*	*S*
1E10	6	0	3
7		1	
1E10		3	
1E10		6	
1E10		*	

after fifth pass

A	*X*	*B*	*S*
1E10	7	0	2
1E10		1	
1E10		3	
1E10		6	
1E10		7	

FIGURE 11.1 (cont'd.)

Note that the inner loop (lines 35–65) determines the smallest value and lets *X* be equal to it and lets *S* be equal to the index; that is, to the position in the array of the smallest element just found.

NUMERICAL SORTING—THE BUBBLE SORT

A much more efficient method of sorting is known as the bubble sort. It requires only one array; that is, the original one, and takes less time to compute. But it is much more difficult to understand.

Program 11.2 accomplishes the same thing as Program 11.1, using the same data. Figure 11.2 illustrates how Program 11.2 works.

PROGRAM 11.2 The Bubble Sort

```
10 FOR I= 1 TO 5
15 READ A(I)
17 PRINT A(I),
20 NEXT I
25 FOR I=2TO 5
30 LET J=I
35 IF A(J)>=A(J-1)  THEN 65
40 LET D=A(J)
45 LET A(J)=A(J-1)
50 LET A(J-1) = D
55 LET J=J-1
60 IF J>=2  THEN 35
65 NEXT I
70 FOR I=1 TO 5
75 PRINT A(I),
80 NEXT I
85 DATA 1,7,6,0,3
90 END
RUN

1              7              6              0              3
0              1              3              6              7
```

			A		
before 1st switch	1	7	6	0	3
after 1st switch	1	6	7	0	3
after 2nd switch	1	6	0	7	3
after 3rd switch	1	0	6	7	3
after 4th switch	0	1	6	7	3
after 5th switch	0	1	6	3	7
after 6th switch	0	1	3	6	7

FIGURE 11.2 The Bubble Sort Illustrated

This routine is called the bubble sort because the smaller numbers "bubble" their way up to the surface by repeated switches with the numbers preceding them.

Case 11.1 illustrates a bubble sort for numeric data.

CASE 11.1 A large manufacturing company asked its employees who were interested in forming car pools to submit their names and addresses to the personnel office. Nearly 500 employees showed an interest. A computer program sorted the last four digits of the supplied zip code and prepared a list for the employees to use in forming their car pools.

Program 11.3 performs a sort on the zip codes of the following *test data*:

Name	Address	Zip Code
Name 1	Add-1	7504
Name 2	Add-2	7501
Name 3	Add-3	6811
Name 4	Add-4	7504
Name 5	Add-5	6812
Name 6	Add-6	7501
Name 7	Add-7	6811
Name 8	Add-8	6799

PROGRAM 11.3 Case 11.1, Car-Pool List Using Numeric Bubble Sort

```
5 DIM N$(1Ø),A$(1Ø),Z(1Ø)
1Ø LET N=8
15 FOR I=1 TO N
2Ø READ N$(I),A$(I),Z(I)
25 NEXT I
3Ø DATA NAME 1, ADD-1,75Ø4,NAME 2,ADD-2,75Ø1
35 DATA NAME 3, ADD-3,6811,NAME 4,ADD-4,75Ø4
4Ø DATA NAME 5, ADD-5,6812,NAME 6,ADD-6,75Ø1
45 DATA NAME 7, ADD-7,6811,NAME 8,ADD-8,6799
6Ø REM SORT OF ZIP CODES FOLLOWS:
7Ø FOR I= 1 TO N-1
8Ø       FOR J=1 TO N-1
9Ø         IF Z(J+1)>Z(J) THEN 13Ø
1ØØ        LET K=Z(J)
1Ø5        LET M$=N$(J)
1Ø6        LET B$=A$(J)
11Ø        LET Z(J)=Z(J+1)
115        LET N$(J)=N$(J+1)
116        LET A$(J)=A$(J+1)
12Ø        LET Z(J+1)=K
125        LET N$(J+1)=M$
126        LET A$(J+1)=B$
13Ø      NEXT J
14Ø NEXT I
145 PRINT "CAR POOL LIST SORTED BY ZIP CODE"
15Ø PRINT "ZIP CODE","NAME","ADDRESS"
16Ø FOR P= 1 TO N
17Ø    PRINT Z(P),N$(P),A$(P)
18Ø NEXT P
19Ø END
RUN
CAR POOL LIST SORTED BY ZIP CODE
ZIP CODE        NAME            ADDRESS
 6799            NAME 8          ADD-8
 6811            NAME 3          ADD-3
 6811            NAME 7          ADD-7
 6812            NAME 5          ADD-5
 75Ø1            NAME 6          ADD-6
 75Ø1            NAME 2          ADD-2
 75Ø4            NAME 4          ADD-4
 75Ø4            NAME 1          ADD-1
```

Program 11.3 not only sorts the numeric zip codes, but also maintains the names and addresses that go along with the sorted zip codes. Otherwise, the end result would be a sorted zip-code list of little value to those wanting to form a car pool.

As each zip-code value in the array Z is sorted and its position in the array changed, so is the position of the name N$ and the address A$. For example, the lowest zip code is 6799 in position Z(8), along with "Name 8" in N$(8), and "Add-8" in A$(8). When the value 6799 in Z(8) is switched into a new position Z(J), the associated items in N$(8) and A$(8) must also be switched into N$(J) and A$(J), respectively. These switches of the items associated with the zip code are accomplished by the following program segments:

```
105 LET M$ = N$(J)
106 LET B$ = A$(J)
115 LET N$(J) = N$(J+1)
116 LET A$(J) = A$(J+1)
125 LET N$(J+1) = M$
126 LET A$(J+1) = B$
```

Once the sort is completed, the program will output—in ascending order—the zip code, name, and address list. Lines 160–180 in Program 11.3 will cause the output listing shown.

Before going on to alphabetic sorting, let us examine the following lines in Program 11.3:

```
 90 IF Z(J+1) > Z(J) THEN 130
100 LET K = Z(J)
110 LET Z(J) = Z(J+1)
120 LET Z(J+1) = K
```

These sort the zip-code values. Two values are tested at a time: one in the J+1 position of the array Z; the other in the J position. If the value in the J+1 position is greater than the value in the J position, no further processing of the values occurs. But if the value in the J+1 position is *not* greater than the value in J position, lines 100–120 are executed. The purpose of these lines is to change the positions of the two values, putting the smaller value in the position of the larger value and vice versa.

The switch of values into different positions is performed by the lines above. The variable *K* is a temporary holding variable. Using the first two zip-code values from Case 11.1, Figure 11.3 illustrates this switching and holding process.

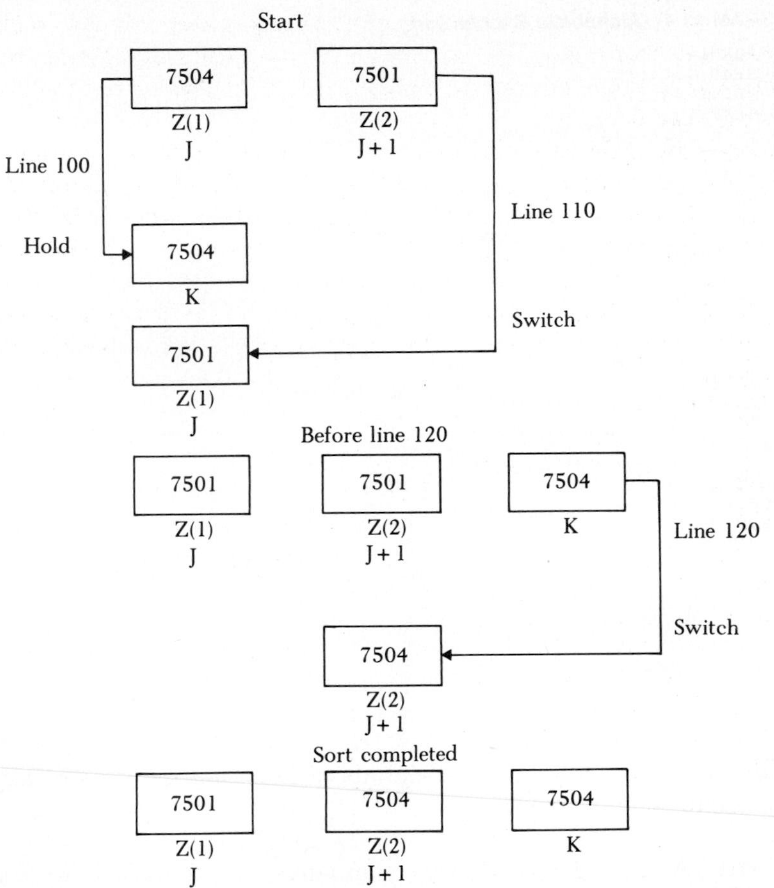

FIGURE 11.3 Switching and Holding Process, Program 11.3, Case 11.1 Numeric

ALPHABETICAL SORTING

Just as we were able to sort numerical arrays, so can we also sort alphabetical arrays. Program 11.4 puts six names into alphabetical order, using a bubble sort technique.

PROGRAM 11.4 Alphabetic Bubble Sort

```
Ø5 FOR I=1 TO 6
1Ø READ N$(I)
12 PRINT N$(I)
15 NEXT I
2Ø DATA JULIE,JOSHUA,EFRAM,BENNET,ARI,ISAAC
22 PRINT
25 FOR I= 2 TO 6
3Ø LET J=I
35 IFN$(J)>=N$(J-1) THEN 65
4Ø LET D$=N$(J)
45 LET N$(J)=N$(J-1)
5Ø LET N$(J-1)=D$
55 LET J=J-1
6Ø IFJ>=2 THEN 35
65 NEXT I
7Ø FOR I=1 TO 6
75 PRINTN$(I)
8Ø NEXT I
85 END
RUN

JULIE
JOSHUA
EFRAM
BENNET
ARI
ISAAC

ARI
BENNET
EFRAM
ISAAC
JOSHUA
JULIE
```

A problem may involve several alphabetic lists that require sorting. Case 11.2 presents such a situation.

CASE 11.2 A catalogue mail-order company has purchased two mailing lists. They may contain duplicate names. The lists are not in alphabetic sequence. To reduce mailing costs, the lists are to be sorted and merged. Any duplicate names are to be deleted.

Program 11.5 uses the following *test data* to develop a third list from the two lists supplied:

List 1	List 2
XYZ	CBA
JKL	BMD
LMN	PDQ
CBA	XXX
YYY	XYA
ABC	LMN
AAA	BBB
XXX	ZZZ
EFG	GFE

PROGRAM 11.5 Case 11.2, Mailing List Using Alphabetic Sort

```
5 DIM N$(20),X$(20)
10 REM READ IN BOTH LISTS
15 LET N= 18
20 FOR I= 1 TO N
25 READ N$(I)
30 NEXT I
35 DATA XYZ,JKL,LMN,CBA,YYY,ABC,AAA,XXX,EFG
40 DATA CBA,BMD,PDQ,XXX,XYA,LMN,BBB,ZZZ,GFE
42 REM SORT BOTH LISTS
45 FOR I= 1 TO N-1
50     FOR J= 1 TO N-1
60        IF N$(J+1)>N$(J) THEN 80
65        LET M$=N$(J)
70        LET N$(J)=N$(J+1)
75        LET N$(J+1)=M$
80     NEXT J
85 NEXT I
87 REM TEST FOR DUPLICATES
90 FOR M= 1 TO N
95    IF N$(M)=N$(M+1) THEN 115
97 REM COUNT ITEMS IN THE LIST
100    LET C=C+1
105    LET N$(C)=N$(M)
110       GO TO 125
112 REM COUNT DUPLICATES FROM BOTH LISTS
115    LET D=D+1
120    LET X$(D)=N$(M+1)
125 NEXT M
130 PRINT "# OF ITEMS IN LIST";C;"    # OF DUPLICATES";D
135 PRINT "NEW LIST","DUPLICATES"
140 FOR M=1 TO C
145 PRINT N$(M),X$(M)
150 NEXT M
200 END
RUN
# OF ITEMS IN LIST 15     # OF DUPLICATES 3
NEW LIST          DUPLICATES
AAA               CBA
ABC               LMN
BBB               XXX
BMD
CBA
EFG
GFE
JKL
LMN
PDQ
XXX
XYA
XYZ
YYY
ZZZ
```

In Program 11.5, the two lists are read in and stored as a single list in the array N$. This process is accomplished by lines 20–30. A bubble sort of the alphabetic list is then performed by lines 45–85. Figure 11.4 illustrates the holding and switching process of the sort sequence after the string test in line 60

60 IF N$(J+1) > N$(J) THEN 80

is *not* true.

Once both lists are sorted into a single list, a test for duplicates is performed by the program section lines 90–125. If a duplicate is found; that is, if line 95

95 IF N$(M) = N$(M+1) THEN 115

is true, the duplicate is removed from the list and placed into a new array designated X$. This placement of duplicates into the new array is performed by line 120

120 LET X$(D) = N$(M+1)

The final phase of the program prints out the new list and any duplicates found. This task is performed by lines 140–150.

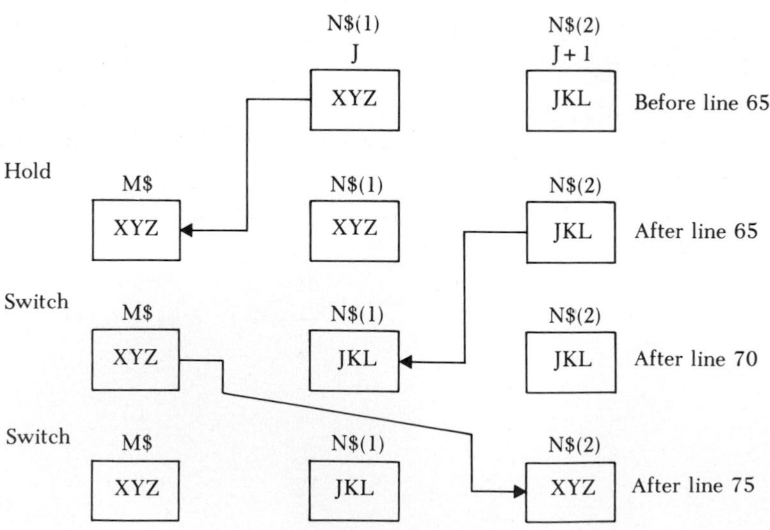

FIGURE 11.4 Switching and Holding Process, Program 11.5, Case 11.2, Alphabetic Sort

SUMMARY

This chapter demonstrated how numerical arrays can be sorted and how alphabetical arrays can be put in alphabetical order. The bubble sort and selection sort techniques were illustrated.

EXERCISES

11.1 Write a selection sort program similar to **Program 11.1,** except that you want to put the numbers in descending order. HINT: In this case, x must be assigned a very small number, such as $-1E10$.

11.2 Write a bubble sort program that puts numbers in descending order. Use the data from **Program 11.1**

11.3 Write a selection sort program to sort an alphabetic array. Use the data from **Program 11.4**

* 11.4 Prepare a diagram similar to Figure 11.1 for the data 0,8,9,3,2.

* 11.5 Prepare a diagram similar to Figure 11.2 for the data 0,8,9,3,2.

* 11.6 Prepare a diagram similar to Figure 11.1, in which the data is still 1,7,6,0,3, but you are sorting in descending order instead.

11.7 To carry out a reconciliation of a checking account, the first step is to put the cancelled checks into a sort sequence from low to high numbers. Write a program to sequence the following check numbers:

1108, 1102, 1098, 1100, 1095, 1110, 1107, 1097, 1104, 1105, 1094

11.8 Redo *exercise 11.7* so that all of the check numbers are sorted from low to high, and the numbers of any missing checks are also printed out as a separate category.

11.9 The Town Food Stores, Inc., has 13 stores in its chain. Yesterday's sales for each store are:

Store	Sales	Store	Sales
1	$3,696	2	$4,281
3	5,650	4	6,969
5	3,854	6	4,955
7	5,724	8	1,695
9	7,864	10	1,947
11	4,417	12	5,092
13	2,611		

Write a program that outputs this data in descending order, with the store with the greatest sales first, down to store with the lowest sales. Store numbers should also be outputted along side the sales data.

11.10 For the regional sales data listed below, write a program that will sort sales from low to high and output the results with their appropriate region.

Region	Sales (million $)
Northeast	20
Atlantic	25
Southern	18
Central	16
Southwest	23
Western	28
Pacific	26

11.11 For the data given in *exercise 11.10* write a program that will sort sales from high to low and output the results for their appropriate region.

11.12 For the data given in *exercise 11.10* write a program that will alphabetize each region and also output their sales.

*11.13 Would **Program 11.5** of **Case 11.2** process three lists of names? Revise the program to process a third list: CCC, XYZ, MNO, BBB, XXX, CBA, MNO, NNN, and then run the program.

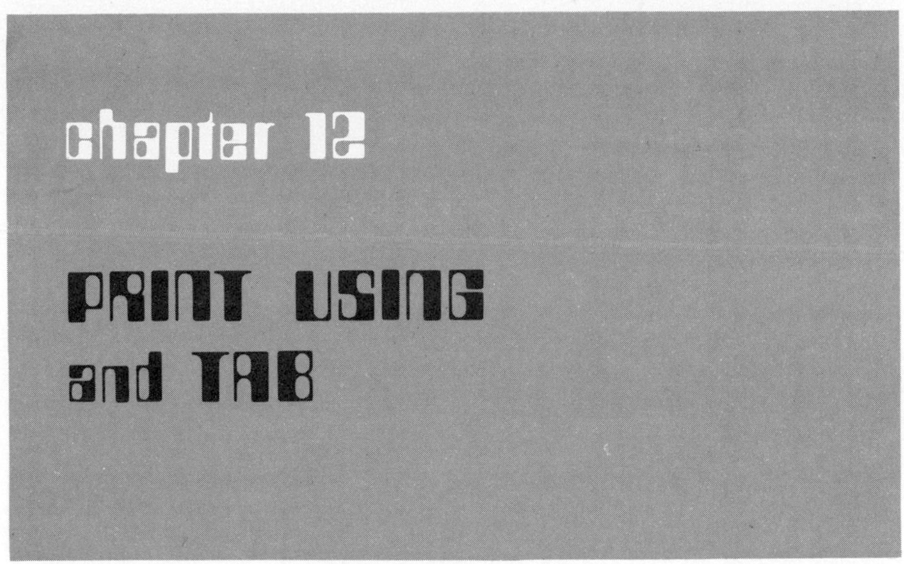

THE PRINT USING STATEMENT

The PRINT USING statement is a very useful feature of many BASIC systems. It allows greater control of the output than the PRINT statement. Note, for example, the output in Program 5.3. Some revised prices are whole numbers and some have several decimal positions. Suppose we wish all of the revised prices to be printed rounded to two decimal places. Also observe that the column containing the item numbers is 15 spaces wide where 8 would be more than enough. Finally, it would be nice if prices over $1000 were printed with commas. These difficulties can be corrected with the PRINT USING statement.

To improve the output in Program 5.3 we replace each PRINT statement with a PRINT USING statement and an associated image statement. Look at Program 12.1.

PROGRAM 12.1 Revising Prices with PRINT USING

```
5 REM PROGRAM TO UPDATE PRICE LIST
10 PRINT USING 60
11 PRINT USING 61
15 READ I,P
20 LET R=P*1.066
30 PRINT USING 62,I,P,R
40 GO TO 15
50 DATA 218,200,233,1456,345,545,367,248,401,225,406,179
55 DATA 407,1000,557,267,679,470,887,359
60 FMT ITEM              CURRENT               REVISED
61 FMT NUMBER            PRICE                 PRICE
62 FMT ###          $##,###.##            $##,###.##
90 END
```

PROGRAM 12.1 continued

```
RUN
 ITEM              CURRENT                REVISED
 NUMBER            PRICE                  PRICE
 218          $     200.00           $     213.20
 233          $ 1,456.00             $ 1,552.10
 345          $     545.00           $     580.97
 367          $     248.00           $     264.37
 401          $     225.00           $     239.85
 406          $     179.00           $     190.81
 407          $ 1,000.00             $ 1,066.00
 557          $     267.00           $     284.62
 679          $     470.00           $     501.02
 887          $     359.00           $     382.69

OUT OF DATA- LN #  15
```

The image statement associated with each PRINT USING statement begins with the letters FMT* and tells the computer how to print the variables (if any) of the PRINT USING statement. The image statement may also contain only headings. Thus lines 10 and 11 which have no variables in them will print everything following the letters FMT in lines 60 and 61, exactly as it appears there. Line 30 will cause the values of the variables *I*, *P*, and *R* to be printed where the fields of the "#"** symbols are in the image statement. That is, the item number, *I*, will be printed in the first three columns, the current price will be printed where the second field of #'s is and with two zeros to the right of the decimal point since there is a decimal point before the last two #'s. Note that the prices are right justified and all of the decimal points are aligned. Finally, the revised prices will appear where the third field of #'s is. Note how the commas are printed only for numbers more than $1,000.00.

The general form of the PRINT USING statement is:

line #1 PRINT USING line #2, V1, V2

where line #2 is some line number (either before or after line #1) that contains the format or FMT statement that should be used to print the variables *V*1, *V*2, etc. If there is no variable list, then the FMT statement should contain a heading.

The form of the FMT statement is:

line #FMT HEADING and/or #,###,##

The variable(s) from the corresponding PRINT USING statement will be printed in the positions of the # symbols.

Some other features of the PRINT USING statement are illustrated in Program 11.2. Note how readable the numeric output appears with the

*In some systems, a full colon is used instead of the letters FMT.

**In some systems, a "9" is used instead of the "#."

commas. Also note that if a field of #'s is surrounded with parentheses, the output will have the parentheses only if the number is negative, as in the profit (loss) column. Note also that all of the decimal points are aligned properly, the numbers are all right justified, and the zeros are filled in all printing positions to the right of the decimal.

PROGRAM 12.2 Profit (Loss) with PRINT USING

```
10 PRINT USING 400
15 FOR J=1 TO 5
20 READ N$,I,E
25 LET P=I-E
30 PRINT USING 401,N$,I,E,P
35 NEXT J
40 DATA HERGOLD REALTY CO.,500000,197000
45 DATA SUNBRITE DAIRY CO.,1209765,1340123
50 DATA ACE RENTAL CO.,546739,467654
55 DATA ARNOLD PAINT CO.,65000,36000
60 DATA CHEFA CATERING CO.,430000,739000
400 FMTCOMPANY                  GROSS INCOME        EXPENSES  PROFIT(LOSS)
401 FMT################### ##,###,###.##  ###,###,###.##  (###,###.##)
999 END
```

```
RUN
COMPANY                 GROSS INCOME          EXPENSES  PROFIT(LOSS)
HERGOLD REALTY CO.        500,000.00        197,000.00    303,000.00
SUNBRITE DAIRY CO.      1,209,765.00      1,340,123.00  (130,363.00)
ACE RENTAL CO.            546,739.00        467,654.00     79,135.00
ARNOLD PAINT CO.           65,000.00         36,000.00  ( 21,000.00)
CHEFA CATERING CO.        430,000.00        739,000.00  (359,000.00)
```

Another very useful feature of the PRINT USING statement is the asterisk protection feature, illustrated in Program 12.3. Note the single asterisk (*) in Line 201.

PROGRAM 12.3 Asterisk Protection Feature

```
10 PRINT USING 200
20 FOR I=1 TO 5
25 READ N$,H,R
30 PRINT USING 201,N$,H,R,H*R
35 NEXT I
200 FMT NAME            HOURS          RATE          SALARY
201 FMT ##########        ###        $###.##     $*#,###.##
300 DATA F.BACK,50,21.00,H.BOOK,25,2.50
310 DATA C.RAICE,31,2.75,K.SHIRA,39,3.72
320 DATA P.SURI,37,3.86
999 END
```

```
RUN
 NAME           HOURS         RATE        SALARY
 F.BACK            50      $ 21.00    $*1,050.00
 H.BOOK            25      $  2.50    $****62.50
 C.RAICE           31      $  2.75    $****85.25
 K.SHIRA           39      $  3.72    $***145.08
 P.SURI            37      $  3.86    $***142.82
```

Observe that the asterisks fill in all blanks between the "$" and the first nonzero figure. This feature effectively prevents any unscrupulous employees from giving themselves a raise in salary by adding a number in the blank space before the existing salary on a paycheck.

The user/programmer must be careful when using the PRINT USING statement to have enough # symbols in the image statement to accommodate the largest number or string that is to be printed in that field. If the number of characters or digits to be printed is less than the number of # symbols in the image statement, no harm is done. Numbers will be printed in the rightmost positions and strings will be printed in the leftmost positions. If the number of characters or digits to be printed is more than the number of # symbols in the image statement, an error message will be printed or, in some systems, the leading characters or digits will not be printed.

An application of PRINT USING is given in Case 12.1

CASE 12.1 A utility company would like to prepare a report summarizing the kilowatts used by its customers and the amounts charged. The rate per kilowatt is .0918829.

Program 12.4 prepares this report. Note that the FMT statement in line 210 directs the computer to print the word TOTALS and the values of the total variables *K*1 and *D*1.

PROGRAM 12.4 Case 12.1, Utility Bills

```
2 LET R=.Ø913329
5 LET D1=Ø
6 LET K1=Ø
1Ø PRINT USING 2ØØ
15 FOR I=1 TO 5
2Ø READ N$,K
25 LET D=R*K
3Ø LET D1=D1+D
35 LET K1=K1+K
4Ø PRINT USING 2Ø5,N$,K,D
45 NEXT I
47 PRINT
5Ø PRINT USING 21Ø,K1,D1
55 DATA G.BAYES,62.3,R.BERSON,45.1
6Ø DATA L.GORDON,53.7,M.KUHR,3Ø.9
65 DATA I.ROBERT,74.Ø
2ØØ FMT      NAME              KILOWATTS             AMOUNT
2Ø5 FMT      ##########            ###.#            #,###.##
21Ø FMT      TOTALS              #,###.#           ##,###.##
999 END
RUN
      NAME              KILOWATTS          AMOUNT
      G.BAYES                62.3            5.72
      R.BERSON               45.1            4,14
      L.GORDON               53.7            5.39
      M.KUHR                 3Ø.9            2.34
      I.ROBERT               74.Ø            6.3Ø

      TOTALS                271.Ø           24.9Ø
```

THE TAB FUNCTION

The TAB feature directs the computer to print output in any column that we like. For example, if we wanted to print "MARCH SALES REPORT" beginning in column 36, we would write the statement:

10 PRINT TAB(35); "MARCH SALES REPORT"

The TAB(35); will skip until the 36th space. Note the semicolon following the TAB(35). A comma there would have caused "MARCH SALES REPORT" to be printed in column 46 (i.e., the fourth column) since the fourth column is the next available column after the 36th position. Thus, the TAB statement should *always be used with a semicolon.*

The parentheses following the word TAB can contain any numerical expression. If the expression has a noninteger value, the number of spaces skipped will be the integer part of the value.

The number in parentheses always refers to the number of spaces skipped from the left-hand margin. Thus the statement:

10 PRINT TAB(10); "*"; TAB(35); "*"

directs the computer to print an "*" in columns 11 and 36, not in columns 11 and 46. Program 12.5 illustrates the TAB feature.

PROGRAM 12.5 The TAB Feature

```
10 FOR I = 1 TO 9
15 PRINT "*";TAB(I);"*";TAB(10);"*"
20 NEXT I
25 END

RUN
**        *
* *       *
*  *      *
*   *     *
*    *    *
*     *   *
*      *  *
*       * *
*        **
```

Note that line 15 prints three asterisks. The first asterisk is in the first column, the second in the (I+1)st column, and the third in column 11.

In Program 10.7, we had in array *G*$ the letters *A, B*+, *C*+, *C, D*+, *D*, and *F*; and in array *N*, the number of students receiving a particular grade. That is, *G*$(1) = "*A*" and *N*(1) = the number of students receiving the grade of *A*, *G*$(2) = "*B* +" and *N*(2) = the number of students receiving the grade of *B*+, and so on.

Suppose we wanted to plot the frequency distribution of grades. The program segment lines 400–415 of Program 12.5 when inserted into Program 10.7 will accomplish this. We have also (1) used the GO SUB and RETURN statements in Program 12.5 to segment the report into sections by underlining, (2) used the STOP statement (lines 499), (3) used the suggestion given in *exercise 10.4,* and (4) used the PRINT USING statements in place of the PRINT statements in lines 30 and 165 to further improve the appearance of the output.

PROGRAM 12.6 The Grade Program with a Plot

```
5 DIM N(8),G$(8)
7 GO SUB 500
10 FOR I=1 TO 8
15 READ G$(I)
16 DATA A,B+,B,C+,C,D+,D,F
20 LET N(I)=0
25 NEXT I
30 PRINT USING 300
35 FOR I= 1 TO 10
40 READ N$,G1,G2,G3,F
45 LET A=((G1+G2+G3)/3+F)/2
50 IF A>94 THEN 70
55 IF A<60 THEN 80
60 LET X=INT((94-A)/5)+1
65 GO TO 160
70 LET X=1
75 GO TO 160
80 LET X=8
160 LET N(X)=N(X)+1
165 PRINT USING 301,N$,A,G$(X)
170 NEXT I
171 PRINT
172 GO SUB 500
175 PRINT "GRADE","NUMBER"
180 FOR I=1 TO 8
185 PRINT G$(I),N(I)
190 NEXT I
195 PRINT
200 DATA J.SAMBORN,65,76,80,90,P.FISHMAN,70,81,95,93,E.GOLD,76,84,68,78
210 DATA A.EINSTEIN,98,97,90,95,B.WEIN,86,88,89,89,S.DACHS,77,76,80,73
220 DATA M.FALIG,81,84,90,80,R.HERMAN,58,74,67,54,E.GILA,70,75,78,79
230 DATA J.LYNN,70,74,65,68
300 FMT NAME              AVERAGE      GRADE
301 FMT #############     ###.##        ###
305 GO SUB 500
400 FOR I=1 TO 8
405 PRINT G$(I);TAB(N(I)*3+5);"*"
410 PRINT
415 NEXT I
420 FOR I=0 TO 10
425 PRINT TAB(4+3*I);I;
430 NEXT I
435 PRINT
440 PRINT TAB(13);"NO. OF STUDENTS"
450 GO SUB 500
499 STOP
500 PRINT
501 PRINT
505 FOR I=1 TO 70
510 PRINT "-";
515 NEXT I
520 PRINT
521 PRINT
525 RETURN
9999 END
RUN
```

PROGRAM 12.6 continued

```
--------------------------------------------------------------------

NAME              AVERAGE       GRADE
J.SAMBORN          81.83        B
P.FISHMAN          87.50        B+
E.GOLD             77.00        C+
A.EINSTEIN         95.00        A
B.WEIN             88.33        B+
S.DACHS            75.33        C+
M.FALIG            82.50        B
R.HERMAN           60.17        D
B.GILA             76.67        C+
J.LYNN             68.83        D+

--------------------------------------------------------------------

GRADE            NUMBER
A                  1
B+                 2
B                  2
C+                 3
C                  0
D+                 1
D                  1
F                  0

--------------------------------------------------------------------

A          *

B+            *

B             *

C+               *

C       *

D+         *

D          *

F       *

        0  1  2  3  4  5  6  7  8  9  10
                 NO. OF STUDENTS

--------------------------------------------------------------------
```

SUMMARY

The PRINT USING statement, along with its associated image statement, is more flexible than the standard PRINT statement.

With the PRINT USING statement, you can

1. round numbers to any number of decimal places,
2. align the decimal points and have numbers right justified instead of left justified,

3. have columns of any width instead of only 15-character width columns,
4. have commas printed indicating thousands, millions, etc., in very large numbers,
5. print and adjust column headings more easily,
6. have negative numbers printed surrounded by parentheses (as in profit/loss statements), and
7. have all leading blanks filled in with asterisks.

The TAB feature allows one to conveniently skip spaces, much the same as the tab key does on a typewriter. It also enables one to draw graphs and frequency distributions.

EXERCISES

*12.1 Write a program using PRINT USING to print the square root of 2 correct to 1, 2, 3, 4, 5, and 10 decimal places.

*12.2 Write a program using PRINT USING to print the powers of 2 between 1 and 26, inclusive. Allow eight digits for your answer. Be sure to have the output printed with commas separating the groups of three numbers.

12.3 Rewrite **Program 10.4** with PRINT USING statements. Have all square roots printed correct to four digits.

12.4 Rewrite **Program 7.9** using PRINT USING statements. The sales projections should all be printed correct to two decimal places. Have the heading also printed with PRINT USING statements.

12.5 Write a program that would print the following letters of the alphabet using asterisks and the TAB feature, as in **Program 12.5.**

*a. *Z*	c. *T*	*e. *P*	*g. *W*
*b. *H*	d. *U*	*f. *V*	

12.6 What will the following program print when it is run:

```
 10 GO SUB 100
 20 GO SUB 200
 30 GO SUB 100
 40 GO SUB 200
 50 GO SUB 100
 60 STOP
100 FOR I = 1 TO 10
105 PRINT "*";
110 NEXT I
115 PRINT
120 RETURN
```

```
200 FOR I = 1 TO 7
205 PRINT"*"
210 NEXT I
215 RETURN
300 END
```

*12.7 Write a program using the subroutines in *exercise 12.6* to print the letter *F*.

*12.8 Write one PRINT statement using TAB to print "NAME" in columns 1–4, "SALARY" in columns 21–26, "DEDUCTIONS" in columns 35–44, and "NET PAY" in columns 50–56.

12.9 Modify **Program 3.14** so that the column for sales for each day is 10 characters in width instead of 15 characters. Use the TAB feature.

chapter 13

Matrices and Matrix Operations

There are many programming situations where large data arrays—lists and/or tables—are involved, or where matrix algebra computations are required. The BASIC language has a set of statements to handle such situations. These *matrix statements** provide the programmer with a convenient and easy way to carry out operations that might require added statements if done in an alternate way.

A matrix can be either a list or a table of data, as covered in Chapter 8. This chapter explains reading, printing, and manipulation of data as matrices.

THE MAT READ STATEMENT

The general form of the MAT READ statement is:

line # MAT READ matrix name(s)

Examples of such statements are:

```
20 MAT READ A
30 MAT READ X1
45 MAT READ K, L, M
```

*Some systems do not have matrix statements.

Assume there is a matrix B:

$$\begin{vmatrix} 27 & 36 & 78 \\ 47 & 14 & 49 \end{vmatrix}$$

Examples of MAT READ and DATA statements to read this data are:

```
10 MAT READ B
20 DATA 27, 36, 78
30 DATA 47, 14, 49
```

or

```
10 MAT READ B
20 DATA 27, 36, 78, 47, 14, 49
```

A MAT READ statement is equivalent to reading with nested FOR/NEXT loops as shown in Program 13.1.

PROGRAM 13.1 Reading a Matrix Using Nested FOR/NEXT Loops

```
5 DIM B(2,3)
10 FOR I=1 TO 2
15 FOR J=1 TO 3
20 READ B(I,J)
25 NEXT J
30 NEXT I
35 DATA 27,36,78,47,14,49
99 END
```

A single statement (line 10, MAT READ B, in Program 13.2) functions like lines 10–30 in Program 13.1. All the values read by MAT READ B in Program 13.2 can be treated as subscripted variables.

In order to specify the size of the matrix being read in, we use a DIM statement.* Such a statement serves in the same way as the outer limits of the FOR statements in Program 13.1. A complete program for reading matrix B is shown in Program 13.2.

PROGRAM 13.2 Reading a 2 × 3 Matrix with MAT READ

```
5 DIM B(2,3)
10 MAT READ B
20 DATA 27,36,78,47,14,49
99 END
```

---

*To declare that matrices start with subscripts having a lower bound of one, it may be necessary to use the OPTION BASE statement (Chapter 8), or some similar BASIC system statement.

The DIM in line 5 indicates the size of the matrix—in this case, two rows and three columns. As a result, Program 13.2 yields the following assignment of data to a subscripted variable:

B(1,1) = 27	B(1,2) = 36	B(1,3) = 78
B(2,1) = 47	B(2,2) = 14	B(2,3) = 49

In Chapter 8 it was pointed out that overdimensioning was permitted, but underdimensioning would generate an error message. The same holds true for matrix reading. If the DIM statement is larger than the matrix actually being read, the correct matrix size must be shown in the MAT READ statement. Program 13.3 is a revision of Program 13.2 illustrating this point.

PROGRAM 13.3 Specifying the Size of the Matrix in MAT READ

```
5 DIM B(10,12)
10 MAT READ B(2,3)
20 DATA 27,36,78,47,14,49
99 END
```

Line 10 in the revised program provides the correct row and column specifications. Two general situations for line 10 can be stated:

1. line # MAT READ matrix name (rows *or* columns)
2. line # MAT READ matrix name (rows, columns)

Examples for these statements are:

10 MAT READ X(5):	a single list of 5 items to be subscripted X(1), X(2), . . . , X(5)
30 MAT READ A(20,5):	a table of 100 items (20 rows and 5 columns) subscripted as A(1,1), . . . , A(1,5) . . . . . . A(20,1), . . . , A(20,5)

THE MAT PRINT STATEMENT

A statement of the following form can be used to print out a matrix:

line # MAT PRINT matrix name(s)

Examples of such statements are:

25 MAT PRINT A
35 MAT PRINT X1;
45 MAT PRINT K, L, M

Line 25 generates output in fields of 15 spaces, 5 fields on each line. Line 35 prints output packed across each line, row by row, because of the "dangling" semicolon. Line 45 prints out each matrix one at a time, first matrix *K*, then *L*, and then *M*, one beneath the other.

Several programs that read in and print out matrices using different MAT PRINT statements follow.

Program 13.4 illustrates handling a single list as a matrix with output generated by line 20.

PROGRAM 13.4 MAT READ and MAT PRINT for a List

```
5 DIM L(12)
10 MAT READ L
20 MAT PRINT L
30 DATA 2,4,6,8,10,1,3,5,7,9,11,13
99 END

RUN

 2              4              6              8              10
 1              3              5              7              9
 11             13
```

Program 13.5 illustrates the single list shown in Program 13.4, with line 20 ending with ";". Note how the output is packed onto a single line.

PROGRAM 13.5 MAT PRINT Ending with a Semicolon

```
5 DIM L(12)
10 MAT READ L
20 MAT PRINT L;
30 DATA 2,4,6,8,10,1,3,5,7,9,11,13
99 END

RUN

 2  4  6  8  10  1  3  5  7  9  11  13
```

Program 13.6 illustrates the reading in and printing out of a simple table, four rows by three columns.

PROGRAM 13.6 MAT READ and MAT PRINT for a Table

```
10 DIM X(4,3)
15 MAT READ X
20 MAT PRINT X
25 DATA 2,2,2,6,6,6,8,8,8,9,9,9
99 END

RUN

 2              2              2
 6              6              6
 8              8              8
 9              9              9
```

Program 13.7 illustrates what happens with a different DIM statement than that used in Program 13.6. Instead of a 4 × 3 table, a 6 × 2 table has been outputted. Note the ";" at the end of line 20 and the resulting output.

PROGRAM 13.7 Changing the DIM Statement and Packing Output

```
10 DIM X(6,2)
15 MAT READ X
20 MAT PRINT X;
25 DATA 2,2,2,6,6,6,8,8,8,9,9,9
99 END

RUN

 2  2
 2  6
 6  6
 8  8
 8  9
 9  9
```

Program 13.8 illustrates a single program with several lists and tables being read in and printed out. The program uses the following:

List *A*:	5, 12, 13, 76, 12, 17			
List *J*:	−32, 68, −41, 68			
Table *N*:	.3	.5	.2	
	.6	.7	.8	
	.2	.1	.9	
Table *P*:	8	1	5	6
	3	2	9	7

Note that the data must be in the precise order that it is to be read. That is, lists *A* and *J*, then tables *N* and *P*, must agree with line 10.

PROGRAM 13.8 Reading and Printing Lists and Tables

```
5 DIM A(6),J(4),N(3,3),P(2,4)
10 MAT READ A,J,N,P
20 MAT PRINT A;J,N,P;
30 DATA 5,12,13,76,12,17,-32,68,-41,68
40 DATA .3,.5,.2,.6,.7,.8,.2,.1,.9
50 DATA 8,1,5,6,3,2,9,7
99 END

RUN

 5  12  13  76  12  17


-32             68              -41             68


 .3             .5              .2
 .6             .7              .8
 .2             .1              .9


 8  1  5  6
 3  2  9  7
```

Program 13.9 illustrates overdimensioning with the MAT READ (line 20) giving the row and column specifications for a 3×5 table.

PROGRAM 13.9 Overdimensioning and Table Specifications in MAT READ

```
10 DIM C(10,20)
20 MAT READ C(3,5)
30 MAT PRINT C;
50 DATA 2,3,6,-7,8,9,1,-3,5,9,2,0,1,-5,8
99 END

RUN

 2  3  6 -7  8
 9  1 -3  5  9
 2  0  1 -5  8
```

Program 13.10 illustrates how the parts of a matrix that have been read in can be printed out. The program will read in the following matrix *M:*

$$\begin{vmatrix} 7 & 3 & 6 \\ -5 & 12 & 8 \\ 9 & 17 & 11 \\ 10 & -8 & 5 \end{vmatrix}$$

PROGRAM 13.10 Printing Parts of a Matrix

```
5 DIM M(4,3)
10 MAT READ M
15 DATA 7,3,6,-5,12,8,9,17,11,10,-8,5
20 PRINT "2ND ROW"
25 PRINT M(2,1);M(2,2);M(2,3)
26 PRINT
30 PRINT "COLUMNS 1 AND 2"
35 FOR I= 1 TO 4
40 FOR J= 1 TO 2
50 PRINT M(I,J),
55 NEXT J
60 PRINT
65 NEXT I
70 PRINT "ROWS 2,3,&4-COLS 2&3"
75 FOR I= 2 TO 4
80 FOR J =2 TO 3
85 PRINT M(I,J),
90 NEXT J
95 PRINT
100 NEXT I
199 END


RUN
2ND ROW
-5  12  8

COLUMNS 1 AND 2
 7              3
-5              12
 9              17
 10            -8
ROWS 2,3,&4-COLS 2&3
 12             8
 17             11
-8              5
```

The first output will be the second row of the matrix, based on line 25. The next output will be columns 1 and 2 based on lines 35–65. The last output (the values in rows 2, 3, and 4 but only columns 2 and 3) is based on lines 75–100.

THE MAT INPUT STATEMENT

In Chapter 3 we saw how data could be supplied to a program in response to an INPUT statement. Such a statement results in the symbol "?" being printed at a user's terminal. Then the computer system pauses so that the user can type data in.

It is also possible to enter a matrix of data using the input approach. The general statement to do this is:

line # MAT INPUT variable list

Specific examples are:

25 MAT INPUT C
40 MAT INPUT S,T,V

When a MAT INPUT statement is executed, the symbol "?" appears for each data line in the matrix. After the first "?", one line of data is to be typed. Then another "?" appears, to be followed by the next line of data, and so on. In the case of line 40 above, where there are several matrices to be inputted, each matrix is entered sequentially; first MAT S, then MAT T, and finally MAT V. All data can then be referred to by means of subscripted variables since we are dealing with matrices.

Matrix C below is a 3×2 table with the following data in it:

$$\begin{vmatrix} 17 & -6 \\ 25 & 7 \\ 20 & -8 \end{vmatrix}$$

Program 13.11 shows this matrix as an input. Line 10 provides for the inputting of the data.

PROGRAM 13.11 MAT INPUT Statement

```
5 DIM C(3,2)
10 MAT INPUT C
15 MAT PRINT C
20 PRINT "COL.1 TOTAL", "COL.2 TOTAL"
25 PRINT C(1,1)+C(2,1)+C(3,1),C(1,2)+C(2,2)+C(3,2)
99 END

RUN
?17,-6
?25,7
?20,-8

17          -6
25           7
20          -8

COL.1 TOTAL     COL.2 TOTAL
 62             -7
```

Note that line 25 in Program 13.11 generates totals based on the subscripted variables of the matrix.

Inputting more than one matrix is illustrated in Program 13.12. The following data is used.

$$S = \begin{vmatrix} 78 & 30 \\ 25 & 62 \end{vmatrix} \qquad T = \begin{vmatrix} 17 \\ 21 \\ 9 \end{vmatrix} \qquad V = \begin{vmatrix} 2 & 6 & 9 \\ 7 & 8 & 1 \end{vmatrix}$$

Note that all of the data for each matrix can be inputted at one time, rather than line by line.

PROGRAM 13.12 MAT INPUT for Several Matrices

```
5 DIM S(2,2),T(3,1),V(2,3)
10 MAT INPUT S,T,V
15 MAT PRINT S;T;V;
20 PRINT "NORTHWEST VALUE IN EACH MATRIX";S(1,1);T(1,1);V(1,1)
25 PRINT "SOUTHEAST VALUE IN EACH MATRIX";S(2,2);T(3,1);V(2,3)
99 END

RUN
?78,30,25,62
?17,21,9
?2,6,9,7,8,1

78   30
25   62



17
21
9



2  6  9
7  8  1

NORTHWEST VALUE IN EACH MATRIX 78   17  2
SOUTHEAST VALUE IN EACH MATRIX 62  9   1
```

Lines 20 and 25 in Program 13.12 show how data items inputted into a matrix can be manipulated using subscripted variables.

MATRIX ADDITION, SUBTRACTION, AND MULTIPLICATION

In general all matrix operations have the form:

line # MAT name = operation

Only one operation is permitted in a statement. This means that no more than two matrices can be manipulated at any time in a statement.

Addition and Subtraction

Matrix addition and subtraction can be illustrated by the following statements using matrices A and B:

$$A = \begin{vmatrix} -2 & 3 \\ 7 & -6 \\ 9 & 1 \end{vmatrix} \quad \text{and} \quad B = \begin{vmatrix} 7 & 6 \\ 5 & -2 \\ 8 & 1 \end{vmatrix}$$

25 MAT C = A + B
35 MAT D = A − B

To perform these operations all the matrices must have the same dimensions. We see that both A and B are 3×2. Appropriate dimensioning must be supplied for the matrices to hold the results of the operations, namely, matrices C and D.

Program 13.13 shows the above matrices being added, then subtracted, and the resulting output. Note that line 5 contains dimensioning for matrices C and D.

PROGRAM 13.13 Adding and Subtracting Matrices Using MAT Operations

```
5 DIM A(3,2),B(3,2),C(3,2),D(3,2)
10 MAT READ A,B
15 DATA -2,3,7,-6,9,1,7,6,5,-2,8,1
20 MAT PRINT A;B;
22 PRINT "C=A+B"
25 MAT C=A+B
30 MAT PRINT C;
32 PRINT "D=A-B"
35 MAT D=A-B
40 MAT PRINT D;
99 END


RUN

-2  3
 7 -6
 9  1


 7  6
 5 -2
 8  1


C=A+B

 5  9
 12 -8
 17  2


D=A-B

-9 -3
 2 -4
 1  0
```

If more than two matrices are to be manipulated, an intermediate step such as line 25 in Program 13.14 is required. This program is adding together matrices X, Y, and Z, which have these values:

$$X = \begin{vmatrix} 2 & 7 \\ 1 & 9 \end{vmatrix} \qquad Y = \begin{vmatrix} 5 & -4 \\ 9 & 0 \end{vmatrix} \qquad Z = \begin{vmatrix} -2 & 8 \\ 7 & 2 \end{vmatrix}$$

First X and Y are added in line 25 to give matrix I. This result is then added to matrix Z in line 40 to produce matrix F, the final answer. Dimensioning for matrices I and F must be provided, as is shown in line 5.

PROGRAM 13.14 Adding Three Matrices

```
5 DIM X(2,2),Y(2,2),Z(2,2),I(2,2),F(2,2)
10 MAT READ X,Y,Z
15 MAT PRINT X;Y;Z;
20 REM LINE 25 INTERMEDIATE STEP
25 MAT I=X+Y
30 PRINT "INTERMEDIATE MATRIX I"
35 MAT PRINT I;
40 MAT F=Z+I
45 PRINT "FINAL RESULT: X+Y+Z"
50 MAT PRINT F;
60 DATA 2,7,1,9,5,-4,9,0,-2,8,7,2
99 END

RUN

 2  7
 1  9


 5 -4
 9  0


-2  8
 7  2

INTERMEDIATE MATRIX I

 7  3
 10  9

FINAL RESULT: X+Y+Z

 5  11
 17  11
```

Program 13.15 illustrates the use of MAT statements and nested FOR/NEXT loops. It generates the desired results for Case 13.1. Figure 13.1 represents the flowchart for Program 13.15.

CASE 13.1 The ABC Company has profit data for the last 2 years, month by month, for its four sales regions. This data is shown below. It is desired to aggregate (add together) the yearly data into one table. Also 2 year regional sales totals are wanted.

ABC Company: Profits by Region
Year 1 and 2—Jan. to Dec.
(All figures in thousand $)

Region	J	F	M	A	M	J	J	A	S	O	N	D
Year 1												
1	7	5	5	8	7	5	6	7	7	6	5	6
2	6	5	7	8	6	5	5	7	6	5	6	4
3	5	8	5	7	7	6	5	6	5	6	7	8
4	9	7	8	6	6	7	8	9	8	7	6	7
Year 2												
1	4	6	5	4	5	6	7	8	8	8	7	6
2	5	6	8	7	8	6	6	7	8	7	5	6
3	6	8	6	8	8	7	6	5	6	8	7	9
4	9	8	8	7	8	9	6	9	9	8	7	10

PROGRAM 13.15 Case 13.1, ABC Company Profits—MAT Statements and Nested FOR/NEXT Loops

```
5 DIM Y1(4,12),Y2(4,12),A(4,12)
10 MAT READ Y1,Y2
15 MAT A=Y1+Y2
20 PRINT "ABC COMPANY-PROFITS BY REGIONS,FOR TWO YEARS"
30 PRINT
40 PRINT "REG J   F   M   A   M   J   J   A   S   O   N   D   TOT"
50 FOR I = 1 TO 4
60 LET T(I)=0
65 PRINT    I;
70     FOR J = 1 TO 12
80     PRINT A(I,J);
85     LET T(I) = T(I) + A(I,J)
90     NEXT J
95 PRINT T(I)
100 NEXT I
150 DATA 7,5,5,8,7,5,6,7,7,6,5,6,6,5,7,8,6,5,5,7,6,5,6,4
155 DATA 5,8,5,7,7,6,5,6,5,6,7,8,9,7,8,6,6,7,8,9,8,7,6,7
160 DATA 4,6,5,4,5,6,7,8,8,8,7,6,5,6,8,7,8,6,6,7,8,7,5,6
165 DATA 6,8,6,8,8,7,6,5,6,8,7,9,9,8,8,7,8,9,6,9,9,8,7,10
199 END


RUN
ABC COMPANY-PROFITS BY REGIONS,FOR TWO YEARS

REG J   F   M   A   M   J   J   A   S   O   N   D   TOT
 1  11  11  10  12  12  11  13  15  15  14  12  12  148
 2  11  11  15  15  14  11  11  14  14  12  11  10  149
 3  11  16  11  15  15  13  11  11  11  14  14  17  159
 4  18  15  16  13  14  16  14  18  17  15  13  17  186
```

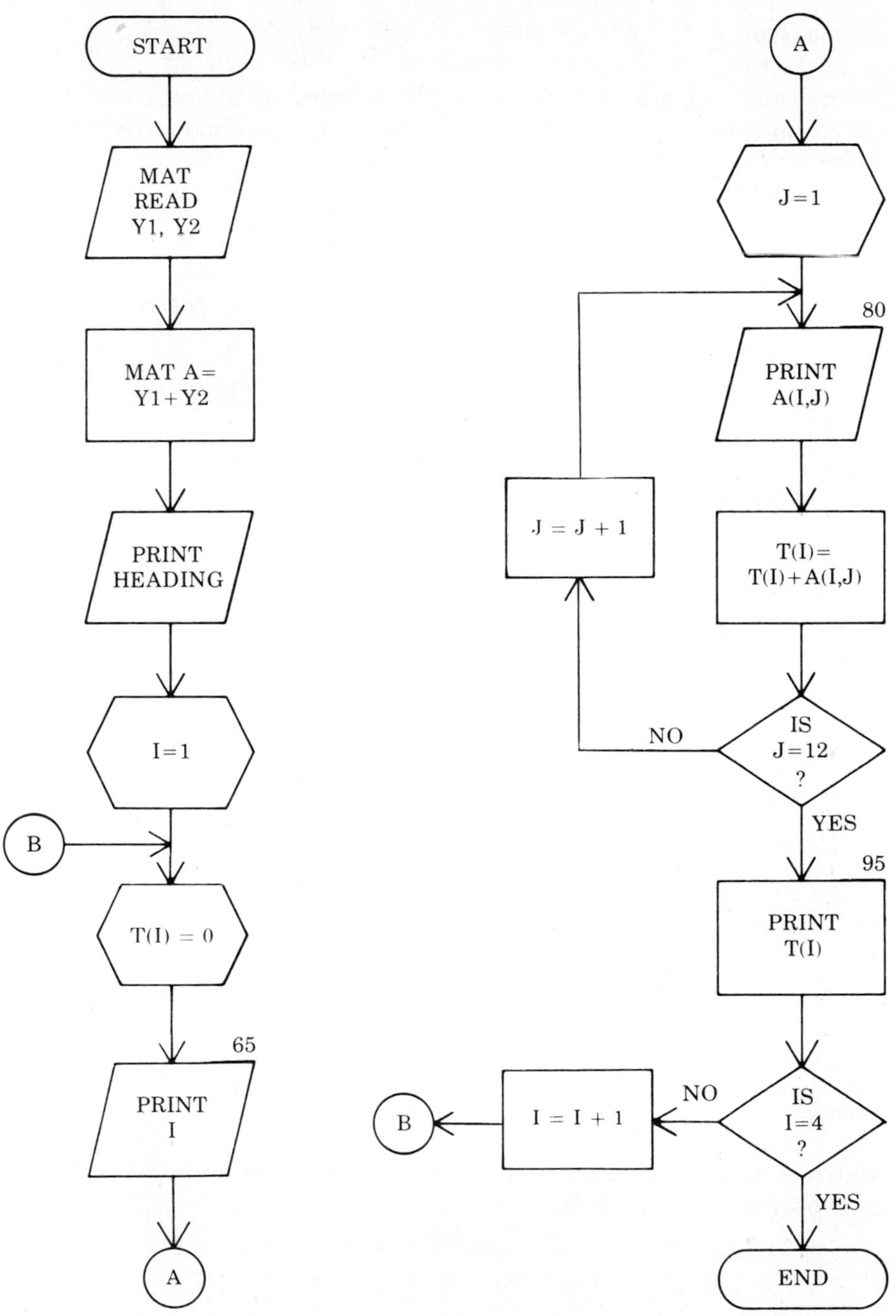

FIGURE 13.1 Flowchart for Program 13.15, Case 13.1, ABC Company Profits

Multiplication

To multiply one matrix by another, the number of columns of the first matrix must be equal to the number of rows in the second matrix. The size of the resulting matrix is a matrix having the number of rows of the first matrix, and the number of columns of the second matrix. In general, if we multiply two matrices, $A \times B$, to get C, we then have

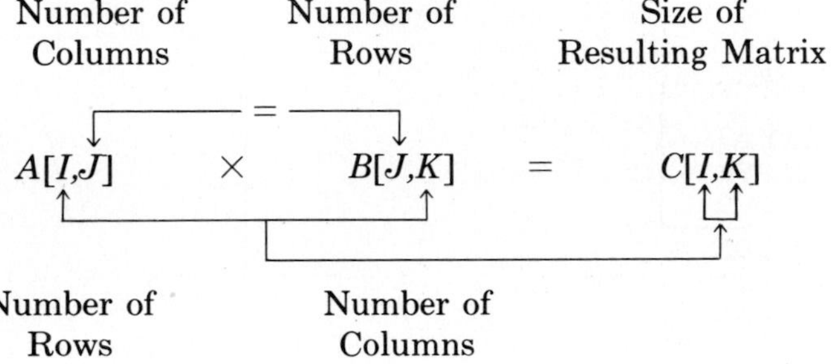

What follows are several examples of matrix multiplication using the following data:

$A = |3\ 2\ 4|$ a 1×3 list or row vector

$$B = \begin{vmatrix} 5 \\ 4 \\ 3 \end{vmatrix}$$ a 3×1 list or column vector

$$C = \begin{vmatrix} 2 & 5 & 1 \\ 1 & 8 & 2 \\ 7 & 3 & 5 \end{vmatrix}$$ a 3×3 table or matrix

$$D = \begin{vmatrix} 2 & 4 & 3 \\ 5 & 4 & 1 \end{vmatrix}$$ a 2×3 table or matrix

Example 1

Matrix A times matrix B (a 1×3 times a 3×1 results in a 1×1). The computation goes like this:

$$|3\ 2\ 4| \begin{vmatrix} 5 \\ 4 \\ 3 \end{vmatrix} = (3 \times 5) + (2 \times 4) + (4 \times 3) = |35|$$

In Program 13.16 this computation is done by line 20

PROGRAM 13.16 Multiplying Matrices: A 1 × 3 Times a 3 × 1 Gives a 1 × 1

```
5 DIM A(1,3),B(3,1),X(1,1)
10 MAT READ A,B
15 MAT PRINT A;B;
20 MAT X=A*B
25 MAT PRINT X
50 DATA 3,2,4,5,4,3
99 END

RUN

 3  2  4


 5
 4
 3


 35
```

Example 2

Matrix B times matrix A (a 3×1 times a 1×3 results in a 3×3). The computation goes like this:

$$\begin{vmatrix} 5 \\ 4 \\ 3 \end{vmatrix} \begin{vmatrix} 3 & 2 & 4 \end{vmatrix} = \begin{vmatrix} (5 \times 3) & (5 \times 2) & (5 \times 4) \\ (4 \times 3) & (4 \times 2) & (4 \times 4) \\ (3 \times 3) & (3 \times 2) & (3 \times 4) \end{vmatrix} = \begin{vmatrix} 15 & 10 & 20 \\ 12 & 8 & 16 \\ 9 & 6 & 12 \end{vmatrix}$$

This computation is carried out by line 20 in Program 13.17.

PROGRAM 13.17 Multiplying Matrices: A 3 × 1 Times a 1 × 3 Gives a 3 × 3

```
5 DIM A(1,3),B(3,1),X(3,3)
10 MAT READ A,B
15 MAT PRINT B;A;
20 MAT X=B*A
25 MAT PRINT X
50 DATA 3,2,4,5,4,3
99 END

RUN

 5
 4
 3


 3  2  4


 15             10             20
 12             8              16
 9              6              12
```

Example 3

Matrix A times matrix C (a 1×3 times a 3×3 results in a 1×3). Line 20 in Program 13.18 does the computation of $A \times C$:

$$\begin{vmatrix} 3 & 2 & 4 \end{vmatrix} \begin{vmatrix} 2 & 5 & 1 \\ 1 & 8 & 2 \\ 7 & 3 & 5 \end{vmatrix} = \left| \begin{pmatrix} (3 \times 2) \\ +(2 \times 1) \\ +(4 \times 7) \end{pmatrix} \begin{pmatrix} (3 \times 5) \\ +(2 \times 8) \\ +(4 \times 3) \end{pmatrix} \begin{pmatrix} (3 \times 1) \\ +(2 \times 2) \\ +(4 \times 5) \end{pmatrix} \right| = \begin{vmatrix} 36 & 43 & 27 \end{vmatrix}$$

PROGRAM 13.18 Multiplying Matrices: A 1 × 3 Times a 3 × 3 Gives a 1 × 3

```
5 DIM A(1,3),C(3,3),X(1,3)
10 MAT READ A,C
15 MAT PRINT A;C;
20 MAT X=A*C
25 MAT PRINT X;
50 DATA 3,2,4,2,5,1,1,8,2,7,3,5
99 END

RUN

 3  2  4


 2  5  1
 1  8  2
 7  3  5


 36  43  27
```

Example 4

Matrix B times matrix C (a 3×3 times a 3×1 results in a 3×1). In Program 13.19, line 20 computes $C \times B$:

$$\begin{vmatrix} 2 & 5 & 1 \\ 1 & 8 & 2 \\ 7 & 3 & 5 \end{vmatrix} \begin{vmatrix} 5 \\ 4 \\ 3 \end{vmatrix} = \begin{vmatrix} ((2 \times 5) + (5 \times 4) + (1 \times 3)) \\ ((1 \times 5) + (8 \times 4) + (2 \times 3)) \\ ((7 \times 5) + (3 \times 4) + (5 \times 3)) \end{vmatrix} = \begin{vmatrix} 33 \\ 43 \\ 62 \end{vmatrix}$$

Program 13.19 Multiplying Matrices: A 3 × 3 Times a 3 × 1 Gives a 3 × 1

```
5 DIM B(3,1),C(3,3),X(3,1)
10 MAT READ B,C
15 MAT PRINT C;B;
20 MAT X=C*B
25 MAT PRINT X;
50 DATA 5,4,3,2,5,1,1,8,2,7,3,5
99 END
```

PROGRAM 13.19 continued

```
RUN

 2  5  1
 1  8  2
 7  3  5



 5
 4
 3



 33
 43
 62
```

Example 5

Matrix D times matrix C (a 2×3 times a 3×3 results in a 2×3). Line 20 in Program 13.20 does the multiplication of $D \times C$:

$$\begin{vmatrix} 2 & 4 & 3 \\ 5 & 4 & 1 \end{vmatrix} \begin{vmatrix} 2 & 5 & 1 \\ 1 & 8 & 2 \\ 7 & 3 & 5 \end{vmatrix} = \begin{vmatrix} \begin{pmatrix} (2 \times 2) \\ +(4 \times 1) \\ +(3 \times 7) \end{pmatrix} & \begin{pmatrix} (2 \times 5) \\ +(4 \times 8) \\ +(3 \times 3) \end{pmatrix} & \begin{pmatrix} (2 \times 1) \\ +(4 \times 2) \\ +(3 \times 5) \end{pmatrix} \\ \begin{pmatrix} (5 \times 2) \\ +(4 \times 1) \\ +(1 \times 7) \end{pmatrix} & \begin{pmatrix} (5 \times 5) \\ +(4 \times 8) \\ +(1 \times 3) \end{pmatrix} & \begin{pmatrix} (5 \times 1) \\ +(4 \times 2) \\ +(1 \times 5) \end{pmatrix} \end{vmatrix} = \begin{vmatrix} 29 & 51 & 25 \\ 21 & 60 & 18 \end{vmatrix}$$

PROGRAM 13.20 Multiplying Matrices: A 2 × 3 Times a 3 × 3 Gives a 2 × 3

```
5 DIM D(2,3),C(3,3),X(2,3)
10 MAT READ D,C
15 MAT PRINT D;C;
20 MAT X=D*C
25 MAT PRINT X;
50 DATA 2,4,3,5,4,1,2,5,1,1,8,2,7,3,5
99 END

RUN

 2  4  3
 5  4  1



 2  5  1
 1  8  2
 7  3  5



 29   51   25
 21   60   18
```

Several cases follow. They illustrate the application of matrix multiplication.

CASE 13.2 The inventory of the Town Car Dealership consists of four models of a small car. Below are the quantities of each model in stock and the cost per car. It is desired to obtain the total dollar value for this inventory.

Car Model	1	2	3	4
Quantity	12	9	8	15
Cost	3150	3400	4100	3800

This case can be completed by letting the cost per model be a row vector, C, of size 1×4; and the quantity of each model a column vector, Q, of size 4×1. Line 35 in Program 13.21 obtains the total dollar value of the inventory by multiplying the cost vector C times the quantity vector Q. A 1×4 times a 4×1 produces a 1×1:

$$\begin{vmatrix} 3150 & 3400 & 4100 & 3800 \end{vmatrix} \begin{vmatrix} 12 \\ 9 \\ 8 \\ 15 \end{vmatrix} = \begin{vmatrix} 158200 \end{vmatrix}$$

PROGRAM 13.21 Case 13.2, Inventory Valuation Using Matrix Multiplication

```
5 DIM C(1,4),Q(4,1),V(1,1)
10 MAT READ C,Q
12 PRINT " ","CAR MODEL"
14 PRINT " 1"," 2"," 3"," 4"
15 PRINT
16 PRINT " ","QUANTITY"
20 PRINT Q(1,1),Q(2,1),Q(3,1),Q(4,1)
22 PRINT " ","COST"
25 MAT PRINT C
26 PRINT
30 MAT V=C*Q
35 PRINT "TOTAL $ VALUE OF INVTY",
40 MAT PRINT V
50 DATA 3150,3400,4100,3300,12,9,3,15
99 END

RUN
                    CAR MODEL
 1                   2                   3                   4

                    QUANTITY

 12                  9                   8                   15


                    COST
 3150                3400                4100                3300

TOTAL $ VALUE OF INVTY
 158200
```

CASE 13.3 Many investors in stocks evaluate their stocks from the price paid when purchased to the present date. Below is a stock portfolio with purchase price for each stock, present market price, and the number of shares of each stock. It is desired to see how the total value of the portfolio has changed over time.

Stock	No. Shares	Purchase Price	Present Price
ABC Co.	4800	39½	37½
AXZ	3800	15⅞	14⅝
BCE	1500	10⅜	11¼
DITO	500	4¾	4¾
KLB	4300	6½	7⅛
LEZY	6700	19⅞	23½
TECH	1600	1½	1¾
LOD	2300	5⅛	6⅛
DZ	900	20½	23⅞
FTC	1900	4	6

Case 13.3 can be completed if the number of shares is treated as a 1×10 matrix, N, and the price information a 10×2 matrix, P. By multiplying matrix N times matrix P, as shown in line 20 of Program 13.22, a 1×2 is obtained. This matrix is the result desired.

PROGRAM 13.22 Case 13.3, Portfolio Valuation Using Matrix Multiplication

```
5 DIM N(1,10),P(10,2),V(1,2)
10 MAT READ N,P
20 MAT V=N*P
30 PRINT "              PORTFOLIO VALUATION"
40 PRINT "PURCHASE VALUE","PRESENT VALUE","GAIN OR LOSS"
50 PRINT V(1,1),V(1,2),V(1,2)-V(1,1)
55 DATA 4800,3800,1500,500,4300,6700,1600,2300,900,1900
60 DATA 39.5,37.5,15.875,14.625,10.375,11.25,4.75,4.75,6.5,7.125
65 DATA 19.875,23.5,1.5,1.75,5.125,6.125,20.5,23.875,4,6
99 END


RUN
          PORTFOLIO VALUATION
PURCHASE VALUE PRESENT VALUE  GAIN OR LOSS
 469213.         492633.        23475
```

Note in line 50 how the results are printed out using subscripted variables, rather than a MAT PRINT statement.

CASE 13.4 The Apex Company manufactures four products. Below is their production cost budget. They want to determine the total costs for each product, as well as the total cost of direct materials, direct labor, and factory overhead.

Apex Company
Production Cost Budget
Current Year

Product	Direct Materials	Direct Labor	Factory Overhead
1	$260,000	$520,000	$400,000
2	292,000	438,000	325,000
3	200,000	400,000	350,000
4	300,000	630,000	385,000

Case 13.4 requires row totals and column totals for the production cost data given. If this data is treated as a matrix *C*, size 4 × 3, it is possible to obtain row and column totals by multiplying matrix *C* by two other matrices. A 1 × 4 matrix of ones times matrix *C* gives a 1 × 3 matrix that represents the column totals. Line 20 in Program 13.23 shows this multiplication as MAT H = K * C. Matrix *K* is a 1 × 4 containing ones. The multiplication looks like this:

$$K(1 \times 4) \quad C(4 \times 3)$$

$$|1\ 1\ 1\ 1| \times \begin{vmatrix} 260000 & 520000 & 400000 \\ \vdots & \vdots & \vdots \\ \vdots & \vdots & \vdots \end{vmatrix}$$

and results in $H(1 \times 3) |\cdots \quad \cdots \quad \cdots|$ column totals.

If matrix *C* is multiplied by a 3 × 1 matrix of ones (line 30), the result is a 4 × 1 matrix that represents the row totals. The multiplication looks like this:

$$\begin{matrix} C(4 \times 3) & & R(3 \times 1) & & V(4 \times 1) \\ \begin{vmatrix} 260000 & 520000 & 400000 \\ \vdots & \vdots & \vdots \\ \vdots & \vdots & \vdots \end{vmatrix} & \times & \begin{vmatrix} 1 \\ 1 \\ 1 \end{vmatrix} & = & \begin{vmatrix} \vdots \\ \vdots \\ \vdots \end{vmatrix} \end{matrix} \quad \text{row totals}$$

The result is matrix *V*, a 4 × 1.

Note in the program that a nested FOR/NEXT loop (lines 40–90) is used to generate the original data and row totals. To generate the column totals, line 100 is used.

PROGRAM 13.23 Case 13.4, Production Cost Budget Using Matrix Multiplication and Nested FOR/NEXT Loops

```
5 DIM C(4,3),K(1,4),R(3,1),H(1,3),V(4,1)
10 MAT READ C,K,R
20 MAT H=K*C
30 MAT V=C*R
32 PRINT "      APEX CO.     "
34 PRINT "  PRODUCTION COST BUDGET"
36 PRINT "       CURRENT YEAR"
38 PRINT "PRODUCT","DIR MAT","DIR LABOR","FAC OH", "TOTAL"
40 FOR I = 1 TO 4
45 PRINT I,
50     FOR J = 1 TO 3
60     PRINT "$"C(I,J),
70     NEXT J
80 PRINT "$"V(I,1)
90 NEXT I
92 FOR U=1 TO 70
95 PRINT "-";
96 NEXT U
97 PRINT
100 PRINT "TOTALS",H(1,1),H(1,2),H(1,3)
140 DATA 260000,520000,400000,292000,438000,325000
145 DATA 200000,400000,350000,300000,630000,385000
150 DATA 1,1,1,1,1,1,1
199 END

RUN
     APEX CO.
  PRODUCTION COST BUDGET
     CURRENT YEAR
PRODUCT          DIR MAT          DIR LABOR        FAC OH           TOTAL
 1               $ 260000         $ 520000         $ 400000         $ 1.18E 6
 2               $ 292000         $ 438000         $ 325000         $ 1.055E 6
 3               $ 200000         $ 400000         $ 350000         $ 950000
 4               $ 300000         $ 630000         $ 385000         $ 1.315E 6
----------------------------------------------------------------------
TOTALS            1.052E 6         1.988E 6         1.46E 6
```

OTHER MATRIX OPERATIONS

Several additional matrix operations are illustrated in this section. If a more detailed explanation is required for any of the illustrations or operations shown, you should refer to an introductory text that covers matrices.*

Multiplication by a Constant

Given a matrix A, to multiply every value in it by a constant K, we can use the following statement:

20 MAT C = (K) * A

*See, for example, E. K. Bowen, Chapter 6, "Compact Notation: Vectors, Matrices, and Summation," *Mathematics with Applications in Management and Economics*, fifth edition, (Homewood, Ill: R. D. Irwin, 1980) or L. J. Goldstein and D. I. Schneider, Chapter 2, "Matrices," *Finite Mathematics and Its Applications,* (Englewood Cliffs, N.J.: Prentice-Hall, 1980).

Suppose A is a 3×2 matrix: $\begin{vmatrix} 180 & 210 \\ 105 & 179 \\ 220 & 260 \end{vmatrix}$

and K is equal to .80. Program 13.24 shows both program and output for a constant times a matrix.

PROGRAM 13.24 Multiplication of a Constant Times a Matrix

```
5 DIM A(3,2),C(3,2)
10 MAT READ A
15 MAT PRINT A;
20 MAT C=(.80)*A
25 PRINT ".80 TIMES MAT A"
30 MAT PRINT C;
40 DATA 180,210,105,179,220,260
99 END

RUN

 180  210
 105  179
 220  260

.80 TIMES MAT A

 144  168
 84  143.2
 176  208
```

Creating an Identity Matrix

An identity matrix has principal diagonal elements equal to one, and all off-diagonal elements equal to zero. Such a matrix can be produced using a statement like this:

$$20 \text{ MAT D} = \text{IDN}$$

Line 20 in Program 13.25 results in a 4×4 identity matrix (D).

PROGRAM 13.25 Identity Matrix

```
10 DIM D(4,4)
20 MAT D=IDN
30 PRINT "A 4 BY 4 IDENTITY MATRIX"
40 MAT PRINT D
99 END

RUN
A 4 BY 4 IDENTITY MATRIX

 1              0              0              0
 0              1              0              0
 0              0              1              0
 0              0              0              1
```

Transposing a Matrix

To interchange the rows and columns of a matrix use the following type of statement:

$$25 \text{ MAT E} = \text{TRN(P)}$$

If P is a 2 by 4,

$$\begin{vmatrix} 12 & 10 & -11 & 13 \\ 16 & 14 & 12 & -4 \end{vmatrix}$$

its transpose would be a 4×2. Program 13.26 illustrates such a transposition of P into E. Note that dimensioning must be provided for matrix E.

PROGRAM 13.26 Transpose of a Matrix

```
10 DIM P(2,4),E(4,2)
15 MAT READ P
18 PRINT "ORIGINAL MATRIX P, 2 BY 4"
20 MAT PRINT P;
25 MAT E=TRN(P)
30 PRINT "TRANSPOSE OF P, E IS A 4 BY 2"
35 MAT PRINT E;
50 DATA 12,10,-11,13,16,14,12,-4
99 END


RUN
ORIGINAL MATRIX P, 2 BY 4

 12  10 -11  13
 16  14  12 -4


TRANSPOSE OF P, E IS A 4 BY 2

 12  16
 10  14
-11  12
 13 -4
```

Inverse of a Matrix

An inverse of a matrix is analogous to obtaining the reciprocal of a quantity. To solve matrix problems that involve division it is necessary to find the inverse of at least one of the matrices in the problem. This is particularly true when solving sets of simultaneous linear equations by matrices (see exercise 13.20).

When it is necessary to use an inverted matrix, such a matrix can be developed using the following type of statement:

$$20 \text{ MAT F} = \text{INV(L)}$$

Assume L is a 2×2 matrix with values as follows:

$$\begin{vmatrix} 7 & 3 \\ 2 & 1 \end{vmatrix}$$

In Program 13.27 the inverse is obtained. The inverse matrix (F) must be dimensioned as shown in line 5.

PROGRAM 13.27 Inverse of a Matrix

```
5 DIM L(2,2),F(2,2)
1Ø MAT READ L
15 PRINT "ORIGINAL MATRIX L"
18 MAT PRINT L;
2Ø MAT F=INV(L)
25 PRINT "INVERSE OF L IS MATRIX F"
3Ø MAT PRINT F;
5Ø DATA 7,3,2,1
99 END


RUN
ORIGINAL MATRIX L

 7  3
 2  1


INVERSE OF L IS MATRIX F

 1.  -3.
-2.   7.
```

Matrices of Zeros or Ones

To set every element of a matrix A to zero, a statement such as this one can be used:

15 MAT A = ZER

Matrix A will be set to zeros. To obtain a matrix B with every element a one, the following statement can be used:

25 MAT B = CON

Matrix B will contain ones. Program 13.28 shows the result of a program creating a matrix of zeros and a matrix of ones.

PROGRAM 13.28 Matrices of Zeros or Ones

```
5 DIM A(5,8),B(7,7)
15 MAT A=ZER
25 MAT B=CON
3Ø MAT PRINT A;B;
99 END
```

PROGRAM 13.28 continued

```
RUN

Ø   Ø   Ø   Ø   Ø   Ø   Ø   Ø
Ø   Ø   Ø   Ø   Ø   Ø   Ø   Ø
Ø   Ø   Ø   Ø   Ø   Ø   Ø   Ø
Ø   Ø   Ø   Ø   Ø   Ø   Ø   Ø
Ø   Ø   Ø   Ø   Ø   Ø   Ø   Ø



1   1   1   1   1   1   1
1   1   1   1   1   1   1
1   1   1   1   1   1   1
1   1   1   1   1   1   1
1   1   1   1   1   1   1
1   1   1   1   1   1   1
1   1   1   1   1   1   1
```

Having a matrix with every element in it set equal to one enables us to easily develop column or row totals for another matrix. For example, if we want to get the column totals for a matrix B, size 4×3, we can multiply it by a matrix A, size 1×4, to produce a matrix C that contains the three column totals. The multiplication looks like this:

$$\underset{A(1 \times 4)}{\begin{vmatrix} 1 & 1 & 1 & 1 \end{vmatrix}} \times \underset{B(4 \times 3)}{\begin{vmatrix} 10 & 15 & 19 \\ 12 & 11 & 10 \\ 11 & 10 & 15 \\ 12 & 15 & 18 \end{vmatrix}} = \underset{C(1 \times 3)}{\begin{vmatrix} 45 & 51 & 62 \end{vmatrix}}$$

In earlier examples, to get row or column totals the matrix of ones was entered as a line of data. Program 13.29 illustrates how the above example can be solved with the matrix of ones obtained by the line

15 MAT A = CON

Note that the size of matrix A is specified by line 10 the dimension statement. The output for the program shows the matrix of ones (A) the matrix of values (B), and the matrix of column totals (C).

PROGRAM 13.29 Column Totals Using a Matrix of Ones

```
1Ø DIM A(1,4),B(4,3),C(1,3)
15 MAT A=CON
2Ø MAT READ B
3Ø MAT C=A*B
4Ø MAT PRINT A;B;C;
5Ø DATA 1Ø,15,19,12,11,1Ø
6Ø DATA 11,1Ø,15,12,15,13
9Ø END
```

PROGRAM 13.24 continued

```
RUN

 1  1  1  1



 10  15  19
 12  11  10
 11  10  15
 12  15  13



 45  51  62
```

The following case (13.5) makes use of a program that incorporates several different matrix operations to process two matrices, *W*1 and *W*2, and a row vector, *R*.

CASE 13.5 The Computer Components Company pays its workers according to the number of units of each type of component (*A*, *B*, or *C*) they have assembled. The piecework rate is as follows:

Component	*A*	*B*	*C*
Rate per unit	$.25	$.35	$.50

Each worker's gross wages are based on a 2-week period. Output for the last 2 weeks is as follows:

	Week 1			Week 2		
	Components			Components		
Worker	*A*	*B*	*C*	*A*	*B*	*C*
1	200	100	20	185	110	22
2	150	125	30	160	115	35
3	320	75	15	275	100	30
4	275	100	15	275	90	20
5	100	200	10	150	150	10

The above case was previously processed in Chapter 8, using Program 8.12 incorporating subscripted variables and FOR/NEXT loops. Program 13.30 simplifies the processing by treating the data as matrices. This program adds two matrices in line 30, MAT A= W1 + W2, then derives the gross wages for each worker by matrix multiplication in line 35, MAT Q= A*R, and finally derives a total for all wages by multiplying a matrix of ones times the gross wage matrix in line 40, MAT S= C*Q.

PROGRAM 13.30 Case 13.5, Computer Components Company, Gross Wage Calculations

```
10 DIM W1(5,3),W2(5,3),A(5,3),R(3,1),Q(5,1)
15 DIM C(1,5),S(1,1)
20 MAT C= CON
25 MAT READ W1,W2,R
30 MAT A=W1+W2
35 MAT Q=A*R
40 MAT S= C*Q
45 PRINT "EMPLOYEE","GROSS WAGE"
50 PRINT "----------------------------"
55 FOR I= 1 TO 5
60 PRINT I,"$";Q(I,1)
65 NEXT I
70 PRINT "----------------------------"
75 PRINT "TOTAL","$";S(1,1)
80 DATA 200,100,20,150,125,30,320,75,15,275,100,15
85 DATA 100,200,10,135,110,22,160,115,25,275,100,30
90 DATA 275,90,20,150,150,10,.25,.35,.50
95 END

READY

RUN
EMPLOYEE        GROSS WAGE
------------------------------
 1              $ 190.75
 2              $ 139
 3              $ 232.5
 4              $ 221.5
 5              $ 195
------------------------------
TOTAL           $ 1023.75
```

SUMMARY

Large arrays of data can be handled easily with matrix operations. In this chapter, reading and printing of matrices have been illustrated. It has been shown how matrices can be added, subtracted, and multiplied.

Since a matrix is a table whose elements are referred to by means of subscripted variables, dimensioning is required.

A matrix can also be inputted. Other matrix operations that can be carried out are multiplication by a constant; creating an identity matrix; transposing a matrix; finding the inverse of a matrix; and creating a matrix of zeros or of ones.

EXERCISES

13.1 Treat the following data first as (a) a one-dimensional list of 20 items; then as (b) a 5×4 table:

1, 4, 5, 6, 7, 4, 1, 7, 9, 10, 6, 0, 8, 1, 7, 0, 4, 6, 8, 1

a. Write a program that reads in the list as a matrix L.

b. Write a program that reads in the table as a matrix T.

*13.2 A 15 × 10 table is to be read in with the program below. The program is not complete. Why not? (The data lines are not shown, but can be assumed correct.)

```
125 MAT READ M
200 DATA........
299 END
```

13.3 A 12 × 30 table is to be read in with the program below. The program is not correct. Why not? (The data lines are not shown, but are correct.)

```
10 DIM (30, 12)
20 MAT READ A (50, 60)
50 DATA.....
99
```

13.4 Write a program that reads in and prints out all of the following matrices:

$$\begin{vmatrix} 68 & 73 & 41 & 12 & 18 & 21 \\ 32 & 47 & 16 & -7 & 12 & 20 \\ 38 & 61 & 62 & 21 & 14 & -9 \end{vmatrix}, \begin{vmatrix} 2 & 7 \\ 3 & 9 \\ 6 & 11 \\ 12 & 8 \\ 14 & 7 \end{vmatrix}, \begin{vmatrix} 1.1 & .6 & .8 & .9 \end{vmatrix}$$

*13.5 Write the program for the matrices in *exercise 13.4* so that the output is "packed."

13.6 Treat the following table as a matrix when it is read in:

	Quiz Grades		
Student	1	2	3
1	9	8	9
2	7	9	8
3	6	7	8
4	7	7	8
5	7	6	9
6	9	7	9
7	8	6	8
8	7	5	6
9	5	8	9
10	6	7	7
11	8	6	6

Write a single program that

a. Prints out the grades for each student with the student number showing in the output.
b. Prints out the grades for students 1–5.
c. Prints out for students 5–10, quiz grades 2 and 3.
d. Prints out for students 9, 10, 11, grades 1 and 3.

13.7 Compute gross pay for each worker in the table below:

Worker	Hours Worked	Rate Per Hour
1	32	$4.25
2	37	3.80
3	40	4.15
4	36	4.20
5	35	4.00
6	37½	3.75

The data should be treated as a matrix with each line an input.

13.8 At the beginning of the week the inventory in stock was as follows:

Item	Beginning Inventory (no. of units)	Units Sold During the Week
1	250	40
2	700	75
3	350	210
4	820	600
5	400	130
6	300	65
7	560	280

Determine what the ending inventory for each item is by treating beginning inventory and units sold as separate matrices. Your results should also be a matrix.

13.9 Below are the number of units shipped each week for each product the XYZ Company manufactures:

	Units Shipped – Product – (000)					
Week	*M*	*N*	*O*	*P*	*Q*	*R*
1	20	17	25	31	30	29
2	22	18	20	28	30	30
3	19	19	26	27	31	31
4	21	20	21	32	31	32

Treat each week as a separate matrix. Write a single program that generates the *total* number of units shipped for each product for (a) weeks 1 and 2, and (b) all 4 weeks.

13.10 Using the weekly data in *exercise 13.9,* compute the remaining inventory of units for the XYZ Company at the end of each week if the initial starting inventory for week 1 is:

Inventory on Hand – Product – (000)					
M	*N*	*O*	*P*	*Q*	*R*
140	210	160	150	195	230

Assume no production has occurred during this 4 weeks.

13.11 Below are the number of units sold for the 10 leading foreign car imports in June of year 1 and year 2. Write a program that gives the total sales for all car types in June of year 1 and June of year 2. Treat the data as a matrix. Output all the data using the numbers 1 to 10 in place of the car names.

Import Sales Leaders

Car	June Year 2	June Year 1
Toyota	28,435	19,549
Datsun	23,867	13,656
Volkswagen	23,268	23,806
Honda	10,061	2,938
Fiat	9,466	7,182
Mazda	9,323	4,999
Colt	5,939	3,300
Volvo	5,629	4,232
Audi	4,789	3,980
Subaru	4,344	1,631

Source: *Automotive News.*

13.12 Use the sales data in *exercise 13.11* and have your program generate total sales for each time period as well as the increase in sales between June of Year 1 and June of Year 2. A total for this difference should also be derived. Output all the data using the numbers 1 to 10 in place of the car names.

13.13 Perform the following matrix multiplications in a single program: A times B, B times A.

$$A = \begin{vmatrix} 4 & 6 & 3 & -1 \\ 0 & 1 & -2 & 1 \end{vmatrix}, \qquad B = \begin{vmatrix} 1 & 2 \\ -1 & 3 \\ 4 & -2 \\ 2 & 1 \end{vmatrix}$$

*13.14 Perform the following matrix multiplications in a single program: C times D, D times C.

$$C = \begin{vmatrix} 1/4 \\ 1/2 \\ -1/2 \\ 3/8 \end{vmatrix}, \qquad D = |16\ 24\ 20\ 36|$$

*13.15 Your stock portfolio contains seven stocks in the following amounts:

Stock	1	2	3	4	5	6	7
No. of Shares	110	200	100	150	200	250	100

Below are the prices for these stocks for three time periods:

Stock	Jan. 2	Price May 1	July 25
1	3	6¼	6⅜
2	6⅞	13¼	17
3	10⅞	16¾	19½
4	2½	5⅞	7⅜
5	3¾	8¼	9⅛
6	2	4⅛	6⅜
7	6	10¾	12

Write a program using matrix operations to find the market value of the stock portfolio for each of the three dates.

13.16 The American Missile Corporation manufactures four antiaircraft missiles. Each missile contains a different number of components. These are as follows:

Component Type	No. of Components per Missile Type 1	2	3	4
X3	20	15	26	19
X4	7	8	11	10
X5	7	7	7	9

A new contract has been received to produce the following quantities of each missile:

Missile	1	2	3	4
Amount to produce	1000	750	800	2000

Write a program to compute and print the total number of X3, X4, and X5 components required to satisfy the new contract.

13.17 Using matrix operations, write a program that will obtain row and column totals for the data below.

Division	Sales by Quarters (million $) 1st	2d	3d	4th
1	2.7	2.6	2.8	2.7
2	1.7	1.5	1.9	2.0
3	4.8	4.9	5.1	5.2
4	1.0	1.1	1.0	.9
5	8.6	8.6	8.7	8.8
6	5.2	5.4	5.6	5.8

13.18 Assume that a 5 percent increase in the sales shown in *exercise 13.17* is required next year by each division. Write a program that generates estimated quarterly sales; i.e., this year's sales increased by 5 percent. Use matrix operations. (*Hint:* This is multiplication by a constant.)

13.19 Below are the production cost elements of the Ajax Company and the quantity of each product to be produced.

	Per Unit Costs	
Cost Elements	Product 1 (200,000)	Product 2 (140,000)
Direct Materials	$2.00	$4.00
Direct Labor	4.00	6.00
Factory Overhead	3.00	4.50

Write a program that uses both matrix operations and FOR/NEXT loops to output:

a. A table with the three cost elements for each product based on the production figures given
b. Total costs for direct materials, direct labor, and factory overhead based on the production figures given
c. Total costs to produce 200,000 units of product 1, and 140,000 units of product 2
d. Total cost for *all* units of products 1 and 2 produced.

13.20 Matrix operations can be used to solve for variables in systems of linear equations.
Suppose we have the two equations

$$3x_1 + 2x_2 = 14 \qquad \text{and} \qquad 6x_1 - 2x_2 = 4$$

where x_1 and x_2 are unknowns. In matrix notation, the solution for this type of system of equation is:

$$X = A^{-1}B$$

where X is a matrix of solution values, A^{-1} is the inverse matrix of the matrix of coefficients of the variables in the equation, and B is a matrix of the values to the right of the equals.
Then for the equations above,

$$\begin{vmatrix} x_1 \\ x_2 \end{vmatrix} = \begin{vmatrix} \text{inverse matrix} \\ \text{of coefficients} \end{vmatrix} \times \begin{vmatrix} 14 \\ 4 \end{vmatrix}$$

where the inverse has not yet been obtained. The matrix of coefficients looks like this:

$$\begin{vmatrix} 3 & 2 \\ 6 & -2 \end{vmatrix}$$

Using matrix operations, write a program that solves for x_1 and x_2.

13.21 Revise **Program 13.29** to obtain row totals using an appropriate matrix of ones.

13.22 For the data in **Case 13.4,** develop a program that will obtain row and column totals using a matrix of constants (ones).

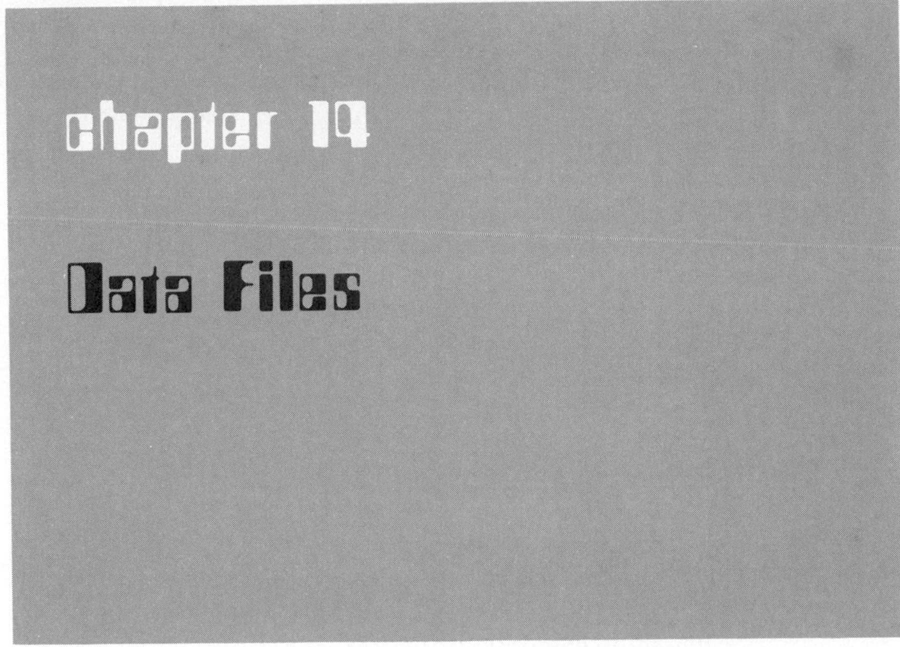

chapter 14

Data Files

Up to this point, we have seen that each program has had its own set of data and data lines as an integral part of the program.

In this chapter we will see how it is possible to place data into a separate and distinct storage entity called a *data file*. Such files are typical of informations systems where data is stored and retrieved as the situation requires. Once we have data in a file, any of numerous programs can then use it as though it were part of the program.*

FILE ACCESS

A file consists of related items or records. Files are typically stored external to the computer in secondary, or auxiliary, storage devices. Such devices make use of magnetic tapes, disks, and drums to actually retain the data files.

---

*The file instructions in this chapter are those of the RAPIDATA System. Refer to your system manual on this topic for exact specifications of statements to be used. It is also suggested that for a better understanding of files students refer to any one of a number of data-processing books that cover this topic. For example, M. R. Gore and J. W. Stubbe, Chapter 6, *Computers and Data Processing* (New York: McGraw-Hill, 1979) or V. T. Dock and E. Essick, Chapters 9 and 10, *Principles of Business Data Processing,* third ed., (Chicago: Science Research Associates, 1978).

Once a file has been stored, data retrieval will depend on what type of storage device was used. In general, there are two methods for accessing data on files. If a particular item is required, data on magnetic tape must be read from the beginning of the tape. Because of this, we refer to data retrieval from magnetic tape storage as *sequential access.* This is in contrast to data retrieval from magnetic disk storage devices.

With disk storage a particular item of data can be obtained by *direct access.* Direct access is sometimes referred to as random access. Any file item can be directly obtained whenever it is needed—without searching through each item from the beginning of the file.

We will examine the storage and access of data by first looking at *sequential access* and then at *direct access.*

CREATING A SEQUENTIAL ACCESS FILE

To create a sequential access data file, the first step is to give the file a name. A file can be up to six characters in length, starting with one of the alphabetic characters *A* to *Z*. Since a file being set up for the first time is like a new program, on many systems the creator of the file has to type in the command NEW, followed by the desired file name. The general form is:

NEW:file name

Specific examples are:

```
NEW:FILEA
NEW:XYZCO
NEW:YR1976
NEW:WAGES
```

After the naming of the file, the actual file creation is done. The structure of one line of a file is a line number, followed by a blank space, and then the data. Data may be either string or numeric. In general, a file line format looks like this:

line # (data list)

Specifically, a file may look like this:

```
NEW:GRADES
15 JACK, 80, 95, 76
20 BILL, 75, 70, 68
30 SALLY, 95, 75, 80
35 JOAN, 100, 80, 75
```

or like this:

```
NEW:PARTS
2 28, X1234
4 17, LM31K
6 101, BC7D
8 81, JA475
```

Notice that nowhere is the word DATA indicated. Since it is understood that a file will contain data, it is not necessary to type DATA on each line of a file. It is also important to remember to leave a blank between the line number and the data list. Otherwise the line number and the first item in the data list may be taken (incorrectly) as the line number. Observe the file named PARTS to see what would result in terms of line numbering if blanks were missing after any of the line numbers 2, 4, 6, 8.

The last step in the creation of a file is the "saving" aspect. After a file has been named and entered, the system command SAV (for save) must be typed.* This command ensures that the file is available for future use or for access by other programs.

If we have sales information for five years, as shown below, we could create a file to save such information.

XYZ Co.–Sales Data

Year	Millions of Dollars
1970	10.3
1971	11.4
1972	12.6
1973	13.7
1974	12.8

Figure 14.1 shows how the file SALESF is created and saved with the above sales data in it.

```
NEW:SALESF

10 1970,10.3
20 1971,11.4
30 1972,12.6
40 1973,13.7
50 1974,12.8

SAV
```

FIGURE 14.1 Creating a Data File

*The system commands SAV and NEW, used to save and name files, are also used to save and name programs. (See Appendix A.)

READING FROM A SEQUENTIAL FILE

To make use of, or gain access to, a sequential data file we use the appropriate BASIC statement in a program. The general format of the statement to read data from a file is:

line # INPUT:file name:data list

Typical file reading statements could be

40 INPUT: GRADES: N$, G1, G2, G3

or

50 INPUT: PARTS: Q, P$

which could be used in programs to deal with the files GRADES and PARTS shown earlier.

Program 14.1 reads each line one at a time and then prints out the entire contents of the previously created file, SALESF (Figure 14.1)

PROGRAM 14.1 Reading the Contents of a Data File

```
15 PRINT "YEAR","SALES(MILL.$)"
20 INPUT:SALESF:Y,S
25 PRINT Y,S
30 GO TO 20
99 END


RUN
YEAR          SALES(MILL.$)
 1970          10.3
 1971          11.4
 1972          12.6
 1973          13.7
 1974          12.8

FILE OUT OF DATA-- LN #  20
```

In the program (line 20), the data list variables *Y* and *S* correspond to the type of data in the file SALES; that is, numerical data for both year and sales. Note that line 25 (PRINT Y,S) is merely the way the programmer wants to have *Y* and *S* outputted. If only the sales data were desired as output, this could have been obtained by 25 PRINT S. Also note that without line 30 (GO TO 20), only the first line of the data file SALESF would be outputted. This is because of the sequential nature of the file process being used. The contents of the file are read from the first line, line by line, until out of data.

When working with files, it is possible to read data from several files. All that is required is additional file INPUT statements in the program. This reading from several files is illustrated in Case 14.1.

CASE 14.1 The XYZ Company has sales data for the years 1970–74 in a file named SALESF (see earlier discussion). Below are the total sales for the industry group that the XYZ Company is a member of. This data is found in a file named INDSF. It is desired to obtain a report that shows XYZ Company sales as a percent of industry sales for the years 1970–74.

Industry Sales Data

Year	Millions of $
1970	150.6
1971	175.2
1972	203.0
1973	230.8
1974	254.5

Program 14.2 reads from previously created data file SALESF and the file INDSF (having the above information in it). The program using both files generates the required output, as diagramed in Figure 14.2.

PROGRAM 14.2 Case 14.1, XYZ Company, Reading Several Data Files in One Program

```
25 PRINT "YEAR","XYZ CO.","INDUSTRY","% OF IND."
30 PRINT "      ","SALES(MILL.$)","SALES(MILL.$)"
35 PRINT "-----------------------------------------------------"
40 INPUT:SALESF:Y,S
50 INPUT:INDSF:N,D
60 PRINT N,S,D,(S/D)*100
65 GO TO 40
99 END

RUN
YEAR            XYZ CO.         INDUSTRY        % OF IND.
                SALES(MILL.$)   SALES(MILL.$)
-----------------------------------------------------
 1970            10.3            150.6           6.83931
 1971            11.4            175.2           6.50685
 1972            12.6            203             6.2069
 1973            13.7            230.8           5.93588
 1974            12.8            254.5           5.02947

FILE OUT OF DATA-- LN #   40
```

Lines 40 and 50 in the program obtain the data from the files SALESF and INDSF, respectively. In line 60 the desired computation is carried out based on the data from the two files. The GO TO in line 65 branches back to the first file INPUT as though branching to a READ/DATA, as in programs without files.

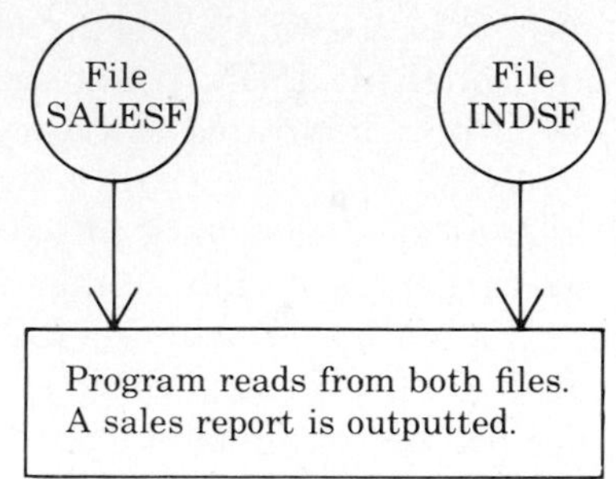

FIGURE 14.2 Case 14.1, XYZ Company, Diagram of Files and Programs

WRITING TO A SEQUENTIAL ACCESS FILE

In addition to reading from a sequential file in a program, it is also possible to take the results of a program and have them placed into a sequential file. To transfer program results to a sequential file requires the following BASIC statement format:

line # PRINT: file name: list structure or expressions

Some typical statements are:

```
 30 PRINT: XFILE: "TOTALS", A, B, C,
 45 PRINT: YEARS: 1975, Y$, M$, L1, L2
170 PRINT: GNP: C + I + G, "YEAR"
185 PRINT: PAY: "HOURS WORKED × RATE"; H * R
```

Before writing to a file, it is important to remember that a file must be in existence to receive program results being sent to it. The file receiving program results could be either an empty one, or one with data already in it.

Figure 14.3 illustrates the creation of an empty file named EMPTY. Program 14.3 (SUMUP) generates output to the terminal as well as transferring results to the file EMPTY.

```
NEW:EMPTY

SAV
```

FIGURE 14.3 Creating an Empty File

PROGRAM 14.3 Writing to an Empty File

```
10 REM THIS PROGRAM ADDS UP VALUES, TRANSFERS THEM TO
11 REM A FILE,'EMPTY', WITH THE SUM OF THE VALUES
15 LET S=0
20 READ X
21 DATA 5,5,10,15,25,40,-999
22 IF X=-999 THEN 60
25 PRINT X
30 LET S=S+X
40 PRINT:EMPTY:"X VALUE";X
50 GO TO 20
60 PRINT "TOTAL=";S
70 PRINT:EMPTY:"TOTAL OF X IS";S
99 END
```

```
RUN
 5
 5
 10
 15
 25
 40
TOTAL= 100
```

In Program 14.3, lines 40 and 70 write to the file EMPTY the items shown, that is, the values *X* and *S* (the total, or sum, of the *X* values). Figure 14.4 is a listing that shows what the file EMPTY now contains.* Such a listing verifies the accuracy of the file.

```
OLD:EMPTY


X VALUE 5
X VALUE 5
X VALUE 10
X VALUE 15
X VALUE 25
X VALUE 40
TOTAL OF X IS 100
```

FIGURE 14.4 Listing Contents of the File EMPTY

A sequential file such as EMPTY is useless in terms of its being used by another program because the file does not have line numbers for the items in it. To provide line numbering for program output being written to a file, the following statement can be used:

line # PRINT: file name: LNM(X); list structure or expressions

*To obtain a listing of a file or program that has been saved the system command OLD followed by the file or program name must be typed before the command LIST. (See Appendix A.)

where the X represents the line number in the file that the items following the semicolon will have. If the file contains more than one item the line numbering will increment by one. If X is less than a line number that already exists in the file, the line number assigned will be one more than the last line number in the file. Some examples of the file line numbering statement are:

```
 45 PRINT: FILE 2:LNM(5); W, H, W*H
 60 PRINT: IVEN: LNM(100); N$, P$, B–E
 75 PRINT: XYZ: LNM(15); 1970 + I
100 PRINT: AB2: LNM(72); "TOTALS"; A + B
```

Program 14.3 has been revised by changing lines 40 and 70 to generate line numbers in the file EMPTY. Program 14.4 shows the revised program SUMUP. Figure 14.5 shows a list of the file EMPTY, now having the line numbers that are a result of program lines 40 and 70.

PROGRAM 14.4 Writing to an Empty File and Providing Line Numbers

```
10 REM THIS PROGRAM ADDS UP VALUES, TRANSFERS THEM TO
11 REM A FILE,'EMPTY', WITH THE SUM OF THE VALUES
15 LET S=0
20 READ X
21 DATA 5,5,10,15,25,40,-999
22 IF X=-999 THEN 60
25 PRINT X
30 LET S=S+X
40 PRINT:EMPTY:LNM(10);"X VALUE";X
50 GO TO 20
60 PRINT "TOTAL=";S
70 PRINT:EMPTY:LNM(20);"TOTAL OF X IS";S
99 END

RUN
 5
 5
 10
 15
 25
 40
TOTAL= 100
```

```
OLD:EMPTY


10 X VALUE 5
11 X VALUE 5
12 X VALUE 10
13 X VALUE 15
14 X VALUE 25
15 X VALUE 40
20 TOTAL OF X IS 100
```

FIGURE 14.5 Listing Contents of the File EMPTY Showing Line Numbers

Case 14.2 illustrates the use of several sequential data files by different programs.

CASE 14.2 The Ajax Company has an employee payroll file named MASTER. The file structure contains employee name, social security number, number of dependents, and wage rate per hour for each person. A second file named HOURS contains employee social security number and the number of hours worked by the employee during the week.

Each week a payroll report for management is generated by a program named REPORT. This program makes use of the contents of the two files. The program REPORT also transfers to a file named GROSS the net wage after deductions of each employee. A summary wage report is required by management. This task is accomplished by using a program named SEGROS.

Below are the tax deductions used by the program REPORT based on an individual's number of dependents.

Number of Dependents	Deduction from Gross
1	10%
2	9
3	8
4	7
5 or more	6

Figure 14.6 shows a diagram of the files and programs in Case 14.2.

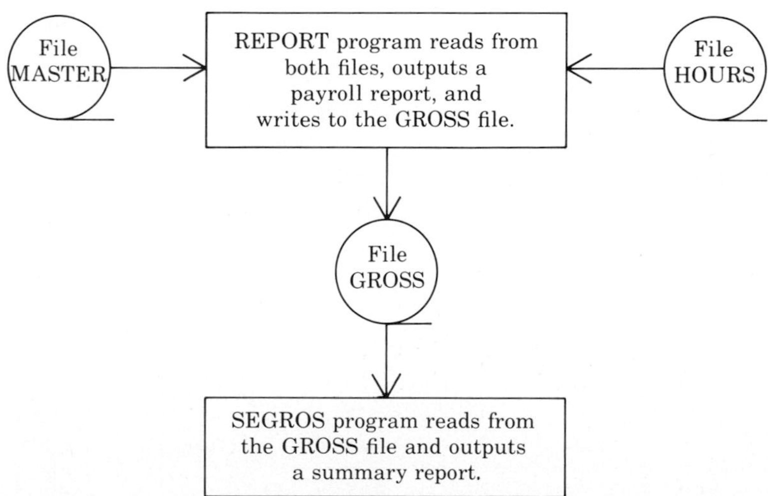

FIGURE 14.6 Case 14.2, Ajax Company, Schematic of Files and Programs

Figure 14.7 shows the two files, MASTER and HOURS, and the empty file GROSS. The contents for this file will be derived from the REPORT program.

The files, MASTER and HOURS, are used by Program 14.5 (REPORT) to generate the weekly payroll report. Line 75 of the REPORT program generates the contents of the GROSS file. This file is then used by Program 14.6 (SEGROS) to provide management with a summary payroll report.

```
NEW:MASTER


10 J. STINE,1234567,2,3.50
20 B. O'HARA,8901234,3,5.25
30 M. BENNETT,5678901,1,4.75
40 J. LAKE,2345678,5,3.75
50 B. FARRONE,9012345,4,4.00
60 C. ERICSON,6789012,3,5.00


SAV

NEW:HOURS


5 1234567,40
10 8901234,35
15 5678901,37
20 2345678,40
25 9012345,30
30 6789012,32


SAV

NEW:GROSS

SAV
```

FIGURE 14.7 Case 14.2, Ajax Company, Data Files MASTER, HOURS, and GROSS

PROGRAM 14.5 Case 14.2, Ajax Company, REPORT Program

```
NEW:REPORT

5 REM PAYROLL REPORT PROGRAM
10 REM READ IN AND STORE TAX RATES
15 FOR I=1 TO 5
20 READ T(I)
25 NEXT I
30 DATA .10,.09,.08,.07,.06
32 REM GENERATE REPORT
35 PRINT TAB(10);"AJAX CO. WEEKLY PAYROLL REPORT"
37 PRINT
40 PRINT "NAME","SOC. SEC. NO.","GROSS WAGE","NET WAGE"
42 PRINT "----------------------------------------------------"
45 FOR A=1 TO 6
50 INPUT:MASTER:N$,S$,D,P
55 INPUT:HOURS:S$,H
60 LET G=P*H
62 IF D>4 THEN 66
64 GO TO 70
66 LET D=5
70 PRINT N$,S$,G,G-G*T(D)
75 PRINT:GROSS:LNM(5);N$;",",H;",",G
```

PROGRAM 14.5 continued

```
80 NEXT A
85 PRINT
90 PRINT TAB(20);"***PAYROLL REPORT COMPLETED***"
99 END

RUN
          AJAX CO. WEEKLY PAYROLL REPORT

NAME           SOC. SEC. NO.  GROSS WAGE      NET WAGE
-----------------------------------------------------
J. STINE       1234567          140             127.4
B. O'HARA      8901234          183.75          169.05
M. BENNETT     5678901          175.75          158.175
J. LAKE        2345678          150             141
B. FARRONE     9012345          120             111.6
C. ERICSON     6789012          160             147.2

                    ***PAYROLL REPORT COMPLETED***
```

PROGRAM 14.6 Case 14.2, Ajax Company, SEGROS Program

```
NEW:SEGROS

5 REM PROGRAM TO GENERATE OUTPUT BASED ON THE GROSS FILE
6 PRINT
7 PRINT "EMPLOYEE,HOURS WORKED THIS WEEK,GROSS PAYROLL"
8 PRINT
10 PRINT "NAME";TAB(12);"HOURS WORKED";TAB(28);"GROSS PAY"
12 PRINT "-----------------------------------------------------"
15 LET W=0
20 LET P=0
25 FOR I=1 TO 6
30 INPUT:GROSS:N$,H,G
35 PRINT N$,H,G
40 LET W=W+H
45 LET P=P+G
50 NEXT I
70 PRINT "------------------------------------------------------"
75 PRINT "AVERAGE HOURS WORKED THIS WEEK";W/6
77 PRINT "TOTAL GROSS PAY THIS WEEK $";P
78 PRINT
80 PRINT TAB(10);"SUMMARY GROSS PAY REPORT COMPLETED"
99 END

RUN

EMPLOYEE,HOURS WORKED THIS WEEK,GROSS PAYROLL

NAME        HOURS WORKED    GROSS PAY
-----------------------------------------------------
J. STINE        40             140
B. O'HARA       35             183.75
M. BENNETT      37             175.75
J. LAKE         40             150
B. FARRONE      30             120
C. ERICSON      32             160
-------------------------------------------------------
AVERAGE HOURS WORKED THIS WEEK 35.6667
TOTAL GROSS PAY THIS WEEK $ 929.5

          SUMMARY GROSS PAY REPORT COMPLETED
```

The following case (14.3) demonstrates the significant advantages of using files.

CASE 14.3 The Atlantic Specialty Company conducts a stock purchase plan for its employees. Each month the employee contributes a part of his or her salary toward the purchase of Atlantic Specialty stock. The company will purchase full (not fractional) shares of the company stock

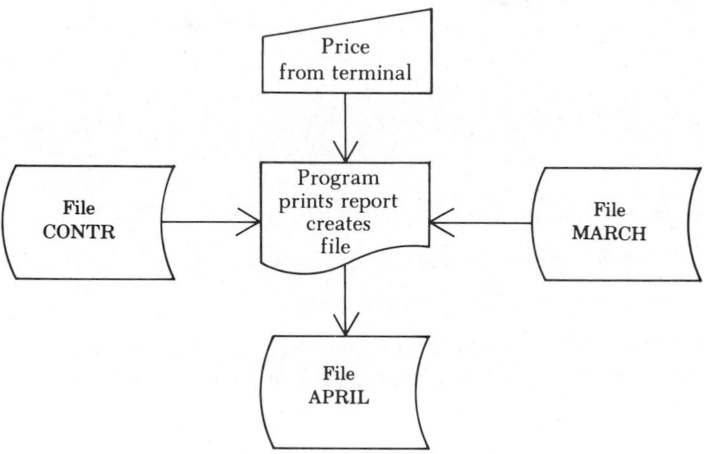

FIGURE 14.8a Case 14.3 Atlantic Specialty Company, Files and Program Run at the End of March

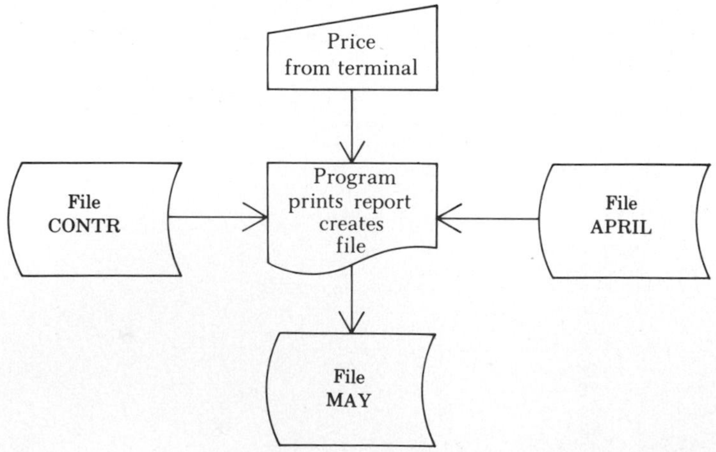

FIGURE 14.8b Case 14.3 Atlantic Specialty Company, Files and Program Run at the End of April

with the employee's contribution, based on the current market value of the shares. The company will also keep a record of the number of shares owned and any dollar balance left. To carry out the stock purchase plan and keep track of all relevant information, a program and several data files are used.

Figure 14.8 shows a diagram of how the program processes the data files.

The data inputs to Program 14.7 consists of two sequential files and one number entered as input from the terminal. The first data file CONTR in Figure 14.9 contains each employee's name, followed by the amount contributed each month. The second data file MARCH in Figure 14.9 contains each employee's name followed by the number of shares owned as of March 1, followed by the amount of money that is left over from the previous stock purchase. The current price per share is input from the terminal when Program 14.7 is run.

The program combines the information from both files and the price of the stock to create a file in Figure 14.10 called APRIL, which is identical in structure to the MARCH file but contains the updated information. Program 14.7 also prints a report that contains the number of shares purchased this month, the number of shares owned by each employee, and the total amount of money in the employee's accounts.

PROGRAM 14.7 Case 14.3, Atlantic Specialty Company, Stock Purchase Plan Program, March

```
10 PRINT"WHAT IS CURRENT PRICE PER SHARE";
20 INPUT P
30 LET S1=0
40 LET B1=0
50 LET N1=0
60 FOR I=1 TO 5
70 INPUT:CONTR:N$,C
80 INPUT:MARCH:M$,S,B
90 LET B=B+C
100 LET N=INT(B/P)
110 LET N1=N1+N
120 LET S=S+N
130 LET S1=S1+S
140 LET B=B-N*P
150 LET B1=B1+B
160 PRINT :APRIL:M$;",";S;",";B
170 NEXT I
180 PRINT "NO. OF SHARES PURCHASED= ";N1
190 PRINT "NO. OF SHARES OWNED= ";S1
200 PRINT "CURRENT TOTAL DOLLAR BALANCE= ";B1
210 END

RUN
WHAT IS CURRENT PRICE PER SHARE ?10
NO. OF SHARES PURCHASED =  4
NO. OF SHARES OWNED =  612
CURRENT TOTAL DOLLAR BALANCE =  22
```

The file MARCH (Figure 14.9) indicates that M. Tendler currently owns 146 shares of stock and has a balance of $7. This month he is contributing $5 (see Figure 14.9 the file CONTR), and the current price per share is $10. Therefore, the company purchases one additional share for M. Tendler for $10, and file APRIL in Figure 14.10 indicates that M. Tendler now owns 147 shares and has a balance of $2; that is, $7 from last month + $5 current contribution − $10 for the one share purchased = $2.

When the month of May arrives, the CONTR file (Figure 14.9) is combined with the APRIL file (Figure 14.10) and then the current price per share ($8) to create a MAY file (Figure 14.11). To carry out this processing, the original program (14.7) is revised by changing lines 80 and 160. This re-

```
CONTR

10 M.TENDLER,5
15 L.ROSS,6
20 G.WIND,4
25 A.RITTER,7
30 M.GOTEL,3

MARCH

10 M.TENDLER,146,7
15 L.ROSS,45,3
20 G.WIND,67,9
25 A.RITTER,250,13
30 M.GOTEL,100,5
```

FIGURE 14.9 Case 14.3, Atlantic Specialty Company, Data Files CONTR and MARCH

```
APRIL

M.TENDLER, 147 , 2
L.ROSS, 45 , 9
G.WIND, 68 , 3
A.RITTER, 252 , 0
M.GOTEL, 100 , 8
```

FIGURE 14.10 Case 14.3, Atlantic Specialty Data File APRIL

```
MAY

M.TENDLER, 147 , 7
L.ROSS, 46 , 7
G.WIND, 68 , 7
A.RITTER, 252 , 7
M.GOTEL, 101 , 3
```

FIGURE 14.11 Case 14.3, Atlantic Specialty Company, Data File MAY

vised program and output are shown as Program 14.8. Each month a similar revision of the program is required to read from the current month file and to write the file for the next month.

PROGRAM 14.8 Case 14.3, Atlantic Specialty Company Stock Purchase Plan Program, April

```
10 PRINT "WHAT IS CURRENT PRICE PER SHARE";
20 INPUT P
30 LET S1=0
40 LET B1=0
50 LET N1=0
60 FOR I=1 TO 5
70 INPUT:CONTR:N$,C
80 INPUT:APRIL:M$,S,B
90 LET B=B+C
100 LET N=INT(B/P)
110 LET N1=N1+N
120 LET S=S+N
130 LET S1=S1+S
140 LET B=B-N*P
150 LET B1=B1+B
160 PRINT:MAY:M$;",";S;",";B
170 NEXT I
180 PRINT"NO. OF SHARES PURCHASED = ";N1
190 PRINT"NO. OF SHARES OWNED = ";S1
200 PRINT"CURRENT TOTAL DOLLAR BALANCE = ";B1
210 END

RUN

WHAT IS CURRENT PRICE PER SHARE ?8
NO. OF SHARES PURCHASED =  2
NO. OF SHARES OWNED =  614
CURRENT TOTAL DOLLAR BALANCE =  31
```

The advantage of using files in this case illustration is evident, since it demonstrates how large amounts of data can be manipulated without using DATA statements. Having the program create a file that can be used as INPUT when the program is run the next time avoids much effort and eliminates the possibilities of errors in repeating the data entry.

DIRECT FILE ACCESS

In order to store data as a file on a disk, the file must first be named and then saved in the way previously described for a sequential access file. We begin by creating an empty file:

NEW:FILEA

SAV

After the file has been named and saved, data can be placed into it. The placement of such data on to the disk and into the file is accomplished through a program—not by line number entry, as was the case with the sequential access file. Within such a program a specification statement that declares a disk is to be used for storage must appear. This statement takes the form:

line # DISK variable name(X,Y):file name:

where *X* represents the number of items or records that may go into the file, and *Y* represents the length of an item or record. For example, the statement

100 DISK A(50,10):FILEA:

indicates that a numeric array A consisting of 50 records each having up to 10 characters will be entering a file named FILEA.

If we want to use an array that will contain string data with disk storage, the statement to use has the form:

line # DISK string variable name(X,Y):file name:

where *X* is the number of records and *Y* is the number of characters in each record. Thus,

10 DISK N$(100,20):FILEA:

indicates that an array with nonnumeric data having up to 100 records, each with a maximum of 20 characters, will be processed through the file named FILEA.

WRITING TO A DISK FILE

Recall that to write to a sequential file we used a statement such as this one:

50 PRINT:XFILE:A,B$

To write to a file on a disk requires a similar statement. It takes the general form of:

line # PUT:string array name(I):variable list

where I is an array subscript. The statement

30 PUT:N$(I):A,B$

placed within an appropriate program will cause data values for variables A and B$ to be written into the Ith record of disk array N$.

Program 14.9 illustrates the writing of five records to a disk file, FILEA, created as described above before this program was processed. Line 30 specifies disk storage is to be used for the data A and B$, to be put into the disk file array N$. The value of I serves as a subscript or address that can be used for data retrieval.

A listing of the contents of FILEA would not produce anything that looks like the data in lines 60 and 70 or the output from Program 14.9. Rather, after the LIST system command we get a message "BINARY FILE",

PROGRAM 14.9 Writing to a Disk File

```
10 DISK N$(100,20):FILEA:
20 FOR I= 1 TO 5
25 READ A,B$
30 PUT:N$(I):A,B$
40 PRINT A,B$
50 NEXT I
60 DATA 25,BLUE,20,RED,30,YELLOW
70 DATA 10,GREEN,16,BROWN
90 END

RUN
 25             BLUE
 20             RED
 30             YELLOW
 10             GREEN
 16             BROWN
```

```
OLD:FILEA

READY
LIST


FILEA

BINARY FILE
```

FIGURE 14.12 Listing of Disk File, FILEA

as shown in Figure 14.12. This message is informing us that the contents of the file we want to list are in machine-language form, that is, in binary shape made up of 0's and 1's, and not in the form of the sequential access files described earlier in the chapter.

READING FROM A DISK FILE

To retrieve a record or line with sequential files, the entire file is read, starting from the first line until the desired record is located. With a disk file we retrieve a record without having to pass through all preceding records in the file. Thus disk storage increases the speed of processing file information and provides us with *direct access* to a specific record when needed.

In order to access data from a disk file, we use a GET statement that has the general form:

line # GET:string array name(I):variable list

where I is an array subscript. Or, as an example,

50 GET:N$(4):A,B$

will retrieve the values of A and B$ from the 4th record of the disk array file N$.

This process of direct (or random) access is shown in Program 14.10. The program does not search the entire disk for the desired array contents of FILEA. Instead the computer is directed to access through the GET statement in line 50 the Ith record as instructed by line 20 READ I. Thus when I = 3, the third record of N$(I) is retrieved without a complete search through the file, FILEA.

Because it provides data retrieval faster than sequential access, direct/random access has found wide application in business systems dealing with customer inqueries. This type of system is used by organizations that typically receive requests for information over the phone. Examples include people requesting information from:

1. Public utility companies, about their bills–gas, electric, or telephone
2. Insurance companies, about policies
3. Airlines, about reservations and flight information
4. Banks, about their checking or saving accounts

Fast retrieval and access to stored information is also a characteristic of many management information systems (MIS). Many inventory systems are predicated on locating items in a hurry or checking to see if an item is in stock. Random access makes such systems a reality.

PROGRAM 14.10 Reading from a Disk File by Direct Access

```
10 DISK N$(100,20):FILEA:
20 READ I
30 DATA 3,2,5,4,1
50 GET:N$(I):A,B$
60 PRINT I;A;B$
70 GO TO 20
90 END

RUN
 3  30 YELLOW
 2  20 RED
 5  16 BROWN
 4  10 GREEN
 1  25 BLUE

OUT OF DATA- LN #  20
```

The case that follows is a rather simple illustration of the disk file concepts described so far.

CASE 14.4 Many banks provide their checking-account customers with overdraft privileges of different amounts. The range of "checking plus" may be from $500 to $2000, depending on the individual. Since a bank may have thousands of accounts, a random access system for credit inquiries is desired because of the minimum delay needed when a transaction takes place. For such a system, two programs will be needed. The first program will be a "Disk File Record Entry Program" that will enter to a disk file such items as the customer account number, name, and credit limit. The second program will be a conversational one that upon entry of the customer's account number will directly access the appropriate disk file and output the desired record. We can call this second program a "Random Access Credit Check Program."

Programs 14.11 and 14.12 illustrate what is needed for Case 14.4. The "Disk File Record Entry Program" (14.11) will be writing to the file named "Credit" into the string A$ (line 20) data first read into the program by line 40 READ C,N$L. Note that the PUT statement,

60 PUT:A$(C):C,N$,L

uses the subscript *C,* which is the checking account number. This is important, because we wish to access from the disk by this number. Therefore, we have to write the initial data to the disk using the same number as a subscript.

PROGRAM 14.11 Case 14.4, Bank Credit Checking, Disk File Record Entry Program

```
10 REM DISK FILE RECORD ENTRY PROGRAM
20 DISK A$(1000,35):CREDIT:
30 FOR R=1 TO 4
40 READ C,N$,L
50 PRINT C;N$,L
60 PUT:A$(C):C,N$,L
70 NEXT R
80 DATA 691, ELAINE ROBBINS, 1500
90 DATA 538, FRED KEENNAN, 2000
100 DATA 134, IRA MORGAN, 500
110 DATA 369, LINDA COHEN, 1000
120 REM TEST ON ACCESS
130 PRINT
140 GET:A$(134):C,N$,L
150 PRINT C;N$;L
160 END

RUN
 691 ELAINE ROBBINS              1500
 538 FRED KEENNAN                2000
 134 IRA MORGAN                  500
 369 LINDA COHEN                 1000

 134 IRA MORGAN 500
```

Also notice that the output of the program consists of the data assigned to the disk and an additional line "134 IRA MORGAN 500." This last line of output results from a "TEST ON ACCESS" included in the program to see if the data has got to the disk and is retrievable. The "TEST" is found in line 140 GET:A$(134):C,N$,L, which requests that the record with account number 134 be directly accessed. It is then printed out by line 150.

PROGRAM 14.12 Case 14.4, Bank Credit Checking, Random Access Credit Check Program

```
10 REM RANDOM ACCESS CREDIT CHECK PROGRAM
20 DISK A$(1000,35):CREDIT:
30 PRINT "TO ACCESS AN ACCOUNT FOR CREDIT CHECKING"
40 PRINT "ENTER THE ACCOUNT NUMBER."
50 PRINT "WHAT IS THE ACCOUNT NUMBER";
60 INPUT C
70 GET:A$(C):C,N$,L
80 PRINT
90 PRINT "ACCOUNT NUMBER:";C
100 PRINT "NAME           :";N$
110 PRINT "CREDIT LIMIT $";L
120 PRINT
130 PRINT "DO YOU WISH ANOTHER CREDIT CHECK?"
140 PRINT "  YES OR NO";
150 INPUT Y$
160 IF Y$ = "YES" THEN 50
170 PRINT
180 PRINT"******* CREDIT CHECK COMPLETED *******"
190 END

RUN
TO ACCESS AN ACCOUNT FOR CREDIT CHECKING
ENTER THE ACCOUNT NUMBER.
WHAT IS THE ACCOUNT NUMBER ?533

ACCOUNT NUMBER: 533
NAME           :FRED KEENNAN
CREDIT LIMIT $ 2000

DO YOU WISH ANOTHER CREDIT CHECK?
  YES OR NO ?YES
WHAT IS THE ACCOUNT NUMBER ?369

ACCOUNT NUMBER: 369
NAME           :LINDA COHEN
CREDIT LIMIT $ 1000

DO YOU WISH ANOTHER CREDIT CHECK?
  YES OR NO ?YES
WHAT IS THE ACCOUNT NUMBER ?134

ACCOUNT NUMBER: 134
NAME           :IRA MORGAN
CREDIT LIMIT $ 500

DO YOU WISH ANOTHER CREDIT CHECK?
  YES OR NO ?NO

******* CREDIT CHECK COMPLETED *******
```

In order to retrieve data from the file "Credit", we can use a direct "Ransom Access Credit Check Program" as shown in Program 14.12. This is a conversational program with the user entering only the account through line 60 INPUT C. The GET statement in line 70:

```
70 GET:A$(C):C,N$,L
```

uses the account number *C*, to locate the desired record and bring it into the program so that it can be outputted by the PRINT statements in lines 90–110. If an account number not in the file is entered, say 678, the output for that number will be nonsense values. This is a case of GIGO: garbage in-garbage out.

SUMMARY

This chapter introduced the concepts of sequential access files and direct access files. For efficiency, such files are usually placed in auxiliary storage so that they can be used by many programs. Before a program can use data in a file, the file must be created and saved as a separate entity. To obtain data from a sequential file, an INPUT file statement is used. To write data to a sequential file, a PRINT file statement is used. Direct, or random, access files make use of magnetic disks. To access data in a disk file, we use a GET statement. To write data onto the disk and into a file, we use a PUT statement.

It is important to study the appropriate system manual when working with files since the statements involved differ from system to system.

EXERCISES

* 14.1 For the following data create a sequential data file. After it has been entered, list it out.

Plant	Units Produced
1	2400
2	3200
3	1800
4	2100
5	3000
6	4500

14.2 For the following data create a sequential data file. After it has been entered, list it out.

Stock	Price
ATT	50¾
CBS	53¾
GNMOT	48½
GTELEL	25⅜
IBM	204
PLAYBOY	5
XEROX	67¼

14.3 For the following data create a sequential data file. After it has been entered, list it out.

City	High Temperature (°F) Yesterday	A Year Ago
Boston	65	61
New York	72	69
Washington, D.C.	71	68
Denver	49	55
Los Angeles	83	88
Honolulu	79	79
Phoenix	101	100

* 14.4 Write a program that reads the data file for *exercise 14.1,* outputs the data with headings, and computes the total units produced for all six plants.

14.5 Do *exercise 14.4* but obtain the average production for the six plants.

14.6 For the data in *exercise 14.1,* assume that each unit produced costs \$3.00, and that revenue per unit assuming all units are sold is \$5.50. Write a program that reads the data in *14.1* from a file and outputs the total cost, total revenue, and net revenue obtained from the output of each plant.

14.7 Modify the **Program** in *exercise 14.6* to transfer all the results to a new file. List out this file to check its contents.

14.8 Write a **Program** that can generate as output the contents of the file created in *exercise 14.7.*

14.9 a. For the data in *exercise 14.2* create a file.
b. Create another file for the number of shares held by the "National Bank."

Stock	No. of Shares
ATT	5000
CBS	4500
GNMOT	6000
GTELEL	2000
IBM	1200
PLAYBOY	2500
XEROX	1500

c. Write a program that reads the files of (a) and (b) and outputs for each stock the market value (price times number of shares).

d. Revise the program in (c) to write the results of the program to a new file.

e. Write a program that reads the file created in (d) and outputs its contents.

*14.10 Suppose there already exist the following two separate data files:

```
10 DIV A, 400, 15        10 DIV E, 380, 13
20 DIV B, 500, 23        15 DIV F, 450, 25
30 DIV C, 430, 20        20 DIV G, 300, 21
40 DIV D, 330, 30
```

Write a program that will read and merge these separate files into a single file with appropriate line numbers. List out the file to check the line numbers. It is suggested that each file be read using subscripted variables to facilitate the merging.

*14.11 Treat the following airline flight schedule as a data file:

747'S FROM NEW YORK TO GENEVA AND ZURICH			
Day of Week	Leaves New York	Arrives Geneva (Nonstop)	Arrives Zurich
Mo/Th/Sa/Su	7:10 P.M. 10:05 P.M.	7:30 A.M.	9:00 A.M. 10:40 A.M. (nonstop)
Tu/We/Fr	8:50 P.M.	9:10 A.M.	10:40 A.M.

Write a program that is conversational in nature, such that for any given day desired, Monday to Sunday, the flight schedule is printed out. Test your program by inputting these days: Wednesday, Monday, Friday, Tuesday, Thursday, Sunday, Saturday, Tuesday, Tuesday, Monday, Sunday. It is suggested that the file be read using subscripted variables. The subscript index can be used as a key to help generate the desired results.

14.12 The following airline schedule shows flight information from Seattle and Portland to various destinations. Treat the schedule as two separate files, one for Seattle and one for Portland.

To	Flt #	Leaves	Remarks
		From Seattle	
Auckland	815	11:45 P.M.	707 Tu/Su
Tokyo	891/831	8:00 A.M.	707/747 Daily
Singapore	893/841	7:35 P.M.	747/707 Mo/We/Fr
Manila	893/841	7:35 P.M.	707/747 Tu/Th/Sa/Su
Sydney	893/811	7:35 P.M.	707 Mo
Melbourne	895	8:00 P.M.	707/747 We/Sa
		From Portland	
Sydney	893/811	6:10 P.M.	707/Su/Mo/Tu
			707/747/We/Th/Fr/Sa
Tokyo	891/831	9:15 A.M.	707/747 Daily
Singapore	893/841	6:10 P.M.	707/747 Mo/We/Fr
Manila	893/841	6:10 P.M.	707/747 Tu/Th/Sa/Su

Write a program that is conversational in nature and that, when given the city of departure (Seattle or Portland) and destination, will print out the other flight information, that is, flight number, leaves, and remarks. (See the suggestion in *exercise 14.11*) Test your program with the following input:

Seattle, Tokyo
" , Auckland
Portland, Manila
" , Tokyo
" , Manila
Seattle, Auckland
" , Melbourne
" , Manila
Seattle, Sydney
" , "
Portland, Sydney
Seattle, Manila

See what happens if you enter Portland, Auckland.

14.13 Below are amounts, due dates, rates, and yields for a new bond issue. Treat this information as a data file. Write a conversational program that, when the due date is inputted, will print out the amount, rate, and yield for that date. (See the suggestion in *exercise 14.11.*) To test your program, input these dates: 1976, 1979, 1979, 1980, 1984, 1977, 1992, 1982, 1989, 1978, 1988. See what happens if you input 1969 or 1955.

Amount	Due	Rate	Yield
$290,000	1976	7.25%	4.25%
315,000	1977	7.25	4.50
335,000	1978	7.25	4.75
355,000	1979	7.25	5.00
385,000	1980	7.25	5.20
410,000	1981	7.25	5.35
440,000	1982	7.25	5.45
470,000	1983	7.25	5.60
505,000	1984	7.25	5.70
540,000	1985	7.25	8.85
580,000	1986	7.00	6.00
620,000	1987	7.00	6.10
665,000	1988	7.00	6.25
710,000	1989	7.00	6.40
755,000	1990	7.00	6.60
810,000	1991	7.00	6.75
1,005,000	1992	7.00	6.90

14.14 For the data in *exercise 14.1,* create a direct access data file. After it has been entered, list it out.

14.15 For the following data, create a direct access file. As part of your file entry program have a test segment to check if the data has been successfully written to the disk file. Use the division number as the file subscript.

Division	Manager's Name	Telephone Number
1	Stan Stern	633-5550
2	Allan Price	711-2345
3	Liz Kent	355-9876
4	Jack Baker	632-6110

14.16 Below is a list of part numbers and the current inventory for each.

a. For the data given, create a direct access numeric file.

b. Develop an interactive program that will output the current inventory for a part after the part number has been entered.

Part Number	Current Inventory
3241	250
1345	75
1432	125
4321	75
3311	80

14.17 Redo *exercise 14.16.* Have the program subtract from inventory the amounts ordered as shown below. The part number and amount ordered are to be entered from the terminal. If there is insufficient inventory, that condition should be printed out.

Part Number:	3241	1345	1432	4321	3311
Order Size:	175	80	100	50	100

14.18 Below is the airline flight schedule from one location to another.
a. For the data given, create a direct access file.
b. Develop a conversational program that, given a flight number, will output the remaining information.

Flight Number	Leave	Arrive	Meals
985	7:10 A.M.	9:13 A.M.	Breakfast
201	9:10 A.M.	11:17 A.M.	Snack
327	12:10 P.M.	2:11 P.M.	Lunch
817	3:00 P.M.	5:17 P.M.	Snack
123	5:00 P.M.	7:03 P.M.	Dinner

chapter 15

Case Application Problems and Programming Projects

In this chapter we will illustrate programs for several longer and more involved case applications than we have so far seen. In addition, the chapter contains programming projects that will give students further opportunities to put their knowledge of BASIC to use.

CASE PROBLEM I PRODUCTION DECISION MAKING

To determine how much of an item should be produced when production of the item is not continuous but in batches, a computer can be used to find which batch size is the most profitable to produce. In this case problem the number of batches to produce is based on total expected profit, which is the average profit that can be obtained given the probability of a demand and multiplying it by the profit for that demand. The total is obtained by summing up each expected profit for each demand. Symbolically, this can be written as

$$EP = \Sigma(P(D) \times \text{profit of } D)$$

where Σ is sum of, EP is expected profit, and $P(D)$ is probability of demand (D).

Program 15.1 is based on the following relevant facts:

1. A company can make 1, 2, 3, 4, or 5 batches of a chemical a day.
2. The daily demand varies from 0 to 5 or more batches.
3. The company gains $3000 for each batch sold and loses $3500 for each batch made but not sold.
4. Actual sales for the last 10 days were 5, 7, 1, 0, 2, 3, 3, 1, 1, and 4 batches.

The program using the above information does the following:

1. Calculates the probability of demand based on the 10 days sales data.
2. Calculates and prints out the profits and expected profits for each day for each production level (that is, 1, 2, 3, 4, and 5 batches).
3. Determines the most profitable number of batches to be produced based on the total expected profit found for each batch size.

PROGRAM 15.1 Case Problem I, Production Decision Making

```
60 REM INITIALIZE PROBABILITIES TO ZERO
70 FOR A=0 TO 5
72 LET X(A)=0
74 NEXT A
75 REM READ PAST DEMAND AND CALCULATE PROBABILITY
100 FOR I=1 TO 10
400 READ A
402 DATA 5,7,1,0,2,3,3,1,1,4
405 REM IF DEMAND IS MORE THAN 5, SET DEMAND = 5
500 IF A<=5 THEN 750
700 LET A=5
750 LET X(A)=X(A)+1
800 NEXT I
801 REM Q STANDS FOR THE BEST PROFIT SO FAR. INITIALIZED TO ZERO
805 LET Q=0
806 REM OUTER LOOP ON NUMBER OF BATCHES PRODUCED
810 FOR B=1 TO 5
820 PRINT "NO. OF BATCHES TO BE MADE";B
830 GO SUB 2000
835 PRINT
836 REM INITIALIZE TOTAL EXPECTED PROFIT TO ZERO
840 LET T=0
850 PRINT "DEMAND","PROB.","PROFIT","EXPECTED PROFIT"
851 REM INNER LOOP ON NUMBER OF BATCHES DEMANDED
900      FOR J = 0 TO 5
910      LET P=3000*B
920      IF J<B THEN 942
940      GO TO 960
942      LET P = 3000*J-3500*(B-J)
960      PRINT J,X(J)/10,P,P*(X(J)/10)
970      LET T = T + P*(X(J)/10)
980      NEXT J
990 GO SUB 2000
993 PRINT
995 PRINT TAB(23);"TOTAL EXPECTED PROFIT";T
996 REM COMPARE TOTAL EXPECTED PROFIT WITH BEST PROFIT SO FAR
997 REM SAVE IN VARIABLE K THE BEST NO. OF BATCHES TO BE MADE
999 IF Q>T THEN 1030
1000 LET Q=T
1010 LET K=B
```

PROGRAM 15.1 continued

```
1030 NEXT B
1040 PRINT "THE MOST PROFITABLE NO. OF BATCHES TO BE MADE IS";K
1050 STOP
2000 FOR I=1 TO 70
2010 PRINT "-";
2020 NEXT I
2030 RETURN
2040 END
```

```
RUN
NO. OF BATCHES TO BE MADE 1
----------------------------------------------------------------------
DEMAND          PROB.           PROFIT          EXPECTED PROFIT
 0               .1             -3500           -350
 1               .3              3000            900
 2               .1              3000            300
 3               .2              3000            600
 4               .1              3000            300
 5               .2              3000            600
----------------------------------------------------------------------
                          TOTAL EXPECTED PROFIT 2350.
NO. OF BATCHES TO BE MADE 2
----------------------------------------------------------------------
DEMAND          PROB.           PROFIT          EXPECTED PROFIT
 0               .1             -7000           -700
 1               .3             -500            -150
 2               .1              6000            600
 3               .2              6000            1200
 4               .1              6000            600
 5               .2              6000            1200
----------------------------------------------------------------------
                          TOTAL EXPECTED PROFIT 2750
NO. OF BATCHES TO BE MADE 3
----------------------------------------------------------------------
DEMAND          PROB.           PROFIT          EXPECTED PROFIT
 0               .1             -10500          -1050
 1               .3             -4000           -1200
 2               .1              2500            250
 3               .2              9000            1800
 4               .1              9000            900
 5               .2              9000            1800
----------------------------------------------------------------------
                          TOTAL EXPECTED PROFIT 2500
NO. OF BATCHES TO BE MADE 4
----------------------------------------------------------------------
DEMAND          PROB.           PROFIT          EXPECTED PROFIT
 0               .1             -14000          -1400
 1               .3             -7500           -2250
 2               .1             -1000           -100
 3               .2              5500            1100
 4               .1              12000           1200
 5               .2              12000           2400
----------------------------------------------------------------------
                          TOTAL EXPECTED PROFIT 950.
NO. OF BATCHES TO BE MADE 5
----------------------------------------------------------------------
DEMAND          PROB.           PROFIT          EXPECTED PROFIT
 0               .1             -17500          -1750
 1               .3             -11000          -3300
 2               .1             -4500           -450
 3               .2              2000            400
 4               .1              8500            850
 5               .2              15000           3000
----------------------------------------------------------------------
                          TOTAL EXPECTED PROFIT-1250.
THE MOST PROFITABLE NO. OF BATCHES TO BE MADE IS 2
```

CASE PROBLEM II PROCESS SIMULATION

Computer simulation is useful for management planning and analysis of certain kinds of operations. This case problem uses Monte Carlo simulation to examine the processing of mail bags in a mail order department.*

Monte Carlo simulation is a technique that generates artificial outcomes that represent the process being examined. The technique requires that the process being studied have probabilistic outcomes. From such information, outcomes can be predicted by random sampling instructions included in the computer program. The results obtained can then be analyzed in terms of the management decisions that must be made.

Program 15.2 is designed to carry out a Monte Carlo simulation. The program is based on these relevant facts:

1. A mail order department has two employees who process bags of mail. The bags are delivered during the night for processing that begins at 9 A.M. the next morning.
2. It takes an employee 1 hour to process the contents of one mail bag.
3. At the end of the day, any unprocessed mail bags are left for processing on the next day.
4. Each employee works 7 hours a day, 5 days a week.
5. Over the last 50 days the distribution of the number of bags arriving has been:

Number of Bags Arriving	Relative Frequency	Cumulative Frequency
12	.13	.13
13	.22	.35
14	.26	.61
15	.30	.91
16	.06	.97
17	.03	1.00
	1.00	

Note: The relative frequency represents the probability distribution. The cumulative frequency was obtained by adding each successive relative frequency value. These values are used in Program 15.2 to do the random sampling of outcomes (numbers of bags arriving).

The purpose of the simulation is to help answer these questions:

1. How many mail bags can arrive each day over a 50-day period?

*A reference for the Monte Carlo simulation technique is given in the opening REM statements of **Program 15.2.**

2. How many mail bags remain unprocessed each day over a 50-day period?
3. On the average, how many bags arrive each day?
4. On the average, how many bags are unprocessed each day?
5. Out of 50 days, on how many days were mail bags unprocessed?

The output of the computer simulation generates answers to these questions. Management can then decide whether to (a) hire additional employees; or (b) put the present employees on overtime; or (c) maintain the present operation.

PROGRAM 15.2 Case Problem II, Process Simulation

```
1 REM MONTE CARLO SIMULATION OF A MAIL ORDER
2 REM DEPARTMENT PROCESSING OPERATION
3 REM REFERENCE FOR TECHNIQUE: DECISION MAKING
4 REM THROUGH OPERATIONS RESEARCH, R.J.THIERAUF
5 REM & R.C.KLEKAMP, 2ND. ED., WILEY, 1975  CHAP. 14
6 PRINT "SIMULATION OF MAIL ORDER DEPARTMENT PROCESSING"
7 PRINT "OPERATION FOR FIFTY DAYS WITH TWO EMPLOYEES"
8 PRINT "EACH WORKING SEVEN HOURS A DAY, PROCESSING ONE"
9 PRINT "MAIL BAG PER HOUR EACH"
10 PRINT
12 PRINT "DAY","# MAIL BAGS","TOT # BAGS TO","NUMBER","MAIL BAGS"
14 PRINT "NUMBER","DELIVERED","BE PROCESSED","PROCESSED","UNPROCESSED"
16 GO SUB 275
20 READ E
22 DATA 2
25 LET C=E*7
30 REM INITIALIZE VARIABLES
35 LET A=0
40 LET U=0
45 LET L=0
48 LET Y=0
50 FOR D=1 TO 50
52 REM PICK A RANDOM NUMBER
54 RANDOMIZE
55 LET N=RND
60 REM TEST OF THE RANDOM NUMBER
65 IF N<=.13 THEN 145
70 IF N<=.35 THEN 135
75 IF N<=.61 THEN 125
80 IF N<=.91 THEN 115
85 IF N<=.97 THEN 105
90 REM MATCH RANDOM # WITH # OF BAGS DELIVERED
95 LET B=17
100 GO TO 160
105 LET B=16
110 GO TO 160
115 LET B=15
120 GO TO 160
125 LET B=14
130 GO TO 160
135 LET B=13
140 GO TO 160
145 LET B=12
150 REM COMPUTATIONS FOLLOW
155 REM ACCUMULATE # BAGS DELIVERED
160 LET A=A+B
165 REM TOTAL TO BE PROCESSED=DELIVERED+UNPROCESSED
170 LET P=B+U
175 REM NUMBER PROCESSED CANNOT EXCEED CAPACITY,C.
180 IF P>C THEN 210
```

PROGRAM 15.2 continued

```
185 LET U=0
190 PRINT D,B,P,P,U
200 GO TO 230
205 REM WHEN CAPACITY,C, IS EXCEEDED
210 LET U=P-C
215 PRINT D,B,P,C,U
218 REM L= TOTAL NUMBER OF BAGS UNPROCESSED
220 LET L=L+U
222 REM COUNT NUMBER OF DAYS THERE ARE UNPROCESSED BAGS
225 LET Y=Y+1
230 NEXT D
255 REM COMPUTE AVERAGES, PRINT TOTALS
260 GO SUB 275
265 PRINT "TOTALS",A,TAB(60);L
270 PRINT "  AVERAGES",A/D,TAB(60);L/D
271 PRINT
272 PRINT "OUT OF";D;"DAYS,";Y;"DAYS HAD MAIL BAGS UNPROCESSED"
273 STOP
275 FOR I=1 TO 71
280 PRINT "-";
285 NEXT I
286 PRINT
287 RETURN
290 END
```

```
RUN
SIMULATION OF MAIL ORDER DEPARTMENT PROCESSING
OPERATION FOR FIFTY DAYS WITH TWO EMPLOYEES
EACH WORKING SEVEN HOURS A DAY, PROCESSING ONE
MAIL BAG PER HOUR EACH
```

DAY NUMBER	# MAIL BAGS DELIVERED	TOT # BAGS TO BE PROCESSED	NUMBER PROCESSED	MAIL BAGS UNPROCESSED
1	15	15	14	1
2	12	13	13	0
3	13	13	13	0
4	14	14	14	0
5	12	12	12	0
6	13	13	13	0
7	13	13	13	0
8	15	15	14	1
9	14	15	14	1
10	14	15	14	1
11	15	16	14	2
12	12	14	14	0
13	15	15	14	1
14	13	14	14	0
15	12	12	12	0
16	13	13	13	0
17	14	14	14	0
18	13	13	13	0
19	13	13	13	0
20	16	16	14	2
21	15	17	14	3
22	14	17	14	3
23	15	18	14	4
24	14	18	14	4
25	14	18	14	4
26	13	17	14	3
27	15	18	14	4
28	16	20	14	6
29	15	21	14	7
30	13	20	14	6
31	15	21	14	7
32	15	22	14	8
33	12	20	14	6

PROGRAM 15.2 continued

```
34           15           21           14           7
35           14           21           14           7
36           13           20           14           6
37           16           22           14           8
38           14           22           14           8
39           15           23           14           9
40           14           23           14           9
41           13           22           14           8
42           15           23           14           9
43           17           26           14           12
44           14           26           14           12
45           15           27           14           13
46           12           25           14           11
47           12           23           14           9
48           13           22           14           8
49           15           23           14           9
50           15           24           14           10
--------------------------------------------------------------------
TOTALS       699                                    229
  AVERAGES   13.98                                  4.58

OUT OF 50 DAYS, 37 DAYS HAD MAIL BAGS UNPROCESSED
```

PROGRAMMING PROJECTS

* Project I Design of a Computerized Billing System

Background The G&E Power Co., Inc. is a public utility that wants to set up a computerized billing system. You have been asked to design a program to meet their needs. Your program will be a prototype to handle two customers. Customer 1 pays all bills on time. Customer 2 fails to pay bills on time. Even though only two customers are being billed here, the program must ultimately be able to handle several thousand customers.

Program Test Data The following information is to be used to test the program:

		Meter Readings				
Customer		Gas (cu. ft.)		Elec. (KWH)		
Name/Address	ID No.	Begin	End	Begin	End	Mo.
Your Name	S. S.	1000	1500	300	400	Jan.
Your Address	No.	1500	2000	400	500	Feb.
		2000	2400	500	625	Mar.
		2400	2800	625	700	Apr.
Mr. Bill Due	999-00-6666	1200	1400	180	210	Jan.
Smogville,		1400	1650	210	290	Feb.
USA		1650	2000	290	350	Mar.
		2000	2400	350	400	Apr.

Four months of test data are to be used so that the logic of the program can be checked. This is necessary because of the "warning" notices that are printed out when bills are not paid (see below).

Computational Information Rates and taxes are as follows:

Gas	\$.10 (10¢) per cu. ft.
Electricity	\$.03 (3¢) per KWH (kilowatt hour)
Taxes	6% of total bill each month

Each month a bill is sent to each customer, based on the following simple computation:

Total without taxes = gas total + electric total
= no. of cu. ft. × gas rate + no. of KWH × electric rate
Amount due = (total without taxes) + (total × tax rate)

Program Operation Each month the meter readings for each customer are fed as data to the computer. The name, address, identification (ID) number, and rates are already available as part of the program.

Output Requirements The following printed output is desired: the present balance due, showing the month and dollar amount for gas and electricity; the meter readings and usage for each item; the customer's name, address, and ID number; any previous balance due; the taxes; and the total amount due. All of this output should appear as a billing statement. The form of it is up to you.

If the customer is in arrears, the following notices must be printed on the statement as appropriate:

1. First Notice (no payment received after two months of service)

   "Warning–No payment after 2 months.
   Your next notice will be for a cutoff of
   gas and electricity. Pay up now"

2. Second Notice (no payment received after three months of service)

   "Your gas and electricity have been cut off.
   Service will be restored when full payment
   is made of the amount due."

(Optional) A company record must also be printed for each customer. This record shows name, address, ID number, all meter readings, and usage for each month; all billing for each month by gas, electricity, and totals; and any warnings or cutoff notices. The company record design is up to you.

Summary Your billing system should consist of the following for four months:

1. A billing statement for each (two) customer for each month; with or without warnings or cutoff notices depending upon the circumstances. *Note:* Customer 1 pays all bills on time; customer 2 does not pay any bills. These facts should be built into your program so that the warning notices can be tested.
2. (Optional) A company record showing all of the above information for each month for each customer. You should have four company files for each customer as your output—one file for each month showing the previous months and then the present update.

Documentation A complete flowchart shold be prepared for the program. Include REM statements where appropriate in your program.

Project II Inventory Control System

Background Your firm, Top Knotch Management Consultants Inc., Jamaica, New York 11439, has been hired by the

Good Toy Co., Inc.
Fun And Games Street
Any City, USA, 10000

to write an inventory system program for their 1000 different products. The final program is one that will allow an inventory clerk at the end of each day to merely inform the computer via a terminal of the number of units of each product sold during the day. Such reporting of daily sales by product will provide a constant inventory updating for each product. When the inventory of any particular item reaches a specified low point, new goods will be ordered to replenish the stock. All new orders will arrive before the inventory level of the products reaches zero. Figure 15.1 shows how a typical system works for *each* product.

Programming Assignment You have been asked to write the prototype program for one of the products kept in the inventory. This program is to be conversational in design. Data is entered by means of INPUT statements.

The product is a small aboveground swimming pool 12 feet in diameter that has an item no. 738. It sells for $198 and has a purchase price of $100 from the wholesaler (Wet Pool Co., Inc., Lakeville, USA 20000). The pool can be ordered only in 50 unit lots. Reordering is required when inventory reaches 20 percent of the order size. There are 25 units now in stock.

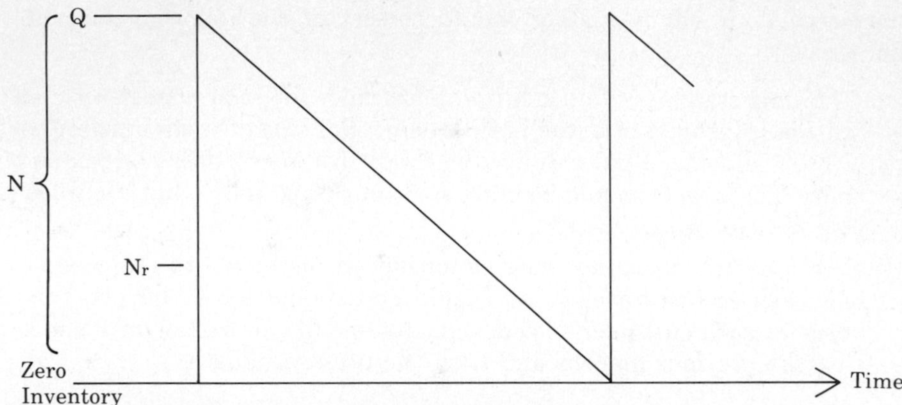

Q = order quantity of some product. New inventory.
N_r = reorder point. Inventory is ordered when the stock level reaches this point. (Q arrives when stock level reaches zero.)
N = inventory stock level as units are sold.

FIGURE 15.1 Inventory System

Generating Sales Data To test the program, data for daily sales for the product are obtained by using two predefined BASIC functions, RND and INT. These functions together will generate random numbers from 0 to 10. For example:

```
10 FOR I = 1 TO 10
20 PRINT INT(11*RND),
30 NEXT I
99 END
```

The 10 numbers generated will represent sales data for each of the 10 days.

Program Requirements The Good Toy Co. would like this program to accomplish the following:

1. The program should "ask" the clerk the item number, description of the item sold from inventory, and the number of units sold during the day.
2. The program should result in the following printouts:
   a. Current inventory *after* the clerk inputs the desired information.
   b. A summary table of the day-by-day inventory for the product at the end of each 5-day week. This table should show the total number of units sold and the dollar value of these sales both day by day and for the whole week.

c. When the reorder point, N_r, is reached, a warning that informs the clerk of this situation.
d. An order form (when the reorder point is reached) that contains the supplier's address, the purchaser's address, the data of the order, the number of units being ordered, the item number, the item description, the retail unit cost, and the total retail cost of the order.

Documentation Throughout your program, use should be made of REM statements so that another programmer can easily follow what you have done. A final flowchart is also desired.

* Project III Design of a Computerized Payroll System

Background The Alpha Co., Inc., wants to set up a computerized payroll accounting system that will be able to handle up to 30 employees. You have been hired to write a computer program to do the weekly payroll. Initially, you will write a test program for only two employees (see below).

Pertinent Information Each employee will have a record containing the following items of information:

1. Employee identification number (social security number)
2. Employee name
3. Number of dependents
4. Hourly pay rate
5. Pay period:
   a. Gross earnings
   b. Federal income tax; state income tax
   c. Social security tax
   d. Net earnings
6. Year-to-date: all items in 5 above

Each weekly pay period, a paycheck is printed out for each employee. Along with the paycheck, the employee gets a stub showing the items in 5 and 6 above.

Weekly time cards are processed for each employee to obtain his or her gross wage (hours worked times hourly wage).

Computational Requirements

1. To compute the paychecks the federal income tax to be withheld is computed as follows:
   a. The tax base is determined by subtracting from gross earnings $30 times the number of dependents.
   b. The amount to be withheld is computed from the following table:

If the amount of the tax base is: Over	But not over	The federal income tax to be withheld is:		
$ 0	$100	14%	of excess over	$ 0
100	200	$ 14 + 15%		100
200	300	29 + 16%		200
300	400	45 + 17%		300
400	800	62 + 19%		400
800		138 + 22%		800

2. To write the paychecks, the state income tax to be withheld is computed based on the following table:
   If the gross wage is:

Over	But not over	The state tax to be withheld is:		
$ 0	$100	2%	of excess over	$ 0
100	300	$2 plus 3%		100
300	500	8 plus 4%		300
500		16 plus 5%		500

3. Social security tax is 10.8 percent of gross earnings, not to exceed $1080 in any one year.
4. Overtime wages are at 1½ times the hourly wage for more than 35 hours worked in one week.
5. Net earnings (the amount of the check) equals gross earnings less federal, state, and social security taxes.
6. Before writing the checks, pay-period figures should be added to year-to-date figures.

Computer Output For each employee, for *each* week the program should generate printouts of the following:

1. A company record for each employee having all of the six items listed under "Pertinent Information."
2. A paycheck for each employee showing name, ID number, company name, week 1 or 2, and the net wage.
3. A check stub having all of the items 5 and 6 listed under "Pertinent Information."

The design of the company record, pay check, and stub is up to you.

Program Test Data The following information for two employees is to be used to test the program:

Name	ID No. (Soc. Sec. No.)	Number of Dependents	Wage/ Hour	Hours Worked Week 1	Week 2
Your name	Your number	1	$14	42	35
Any worker	111-88-9669	4	7	35	32

Documentation A flowchart must be included with the final program, as well as a liberal number of REM statements describing the various parts of it.

Project IV Hotel-Reservation System Simulation

Background The Always Have A Room Motel Co., Inc., has motels in nine locations:

Atlanta, Ga.
Baltimore, Md.
Boston, Mass.
Jacksonville, Fla.
Miami, Fla.
New York, N.Y.
Raleigh, N.C.
Richmond, Va.
Washington, D.C.

A person phones for a reservation in a certain city. Depending on the number of persons in the party, there may or may not be a vacancy. If there is no vacancy, he is told the two closest cities to the desired location—one north of it and the other south of it.

Programming Assignment Using the Monte Carlo technique, write a program that will simulate the system. The program should simulate 20 telephone calls. Assume that a call for each of the nine cities is equally likely (a one-ninth probability for each).

Data for the Program All data for the program is generated internally, using a random number function. This function is used to simulate the city desired by the caller, the number of people in the party (1 to 6), and whether or not there is a vacancy.

Use the following information (based on historical data) to simulate the number of persons in the party and whether or not there is a vacancy:

If the no. of persons is:	The probability of *no* vacancy is:
1	.00 to .30
2	.00 to .40
3	.00 to .50
4 to 6	.00 to .60

Output Format Your printed output might look like this: (as an illustration only)

Call	City Desired*	No. in Party	Vacancy Yes/No	Nearest Other Cities
1	NYC	5	No	XYZ and ABC
____	________	______	________	______________
____	________	______	________	______________
____	________	______	________	______________
20	________	______	________	______________

Documentation A flowchart should be prepared for the program. REM statements should be used throughout the program to explain relevant segments of it.

*This list of cities is not in geographical sequence. Consult a map or atlas for the correct location of each one.

Answers and Solutions to Selected Exercises

CHAPTER 2

2.1 a. 20 PRINT "EARNINGS FOR 3RD QUARTER"
b. 30 PRINT " ", "DIVISION", " ", "SALES"
c. 40 PRINT "NAME", "S.S.#", "DATE OF BIRTH", "NO. OF DEP."

2.3 a. .00000528 c. 4,680,000. e. 75,310,000,000.
b. .000000153 d. .0341791 f. −.0123658

2.4
```
5 PRINT "ANY STUDENT'S NAME"
10 PRINT "124 UNIVERSITY PL."
15 PRINT "ANY TOWN, ANY STATE  ZIP CODE"
20 PRINT "COURSE IS - BUS 10"
99 END


RUN
ANY STUDENT'S NAME
124 UNIVERSITY PL.
ANY TOWN, ANY STATE  ZIP CODE
COURSE IS - BUS 10
```

2.7 Numerical solutions:
a. $\frac{1}{7}$ c. −19 e. $1\frac{1}{2}$ g. −240
b. $15\frac{4}{7}$ d. 80 f. 20 h. 360

2.10
```
10 PRINT "SALES","TAX","TOTAL"
12 PRINT "----------------------------------------"
15 PRINT "$";5,"$";5*.05,"$";5+5*.05
20 PRINT "$";10,"$";10*.05,"$";10+10*.05
25 PRINT "$";15,"$";15*.05,"$";15+15*.05
99 END

RUN
SALES          TAX            TOTAL
----------------------------------------
$ 5            $ .25          $ 5.25
$ 10           $ .5           $ 10.5
$ 15           $ .75          $ 15.75
```

2.15 Expressions have the following values:
a. 5; b. 3; c. 27; d. 11

2.18
```
1 REM  THIS PROGRAM FINDS THE AREA OF A TRIANGLE.
2 REM  NOTE THE USE OF COMPUTATIONAL PRINT.
5 PRINT "BASE","HEIGHT","AREA"
10 PRINT 5,7,5*7/2
15 PRINT 10.5,6.2,10.5*6.2/2
20 PRINT 100,78,100*78/2
99 END

RUN
BASE           HEIGHT         AREA
 5              7              17.5
 10.5           6.2            32.55
 100            78             3900
```

CHAPTER 3

3.1 Unacceptable BASIC variables are:
a. X11; c. −M5; d. C.2; e. PI; h. D+8

3.3 (2*R*C/(U*P))↑.50

3.5 69
304

3.7 a.
```
10 PRINT "SALES","TAX","TOTAL"
15 DATA 5,10,15
20 READ S1,S2,S3
25 PRINT S1,.05*S1,.05*S1+S1
30 PRINT S2,.05*S2,.05*S2+S2
35 PRINT S3,.05*S3,.05*S3+S3
99 END

RUN
SALES          TAX            TOTAL
 5              .25            5.25
 10             .5             10.5
 15             .75            15.75
```

3.15
```
5 REM UNITED COMPUTER COMPANY
7 INPUT S1,P1,W1,S2,P2,W2,S3,P3,W3,S4,P4,W4
10 PRINT "SALESPERSON","AMOUNT SOLD","SALARY"
20 PRINT "1",S1,W1+P1*S1
25 PRINT "2",S2,W2+P2*S2
30 PRINT "3",S3,W3+P3*S3
35 PRINT "4",S4,W4+P4*S4
99 END

RUN
 ?13500,.015,1000,21000,.015,1000,9600,.015,1000,24400,.015,1000
SALESPERSON     AMOUNT SOLD    SALARY
1                13500          1202.5
2                21000          1315
3                9600           1144
4                24400          1366
```

3.20
```
10 REM THIS PROGRAM ILLUSTRATES THE PROPERTY OF THE SUM OF THE
15 REM DEVIATIONS ABOUT THE MEAN IS EQUAL TO ZERO
20 INPUT U
25 READ X1,X2,X3,X4,X5
30 PRINT "SUM OF THE DEVIATIONS ABOUT THE MEAN IS";
35 PRINT (X1-U)+(X2-U)+(X3-U)+(X4-U)+(X5-U)
40 DATA 5,-3,7,8,-2
45 END

RUN
 ?3
SUM OF THE DEVIATIONS ABOUT THE MEAN IS 0
```

CHAPTER 4

4.1	15.25	4	4	3
4.2	−2.75	.25	4	3

4.11
```
5 REM PROGRAM TO FIND TOTAL PROFITS. TOTAL PROFITS = TOTAL REVENUE-
10 REM TOTAL COST. WHERE T=TOTAL PROFIT, P=PRICE PER UNIT, C=COST
15 REM PER UNIT, U=# UNITS SOLD AND BOUGHT,T1=TOTAL REV.(P X U),
20 REM AND T2=TOTAL COST(C X U).
30 READ P,C,U
40 LET T1= P*U
50 LET T2= C*U
60 LET T = T1-T2
70 PRINT "TOTAL PROFIT REPORT"
75 PRINT
80 PRINT "NUMBER OF UNITS SOLD";U
85 PRINT "PRICE PER UNIT";P,"COST PER UNIT";C
86 PRINT "TOTAL REVENUE";T1
92 PRINT "LESS TOTAL COST";T2
95 PRINT "-----------------------------------"
100 PRINT "TOTAL PROFIT";T
150 DATA 10,6.50,225
199 END

RUN
TOTAL PROFIT REPORT

NUMBER OF UNITS SOLD 225
PRICE PER UNIT 10             COST PER UNIT 6.5
TOTAL REVENUE 2250
LESS TOTAL COST 1462.5
-----------------------------------
TOTAL PROFIT 787.5
```

CHAPTER 5

5.1 a. The program would loop infinitely, printing out the same first line of results.
b. Only the first line of output would result.

5.6 b. Variable S would always be set equal to zero, and the last column of output would have the values of X. The heading is repeated each time.
e. Only the heading and the first line of output result. No "OUT OF DATA" occurs.
i. Same as e.
j. The variable S is not accumulated. Since S is equal to zero, the values in the last column of output will be zero.

5.9
```
10 REM GO TO SOLUTION
12 PRINT "SALESPERSON","AM'T.SOLD","SALARY+COMM."
13 PRINT "-----------","---------","------------"
15 LET P=0
20 READ A
30 DATA 13500,21000,9600,24400
40 LET P=P+1
50 PRINT P,"$";A,"$";1000+.015*A
60 GO TO 20
90 END

RUN
SALESPERSON     AM'T.SOLD       SALARY+COMM.
-----------     ---------       ------------
 1              $ 13500         $ 1202.5
 2              $ 21000         $ 1315
 3              $ 9600          $ 1144
 4              $ 24400         $ 1366

OUT OF DATA- LN #  20
```

CHAPTER 6

6.2 a. The output would not change.
b. Omitting line 35 would not cause the output to change, because A is greater than B. If A was less than B, both the B and A values would be printed out, each on a separate line.

6.6 The data value 999 would be processed in lines 60, 65, and 70. An additional line of output results with these values: 999 and 998001. The column totals become: 1016 and 998080.

6.22

```
10 LET S1=25
20 LET S2=15
30 LET S3=30
40 LET H=0
45 READ H
46 PRINT"FOR THE HOUR ";H
50 PRINT,"FLIGHT 381","FLIGHT 402","FLIGHT 283"
55 PRINT"::::::::::::::::::::::::::::::::::::::::::::::::::::::::::::::::::"
60 PRINT"SEATS AVAILABLE";;S1,S2,S3
70 PRINT"WHEN ? APPEARS TYPE RES. FOR THIS HOUR"
80 INPUT F1,F2,F3
90 LET S1=S1-F1
100LET S2=S2-F2
110LET S3=S3-F3
120LET H =H+1
130IF H=5 THEN 299
140IF S1<=10 THEN 180
150IF S2<=10 THEN 200
160IF S3<=10 THEN 220
170GO TO 46
180PRINT"WARNING, FLIGHT 381 HAS 10 OR LESS SEATS AVAILABLE"
190GO TO 150
200PRINT"WARNING, FLIGHT 402 HAS 10 OR LESS SEATS AVAILABLE"
210GO TO 160
220PRINT"WARNING, FLIGHT 283 HAS 10 OR LESS SEATS AVAILABLE"
230GO TO 46
240 DATA 1
299END
```

6.23

```
5 REM CREDIT CARD APPLICATION
7 LET I=0
8 LET I=I+1
10 IF I>10 THEN 999
15 READ N,S,R,Y,L
20 IF S>=25000 THEN100
30 IF S>=20000 THEN 55
40 IF S>=15000 THEN 70
45 IF S>=10000 THEN 80
50 GO TO 8
55 IF R<.25*S/12 THEN 100
60 GO TO 40
70 IF L>5 THEN 100
75 GO TO 8
80 IF L>5 THEN 90
85 GO TO 8
90 IF Y>=3 THEN100
95 GO TO 8
100 PRINT N
200 GO TO 8
900 DATA 605,21000,560,4,5,610,18000,500,10,14
910 DATA 614,35000,750,2,10,656,11000,280,20,19
920 DATA 678,15500,400,6,2,692,8000,200,10,11
930 DATA 694,32000,850,3,3,697,12500,375,4,6
940 DATA 698,40000,950,15,8,700,20000,395,5,5
999 END

RUN
 610
 614
 656
 694
 697
 698
 700
```

6.34 If Y is not greater than or equal to 25, we can go directly to line 60 and test if Y is greater than or equal to 20, since we already know from line 25 that A is over 60. Thus it is not necessary to first test if A is greater than 55.

CHAPTER 7

7.1 1 2 3 4 5 6 7 8 9 10

7.5b
```
7 FOR J=1 TO 10
10 READ N,A,Y,S
15 IF A>=62 THEN 40
20 IF Y>=25 THEN 40
25 IF A>=60 THEN 50
30 IF A>=55 THEN 60
35 GO TO 75
40 PRINT N
45 GO TO 75
50 IF Y>=20 THEN 40
55 GO TO 75
60 IF Y>=20 THEN 70
65 GO TO 75
70 IF S>=25000 THEN 40
75 NEXT J
80 DATA 1234,40,5,12500,1235,61,25,15000
85 DATA 1236,56,21,30000,1237,71,15,13000
90 DATA 1238,62,19,41000,1239,59,30,11000
95 DATA 1240,20,10,10000,1241,56,22,29000
100 DATA 1242,57,18,31000,1243,62,24,35000
999 END

RUN
 1235
 1237
 1238
 1239
 1243
```

7.18
```
5 REM TABLE OF ZEROS
10 FOR I=1 TO 10
15 FOR J=1 TO 10
20 LET X=0
25 IF I=J THEN 40
30 IF I+J=11 THEN 40
35 GO TO 45
40 LET X=1
45 PRINT X;
50 NEXT J
55 PRINT
60 NEXT I
65 END
```

CHAPTER 8

8.8
```
5 REM TWO WEEK TOTALS FOR PRODUCTION
7 DIM W1(5,3),W2(5,3),A(5,3)
10 FOR I=1 TO 5
15 FOR J=1 TO 3
20 READ W1(I,J)
30 NEXT J
35 NEXT I
40 FOR I=1 TO 5
45 FOR J=1 TO 3
50 READ W2(I,J)
52 LET A(I,J)=W1(I,J)+W2(I,J)
55 NEXT J
60 NEXT I
65 FOR I=1 TO 5
70 LET B(I)=0
75 FOR J=1 TO 3
80 LET B(I)=B(I)+A(I,J)
85 NEXT J
90 NEXT I
100 PRINT "WORKER","  A","  B"," C","# UNITS"
110 FOR I=1 TO 5
120 PRINT I,
130 FOR J=1 TO 3
140 PRINT A(I,J),
150 NEXT J
160 PRINT B(I)
170 NEXT I
180 PRINT
190 FOR K=1 TO 65
200 PRINT "-";
210 NEXT K
212 PRINT
215 LET G=0
220 FOR J=1 TO 3
230 LET D(J)=0
240 FOR I=1 TO 5
250 LET D(J)=D(J)+A(I,J)
260 NEXT I
270 NEXT J
275 PRINT "TOTALS",
280 FOR J=1 TO 3
285 PRINT D(J),
290 LET G=G+D(J)
300 NEXT J
310 PRINT G
320 PRINT
400 DATA 200,100,20,150,125,30,320,75,15,275,100,15
410 DATA 100,200,10,185,110,22,160,115,25,275,100,30
420 DATA 275,90,20,150,150,10
999 END
```

```
RUN
WORKER          A          B          C          # UNITS
 1             385        210         42          637
 2             310        240         55          605
 3             595        175         45          815
 4             550        190         35          775
 5             250        350         20          620

-----------------------------------------------------------------
TOTALS         2090       1165        197         3452
```

8.9
```
5 REM DOLLAR VALUE FOR SALE OF MINI-COMPUTERS
10 PRINT"SALESPERSON",,"TOTAL DOLLAR VALUE"
20 DIM S(5,4)
30 FOR J=1 TO 4
40 READ P(J)
50 NEXT J
60 FOR I=1 TO 5
70 LET T(I)=0
80 FOR J=1 TO 4
90 READ S(I,J)
100 LET T(I)=S(I,J)*P(J)+T(I)
120 NEXT J
140 PRINT I,,T(I)
160 NEXT I
900 DATA 10000,12500,17200,20000
950 DATA 6,8,2,1,5,4,3,1,7,6,1,2,3,9,5,0,4,2,4,3
999 END

SALESPERSON                         TOTAL DOLLAR VALUE
 1                                   214400
 2                                   171600
 3                                   202200
 4                                   228500
 5                                   193800
```

CHAPTER 9

9.1 b. 63, c. .4, g. 45.01

9.2 40

9.6 b. between zero and 2.5
d. from zero to 9, inclusive
f. from 50 to 150, inclusive

9.8
```
1 RANDOMIZE
5 REM PICKING A RANDOM NUMBER FROM 001 TO 500
10 LET W = INT(500*RND + 1)
15 PRINT "THE WINNING IS"; W
20 END

RUN
THE WINNING NUMBER IS 250
```

9.15
```
10 READ A,B,C
15 DATA 2,3,1,4,2,1
20 GO SUB 500
25 PRINT A,B,C,D
30 READ A,B,C
35 GO SUB 500
40 PRINT A,B,C,D
45 STOP
500 LET D=A
510 IF D>B THEN 525
515 IF D>C THEN 535
520 RETURN
525 LET D=B
530 GO TO 515
535 LET D=C
540 RETURN
999 END
```

9.15 continued

```
RUN
 2                 3                 1                 1
 4                 2                 1                 1
```

CHAPTER 10

10.1

```
5 DIM N$(5),P(5),Q(5)
10 PRINT "PRODUCT NAME","PRICE","QUANTITY","AMOUNT"
15 PRINT "------------","-----","--------","------"
20 LET A=0
25 FOR I=1 TO 5
30 READ N$(I),Q(I),P(I)
35 LET A=A+P(I)*Q(I)
40 PRINT N$(I),"$";P(I),Q(I),"$";P(I)*Q(I)
45 NEXT I
50 PRINT
55 PRINT "THE TOTAL AMOUNT IS ";"$";A
60 DATA HAND SOAP,24,.69,TOOTH PASTE,35,.76
62 DATA BROWN SUGAR,16,1.25
65 DATA COLA,24,.55,RYE BREAD,50,.20
99 END

RUN
PRODUCT NAME    PRICE           QUANTITY        AMOUNT
------------    -----           --------        ------
HAND SOAP       $ .69            24             $ 16.56
TOOTH PASTE     $ .76            35             $ 26.6
BROWN SUGAR     $ 1.25           16             $ 20
COLA            $ .55            24             $ 13.2
RYE BREAD       $ .2             50             $ 10

THE TOTAL AMOUNT IS $ 86.36
```

10.2

```
10 REM INVENTORY PROGRAM
15 PRINT "WHAT IS THE PRODUCT NAME ";
20 INPUT N$
25 IF N$="STOP" THEN 999
30 FOR I=1 TO 10
35 READ P$,A
40 IF P$=N$ THEN 60
45 NEXT I
50 PRINT "NO SUCH PRODUCT NAME AS ";N$;" TRY AGAIN"
55 GO TO 65
60 PRINT "THE AMOUNT OF ";P$;" IN INVENTORY IS ";A
65 RESTORE
70 GO TO 15
75 DATA SOAP,100,TISSUE,150,BREAD,50
77 DATA BRUSHES,25,ASPIRIN,12,SODA,250
80 DATA CHEESE,80,CEREAL,200,BEANS,500,SOUP,75
999 END

RUN
WHAT IS THE PRODUCT NAME  ?CHEESE
THE AMOUNT OF CHEESE IN INVENTORY IS  80
WHAT IS THE PRODUCT NAME  ?TISSUE
THE AMOUNT OF TISSUE IN INVENTORY IS  150
WHAT IS THE PRODUCT NAME  ?ASPIRIN
THE AMOUNT OF ASPIRIN IN INVENTORY IS  12
WHAT IS THE PRODUCT NAME  ?CAVIAR
NO SUCH PRODUCT NAME AS CAVIAR TRY AGAIN
WHAT IS THE PRODUCT NAME  ?SOUP
THE AMOUNT OF SOUP IN INVENTORY IS  75
WHAT IS THE PRODUCT NAME  ?STOP
```

10.6
```
5 DIM N$(11)
10 FOR I=1 TO 11
15 INPUT N$(I)
20 NEXT I
25 FOR I=1 TO 11
30 PRINT N$(12-I);
35 NEXT I
36 PRINT
40 END

RUN
 ?P
 ?R
 ?O
 ?G
 ?R
 ?A
 ?M
 ?M
 ?E
 ?R
 ?.
.REMMARGORP
```

CHAPTER 11

11.4

	A	X	B	S
Before first pass	A	X	B	S
	0	1E10	*	*
	8		*	
	9		*	
	3		*	
	2		*	
After first pass	A	X	B	S
	1E10	0	0	1
	8		*	
	9		*	
	3		*	
	2		*	
After second pass	A	X	B	S
	1E10	2	0	5
	8		2	
	9		*	
	3		*	
	1E10		*	

*means not yet defined

11.4 continued

After third pass	*A*	*X*	*B*	*S*
	1E10	3	0	4
	8		2	
	9		3	
	1E10		*	
	1E10		*	

After fourth pass	*A*	*X*	*B*	*S*
	1E10	8	0	2
	1E10		2	
	9		3	
	1E10		8	
	1E10		*	

After fifth pass	*A*	*X*	*B*	*S*
	1E10	9	0	3
	1E10		2	
	1E10		3	
	1E10		8	
	1E10		9	

11.5

Before 1st switch	0	8	9	3	2
After 1st switch	0	8	3	9	2
After 2nd switch	0	3	8	9	2
After 3rd switch	0	3	8	2	9
After 4th switch	0	3	2	8	9
After 5th switch	0	2	3	8	9

11.6

Before first pass	*A*	*X*	*B*	*S*
	1	−1E10	*	*
	7		*	
	6		*	
	0		*	
	3		*	

After first pass	*A*	*X*	*B*	*S*
	1	7	7	2
	−1E10		*	
	6		*	
	0		*	
	3		*	

*means not yet defined

11.6 continued

	A	X	B	S
After second pass	1	6	7	3
	−1E10		6	
	−1E10		*	
	0		*	
	3		*	
After third pass	*A*	*X*	*B*	*S*
	1	3	7	3
	−1E10		6	
	−1E10		3	
	0		*	
	−1E10		*	
After fourth pass	*A*	*X*	*B*	*S*
	−1E10	1	7	1
	−1E10		6	
	−1E10		3	
	0		1	
	−1E10		*	
After fifth pass	*A*	*X*	*B*	*S*
	−1E10	0	7	0
	−1E10		6	
	−1E10		3	
	−1E10		1	
	−1E10		0	

11.13 Yes. Revisions needed:

```
 5 DIM N$(30), X$(30)
15 LET N = 26
41 DATA CCC, XYZ, MNO, BBB, XXX, CBA, MNO, NNN
```

CHAPTER 12

12.1

```
10 PRINT USING 55
15 PRINT USING 50
20 PRINT USING 60,2,SQR(2)
25 PRINT USING 65,2,SQR(2)
30 PRINT USING 70,2,SQR(2)
35 PRINT USING 75,2,SQR(2)
40 PRINT USING 80,2,SQR(2)
45 PRINT USING 85,2,SQR(2)
50 FMT ---   -----------
55 FMT TWO   SQUARE ROOT
60 FMT #       #.#
65 FMT #       #.##
70 FMT #       #.###
75 FMT #       #.####
80 FMT #       #.#####
85 FMT #       #.##########
90 END
```

12.1 continued

```
RUN
 TWO   SQUARE ROOT
 ---   -----------
 2       1.4
 2       1.41
 2       1.414
 2       1.4142
 2       1.41421
 2       1.4142135624
```

12.2

```
1 PRINT USING 100
5 FOR I=1 TO 26
10 LET P=2↑I
15 PRINT USING 105,P
20 NEXT I
100 FMT POWERS OF 2 BETWEEN 1 AND 26 INCLUSIVE
105 FMT ##,###,###
199 END

RUN
 POWERS OF 2 BETWEEN 1 AND 26 INCLUSIVE
          2
          4
          8
         16
         32
         64
        128
        256
        512
      1,024
      2,048
      4,096
      8,192
     16,384
     32,768
     65,536
    131,072
    262,144
    524,288
  1,048,576
  2,097,152
  4,194,304
  8,388,608
 16,777,216
 33,554,432
 67,108,864
```

12.5a

```
5 FOR I=1 TO 10
10 PRINT "*";
15 NEXT I
20 PRINT "*"
25 FOR I=1 TO 9
30 PRINT TAB(10-I);"*"
35 NEXT I
40 FOR I=1 TO 10
45 PRINT "*";
50 NEXT I
55 PRINT "*"
99 END
```

12.5a continued

```
RUN
***********
         *
        *
       *
      *
     *
    *
   *
  *
 *
***********
```

12.5b

```
5 FOR I=1 TO4
10 PRINT "*";TAB(10);"*"
15 NEXT I
20 FOR I=1 TO 9
25 PRINT "*";
30 NEXT I
35 FOR I=1 TO 5
40 PRINT "*";TAB(10);"*"
45 NEXT I
99 END

RUN
*         *
*         *
*         *
*         *
***********
*         *
*         *
*         *
*         *
```

12.5e

```
10 FOR I=1 TO 4
15 PRINT "*";
20 NEXT I
25 PRINT
30 PRINT "*";TAB(4);"*"
35 PRINT "*";TAB(5);"*"
40 PRINT "*";TAB(4);"*"
45 FOR I=1 TO 4
50 PRINT "*";
55 NEXT I
56 PRINT
60 FOR I=1 TO 4
65 PRINT "*"
70 NEXT I
75 PRINT
99 END

RUN
****
*   *
*    *
*   *
****
*
*
*
*
```

12.5f

```
5 PRINT "*";TAB(16);"*"
10 FOR I=1 TO 7
15 PRINT TAB(I);"*";TAB(16-I);"*"
20 NEXT I
25 PRINT TAB(8);"*"
99 END

RUN
*               *
 *             *
  *           *
   *         *
    *       *
     *     *
      *   *
       * *
        *
```

12.5g

```
5 FOR I=1 TO 4
10 PRINT TAB(I);"*";TAB(26-I);"*"
15 NEXT I
20 PRINT TAB(5);"*";TAB(13);"*";TAB(21);"*"
25 FOR I=1 TO 3
30 PRINT TAB(5+I);"*";TAB(13-I);"*";TAB(13+I);"*";TAB(21-I);"*"
35 NEXT I
40 PRINT TAB(9);"*";TAB(17);"*"
99 END
```

12.7

```
10 GO SUB 100
20 GO SUB 200
30 GO SUB 100
40 GO SUB 200
60 STOP
100 FOR I=1 TO 10
105 PRINT "*";
110 NEXT I
115 PRINT
120 RETURN
200 FOR I=1 TO 7
205 PRINT "*"
210 NEXT I
215 RETURN
300 END
```

12.7 continued

```
RUN
**********
*
*
*
*
*
*
*
**********
*
*
*
*
*
*
*
```

12.8

```
5 PRINT "NAME";TAB(20);"SALARY";TAB(34);"DEDUCTIONS";TAB(49);"NET PAY"
10 END

RUN
NAME                SALARY        DEDUCTIONS     NET PAY
```

CHAPTER 13

13.2 A dimension statement is needed.

13.5

```
05 REM MATRICES:PACKED OUTPUT
10 DIM A(3,6), B(5,2), C(4)
20 MAT READ A,B,C
30 MAT PRINT A; B; C;
40 DATA 68,73,41,12,18,21,32,47,16,-7,12,20,38,61,62,21,14,-9
50 DATA 2,7,3,9,6,11,12,8,14,7,1.1,.6,.8,.9
68  73
99 END

RUN

 68  73  41  12  18  21
 32  47  16 -7  12  20
 38  61  62  21  14 -9


 2  7
 3  9
 6  11
 12  8
 14  7


 1.1  .6  .8  .9
```

13.7
```
05 REM MAT INPUT:GROSS PAY
10 DIM H(6,1),R(1,6),P(6,6)
20 MAT INPUT H,R
30 MAT P=H*R
40 PRINT
50 PRINT "WORKER","HOURS WORKED","RATE PER HOUR","GROSS PAY"
60 PRINT "------","------------","-------------","---------"
70 FOR I=1 TO 6
80 PRINT I,H(I,1),"$";R(1,I),"$";P(I,I)
90 NEXT I
99 END

RUN
 ?32,37,40,36,35,37.5
 ?4.25,3.80,4.15,4.20,4.00,3.75

WORKER         HOURS WORKED   RATE PER HOUR  GROSS PAY
------         ------------   -------------  ---------
 1              32            $ 4.25         $ 136
 2              37            $ 3.8          $ 140.6
 3              40            $ 4.15         $ 166
 4              36            $ 4.2          $ 151.2
 5              35            $ 4            $ 140
 6              37.5          $ 3.75         $ 140.625
```

13.11
```
05 REM CAR SALES:MATRIX
10 DIM S(10,2),K(1,10),H(1,2)
20 MAT READ S,K
30 MAT H=K*S
40 PRINT " ","IMPORT SALES LEADERS"
50 PRINT " ","--------------------"
60 PRINT " ","JUNE","JUNE"
70 PRINT "NUMBER","1975","1974"
80 PRINT "------------------------------------"
90 FOR I=1 TO 10
100PRINT I,S(I,1),S(I,2)
110NEXT I
120PRINT "------------------------------------"
130PRINT "TOTAL",H(1,1),H(1,2)
140DATA 28435,19549,23867,13656,23268,23806,10061,2938,9466,7182
150DATA 9323,4999,5939,3300,5629,4232,4789,3980,4344,1631
160DATA 1,1,1,1,1,1,1,1,1,1
999END

RUN
               IMPORT SALES LEADERS
               --------------------
               JUNE           JUNE
NUMBER         1975           1974
------------------------------------
 1              28435          19549
 2              23867          13656
 3              23268          23806
 4              10061          2938
 5              9466           7182
 6              9323           4999
 7              5939           3300
 8              5629           4232
 9              4789           3980
 10             4344           1631
------------------------------------
TOTAL           125121         85273
```

13.14
```
05 REM MATRIX MULT.
10 DIM C(4,1),D(1,4),M1(4,4),M2(1,1)
20 MAT READ C,D
30 MAT M1=C*D
40 MAT M2=D*C
50 MAT PRINT M1,M2
60 DATA .25,.5,-.5,.375,16,24,20,36
99 END

RUN

 4              6              5              9
 8              12             10             18
-8             -12            -10            -18
 6              9              7.5            13.5


 19.5
```

13.15
```
05 REM STOCK VALUE:MATRIX
10 DIM N(1,7), P(7,3), V(1,3)
20 MAT READ N,P
30 MAT V=N*P
40 PRINT " ","PORTFOLIO EVALUATION"
50 PRINT " ","--------------------"
60 PRINT "JAN.2","MAY 1","JUL Y 25"
70 PRINT "-----","-----","--------"
80 MAT PRINT V
90 DATA 110,200,100,150,200,250,100
100 DATA 3,6.25,6.375,6.875,13.25,17,10.875,16.75,19.5
110 DATA 2.5,5.875,7.375,3.75,8.25,9.125,2,4.125,6.375,6,10.75,12
120 END

RUN
               PORTFOLIO EVALUATION
               --------------------
JAN.2          MAY 1          JUL Y 25
-----          -----          --------

 5017.5         9650           11776.3
```

CHAPTER 14

14.1
```
NEW:UNITF


5 1,2400
10 2,3200
15 3,1800
20 4,2100
25 5,3000
30 6,4500

SAV
```

14.4
```
5 PRINT "PLANT","UNITS PRODUCED"
10 PRINT "-----","--------------"
15 LET T=0
20 LET N=0
25 INPUT:UNITF:P,U
30 LET N=N+1
35 PRINT P,U
40 LET T=T+U
45 IF N=6 THEN 55
50 GO TO 25
55 PRINT "------------------------------"
60 PRINT "TOTAL",T
99 END

RUN
PLANT          UNITS PRODUCED
-----          --------------
 1              2400
 2              3200
 3              1800
 4              2100
 5              3000
 6              4500
------------------------------
TOTAL           17000
```

14.10 Data Files

```
NEW:DIV1


10 DIV A,400,15
20 DIV B,500,23
30 DIV C,430,20
40 DIV D,330,30
SAV

NEW:DIV2


10 DIV E,380,13
15 DIV F,450,25
20 DIV G>300,21
SAV
```

Program Listing

```
NEW:MERGEF


SAV


5 FOR I=1 TO 4
10 INPUT:DIV1:D$,A,B
15 PRINT:MERGEF:LNM(10);D$;",";A;",";B
20 NEXT I
25 FOR I=1 TO 3
30 INPUT:DIV2:D$,A,B
35 PRINT:MERGEF:LNM(10);D$;",";A;",";B
40 NEXT I
99 END
```

14.10 continued

```
RUN

USED:     3.Ø UNITS


OLD:MERGEF


LIST
1Ø DIV A, 4ØØ , 15
11 DIV B, 5ØØ , 23
12 DIV C, 43Ø , 2Ø
13 DIV D, 33Ø , 3Ø
14 DIV E, 38Ø , 13
15 DIV F, 45Ø , 25
16 DIV G, 3ØØ , 21
```

14.11 Data File

```
NEW:SCHED


1Ø MONDAY     , 7:1ØPM, 7:3ØAM, 9:ØØAM
11            ,1Ø:Ø5PM,        ,1Ø:4ØAM NON STOP
12 TUESDAY    , 8:5ØPM, 9:1ØAM,1Ø:4ØAM
13  , , , ,
14 WEDNESDAY  , 8:5ØPM, 9:1ØAM,1Ø:4ØAM
15  , , , ,
16 THURSDAY   , 7:1ØPM, 7:3ØAM, 9:ØØAM
17            ,1Ø:Ø5PM,        ,1Ø:4ØAM NON STOP
18 FRIDAY     , 8:5ØPM, 9:1ØAM,1Ø:4ØAM
19  , , , ,
2Ø SATURDAY   , 7:1ØPM, 7:3ØAM, 9:ØØAM
21            ,1Ø:Ø5PM,        ,1Ø:4ØAM NON STOP
22 SUNDAY     , 7:1ØPM, 7:3ØAM, 9:ØØAM
23            ,1Ø:Ø5PM,        ,1Ø:4ØAM NON STOP
SAV
```

Program

```
1Ø FOR I=1 TO 7
15 INPUT:SCHED:D$(I),N$(I),G$(I),Z$(I)
2Ø INPUT:SCHED:S$(I),T$(I),U$(I),V$(I)
25 NEXT I
3Ø PRINT "TYPE IN 1 FOR MONDAY, 2 FOR TUESDAY, 3 FOR WEDNESDAY,"
35 PRINT "..., 7 FOR SUNDAY, AND Ø TO TERMINATE, AFTER THE ? MARK"
4Ø PRINT "APPEARS";
45 INPUT N
5Ø IF N=Ø GO TO 11Ø
55 PRINT "747'S FROM NEW YORK TO GENEVA AND ZURICH"
6Ø PRINT "DAY","LEAVES N.Y.","ARRIVES GENEVA","ARRIVES ZURICH"
65 PRINT "---","-----------","--------------","--------------"
7Ø GO TO 85
75 INPUT N
8Ø IF N=Ø THEN 11Ø
85 PRINT D$(N),N$(N),G$(N),Z$(N)
9Ø PRINT S$(N),T$(N),U$(N),V$(N)
95 PRINT
1ØØ PRINT
1Ø5 GO TO 75
11Ø END
```

CHAPTER 15

Project I

The following results should be computed as the amount due at the end of each month:

Month	Account 12442	Account 999-00-6666
Jan.	56.18	22.15
Feb.	56.18	51.19
Mar.	46.75	90.20
Apr.	44.78	134.19

Project III

The following results should be derived for the net pay of each employee:

	Employee Number	
Week	123-45-6789	111-88-9669
1	444.02	194.44
2	348.08	179.48

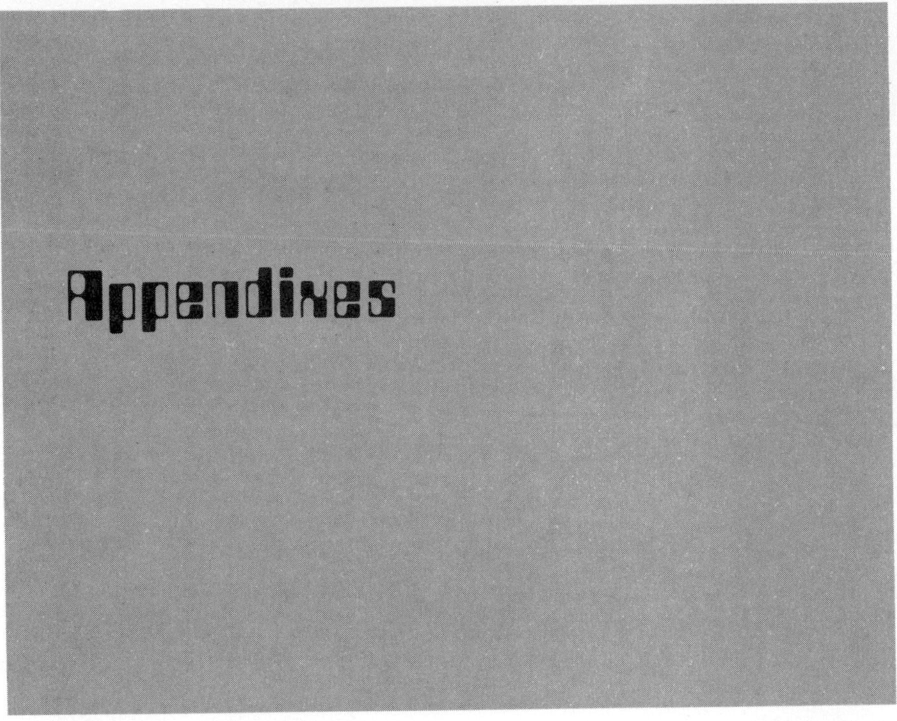

APPENDIX A SYSTEM COMMANDS

This appendix summarizes many of the most widely used timesharing system commands. They are listed in alphabetical order for easy reference. In many systems, only the first three letters of any word must be entered.

1. BYE or GOODBYE disconnects the terminal from the timesharing system. The amount of connect and/or CPU time used this session may also be printed at this time.
2. GOOD BYE (same as BYE, item 1).
3. LIST causes the most current version of the program or file to be printed on the teletype.
   LISTNH stands for LIST NO HEADING and means just what it says—it will do everything that LIST will do but will not print the heading, which includes the name of the program, if any, the time, and the date. Some timesharing systems include the name of the timesharing company as well.

4. NEW allows a new program to be entered into the timesharing system, while it erases the working copy of the current program. The system responds to the NEW command with a request for the NAME of the new program. If you wish to create a new program without naming it, you could just type SCR (see 8) and then begin typing the new program. Such an unnamed program could not be SAVEd until it was NAMEd.
5. OLD introduces a new program that was previously saved (see 7) and destroys the working copy of the current program. The system responds to the OLD command with a request for the NAME of the OLD program that is to be loaded in.
6. RUN compiles and executes the current program. If there are any syntax errors in the program they will be indicated at this time. RUNNH is the same as RUN, but no heading will be printed.
7. SAVE saves the working copy of the current program by writing it onto a disk file. This program can then be recalled by typing OLD and then the name of the program.
8. SCRATCH erases the working copy of the current program. It is useful when you have run one program and then wish to create a new one. There will be no leftover line numbers from the previous program.
9. UNSAVE removes the current SAVEd program from the disk storage. After this command, the program can no longer be recalled by the OLD command.

APPENDIX B A COMPARISON OF BASIC FOR BUSINESS WITH TRS-80* LEVEL II BASIC

Of the many microcomputer systems currently available, the TRS-80 system of Radio Shack is the most widely purchased for small business, home, and personal use. This appendix indicates the few areas of the BASIC language described in this text that *cannot* be implemented/processed on TRS-80 systems with Level II BASIC.

Chapter	Exceptions
2 END,PRINT, and REM	None
3 READ/DATA, RESTORE, and INPUT	None
4 LET	None
5 The GO TO Statement	None
6 IF/THEN, Computed GO TO and STOP	None
7 FOR/NEXT	None
8 Subscripted Variables and Dimensioning	None
9 Functions and Subroutines	Yes
10 String Variables	None
11 Sorting	None
12 PRINT USING and TAB	Yes
13 Matrices and Matrix Operations	Yes
14 Data Files	Yes

Description of Exceptions

Chapter 9 Functions and Subroutines

Statements needed to produce random numbers follow a slightly different syntax. As an illustration, programs to generate integers, that are random numbers in the range of 1 to 100 follow.

ANSI BASIC

```
10 RANDOMIZE
20 PRINT INT(100*RND + 1)
30 END
```

LEVEL II BASIC

```
10 RANDOM
20 PRINT RND(100)
30 END
```

*Trademark of Radio Shack, A Division of Tandy Corporation, Fort Worth, Texas 76102

Level II BASIC requires a "seed" in the argument, depending on the type of random numbers needed. The ANSI random number function requires no argument.

The syntax specification for the subroutine statement differs slightly. ANSI BASIC will process the following:

a. 10 GO SUB 250

or

b. 10 GOSUB 250

Both (a) and (b) are considered the same, even though in(a) there is a space between the Go and SUB. Level II BASIC will not accept (a). An error message is generated upon execution of the statement. The syntax in (b) is the accepted form in Level II BASIC.

Chapter 12 PRINT USING and TAB

In this text an FMT statement is used to specify a format for the PRINT USING statement. LEVEL II BASIC does not accept FMT. Rather the format for a PRINT USING is specified in a string variable which is then referenced by the PRINT USING statement. As an example, the number 1250 is printed as 1,250.00 below.

Text BASIC

```
10 LET N = 1250
20 FMT #,###.##
30 PRINT USING 20,N
40 END
```

Level II BASIC

```
10 LET N = 1250
20 LET A$ = "#,###.##"
30 PRINT USING A$;N
40 END
```

or

```
10 LET N = 1250
20 PRINT USING "#,###.##";N
30 END
```

Chapter 13 Matrices and Matrix Operations

TRS-80 Level II BASIC does not include the matrix statements described in Chapter 13.

Chapter 14 Data Files

The statements shown in this chapter dealing with data files are not included in the TRS-80 Level II BASIC.

OUTPUT SPACING

In Chapter 2 we pointed out that not all computer systems have the same output space available. This is often the case with microcomputers and minicomputers that show output on a CRT. The TRS-Model I screen will display four 16-character print fields per line when a comma is used in the PRINT statement. This is shown in (a), which illustrates a screen display of a program and output similar to Program 2.11 in the text.

a.
```
10 PRINT "FIELD 1","FIELD 2","FIELD 3","FIELD 4","FIELD 5"
20 END
RUN
FIELD 1         FIELD 2         FIELD 3         FIELD 4
FIELD 5
```

The TRS-80 Model II will display five 14-character print fields per line when a comma is used in the PRINT statement. This is shown in (b).

b.
```
10 PRINT "FIELD 1","FIELD 2","FIELD 3","FIELD 4","FIELD 5"
20 END
RUN
FIELD 1       FIELD 2       FIELD 3       FIELD 4       FIELD 5
```

Packed output using the semicolon follows the discussion presented in Chapter 2; in particular Programs 2.14 and 2.18. A semicolon in a PRINT statement will produce a screen display for the TRS-80, as shown in (c). Only a semicolon after a numeric will produce an extra space. This is seen by studying the output produced by lines 16 and 17.

c.
```
15 PRINT "123456789012345"
16 PRINT  1;2;-3
17 PRINT "A";"B";1;"C";-2
20 END
RUN
1234567890
 1  2 -3  4
AB 1 C-2
```

ERRORS

Throughout the text we have pointed out that there are differences in how BASIC will perform from system to system. Such differences are also found with the BASIC of the TRS-80. Specifically the TRS-80 will permit a program to execute with syntax errors that you would normally expect to stop execution. Several examples follow.

a. One syntax error that occurs frequently is the open quote at the end of a PRINT statement. Usually such a missing quote produces an error message as described in Chapter 2. Such errors are not "flagged" on the TRS-80. A PRINT statement like the one in line 10 with an open quote at the end is processed as though it had the missing quote.

```
10 PRINT "ABC CO. 1981
90 END
RUN
ABC CO. 1981
```

b. In Chapter 7 we pointed out that the variable in a FOR statement must also exist in a NEXT statement. That is:

   10 FOR A = 1 TO 5

   is matched with a statement,

   50 NEXT A

   If statement 50 was missing the *A*, an error message "FOR NOT MATCHED WITH NEXT" would result, and the program execution stopped. As the following illustration shows, the TRS-80 will process a program that does not have the variable in the NEXT statement.

```
10 FOR A= 1 TO 5
20   PRINT A
30 NEXT
90 END
RUN
 1
 2
 3
 4
 5
```

   The TRS-80 will also process a program containing nested loops, where the NEXT statements do not have the variable of the FOR statements. This is shown in the illustration that follows.

```
10 FOR A= 1 TO 3
15     FOR B= 1 TO 2
20        PRINT A,B,A+B
25     NEXT
30 NEXT
90 END
RUN
 1             1             2
 1             2             3
 2             1             3
 2             2             4
 3             1             4
 3             2             5
```

Every BASIC program should have as its last statement an END statement to show the physical termination of the program. A program listing without and END statement may lead the reader to believe that the listing is incomplete. Many systems will not execute a program that does not have an END statement. Usually an error message "END IS NOT LAST" occurs when such a program is run.

Microcomputers like the TRS-80 will process a program without an END statement. Such processing is illustrated in the following example. Note the absence of an END statement.

```
10 READ A
20 LET B=A*2
30 PRINT A,B
40 DATA 10
RUN
 10            20
```

A WORD OF CAUTION

Because many microcomputers will process programs having errors like those described above, it is easy to accept the programs as being complete and correct. Such programs if entered into another computer with BASIC, will probably "bomb" out. Therefore we urge you not to take shortcuts merely because you know the program will produce the desired output. Your program should be acceptable to as many systems as possible. Thus you should include the word END, closing quotes on the PRINT, etc., even though it may not be required on the system you use.

TRS-80 SYSTEM COMMANDS

We will examine three TRS-80 system commands: LIST, NEW, and RUN.

1. LIST After a program has been entered and stored in the computer, a display of all program lines can be obtained by entering the command LIST. The entire program will scroll up the display screen continuously, leaving only the last fourteen lines displayed. The automatic scrolling can be stopped by pressing the SHIFT and @ keys together on the TRS-80 Model I, or the HOLD key on the Model II. Scrolling can be restarted by pressing any key. A single line can be listed using LIST followed by the line number. A sequence of lines can be displayed by typing the first-last line number after the command list. Other examples follow:

LIST 25	displays line 25
LIST 25-	displays line 25 and all lines thereafter
LIST -50	displays all lines up to and including line 50
LIST 25–50	displays lines 25 to 50 inclusive
LIST.	displays the current line just entered

2. NEW Erases all the lines of the current program stored in memory. Allows a new program to be entered.
3. RUN This command, when entered, will cause the program stored to be executed. Any syntax errors recongnized by the computer will be indicated at this time.

References Lien, D. A., *User's Manual for LEVEL I, TRS-80* (Fort Worth, Texas: Radio Shack, 1978). Tandy Corporation, *LEVEL II BASIC Reference Manual* (Fort Worth, Texas: Radio Shack, 1978).

Index